IMMORTAL

SIDNEY.

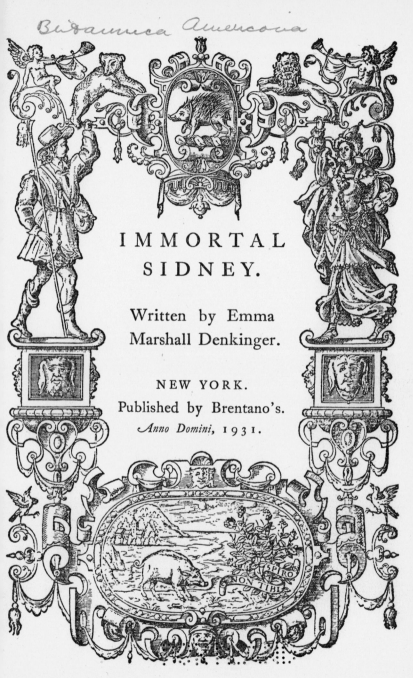

IMMORTAL SIDNEY.

Written by Emma
Marshall Denkinger.

NEW YORK.
Published by Brentano's.
Anno Domini, 1931.

TO A.M.D.

"There is none proceedes either so thoroly or so wysely as my Lady my mother. For myne owne parte I have had onely lighte from her. . . .

AND TO J.A.D.

"There never was so good a father."

A LIST OF THE CHAPTERS.

A List of the Chapters.

A LIST OF THE ILLUSTRATIONS.

The miniature at Windsor Castle is used here with the permission of His Majesty the King. The Archbishop of Canterbury has allowed the reproduction of Lady Rich's portrait from the collection at Lambeth Palace. The photograph of the Great Hall at Penshurst Place appears by consent of the Lord de Lisle and Dudley. The Lant Funeral Roll is in the British Museum. With the exception of Holland's picture of Sir Francis Walsingham, all other portraits are in the National Portrait Gallery, to the Director of which the author is under deep obligation for extraordinary privileges.

IMMORTAL

SIDNEY.

THE FIRST CHAPTER ENTITLED
PROLOGUE IN
PURGATORY.

I F PHILIP SIDNEY was not born of the Blood Royal, it was no fault of his grandfather, John Dudley, Duke of Northumberland.

In the late spring of 1553, in the year before Philip was born, the Duke was about to complete his bold plans. Already he had successfully brought to the scaffold his rival, the Lord Protector Somerset. He had possessed himself of the Lord Protector's houses of Durham and Sion. If he had not taken the title as well, it was purely because he could manage better without it. What was the use of whetting the jealousy of the other nobles before it was necessary? Now he had crowned all by wedding his youngest son, Guildford Dudley, to the Lady Jane Grey.

Northumberland had not chosen the bride for her devotion to the reformed religion, though at the moment he inclined to that comparatively recent schism himself. Still less because she read Greek with Roger Ascham and was darkly rumored to know Hebrew and Chaldee. More useful to him was a certain sweet conformity to which he — *She ?* had been trained by a system of " pinches, nips and bobs and other things " which had formed the practical part of her education. His prime motive for the match was dynastic. The fifteen-year-old king, Edward VI, frail and soon to die, had named as successors to the crown, the heirs male of his cousin, the same Lady Jane. In so doing the lad had set aside his sister Mary, now thirty-seven, known for a resolute character and a determined Catholic; set aside, too, his sister Elizabeth, twenty, and, singularly enough, famous for " a marvellous meek stomach." But after all, both were princesses who must, if they married, take to them royal lords. That, in the days when some degree of domination was conceded to the consort, meant the foisting upon true Britons of hated " foreign " kings. And if heirs female did not marry, what of the succession? Who could guess that the demure Elizabeth, greatest of English queens, would make of the very claims of Virginity, the most successful career on record? Certainly not her little brother, so wan and wasted under the fetching little velvet cap with its bit of white feather. On the day of Cousin Jane's wedding he had been too ill to attend, but he sent his blessing and some handsome gold plate. The festivities were gorgeous enough without him, thanks to the raiment and jewels of the departed Somerset. To the populace that surged up the Strand to Durham House, the bride was " fair though freckled " and looked very tiny beside her tall young husband, bright as Apollo in his golden curls. Handsome as a king, they said. Poor Guildford! And poor Jane!

By mid-June, it became evident that the business of waiting for heirs male might be dangerous. The Lady Jane showed a propensity for living with her mother. The King was growing weaker and weaker. At this juncture Northumberland suggested to Edward a change in his former " Devise." A very simple change. His Majesty should leave the crown not " to the l'Jane*s* heires masles " as the phrasing had originally run, but " to the l'Jane *and her* heires masles." Edward approved, with an invalid's insistence that the " book " be immediately engrossed. The nobles were not so ductile. They saw, as clearly as Northumberland,

Philip Sidney from the Miniature at Windsor.

that by the new arrangement, the house of Dudley would not need to wait a generation to feel upon its brows the circlet royal. It would be " King Guildford " just as soon as God in His mercy saw fit to take King Edward. Further, there were those like the Lord Chief Justice who remembered the will made by Henry VIII at the close of his picturesque career. In it he had so ordered the succession as to take cognizance of every possibility. First in line he named Edward. Second, any heirs male which he, Henry, might yet have by Katherine Parr — " or any other wife that I may have " ! Third, the Princess Mary. Fourth, the Princess Elizabeth. However, Edward's sainted father had married so often and so righteously that at one time or another he had managed to stigmatize both his daughters as illegitimate. Northumberland could, therefore, support the findings of the little king as only properly filial. Besides, was it not disloyal to question the judgment of the ruling prince? Furious at the inability of the Lord Chief Justice to see a subject's duty, Northumberland offered to fight him, or any other objector " in his shirt." The Lord Chief Justice signed the Devise. So, too, did Cranmer and more than a hundred others. Never was illegal instrument more legal than this of Northumberland's planning. A certain William Cecil had a sensitive nose that smelled treason to the windward. Too weak to wield a pen, he took to his bed. Long after Northumberland and Guildford and the gentle Jane had gone their ways to the scaffold, Cecil lived on and became the great Lord Burleigh. His triumph is, however, quite without moral. Robert Dudley, though deeper in these very plans to defraud Elizabeth of her heritage which offended the nice William, managed to live, too. Survived to be Elizabeth's favorite and that " Sweet Robin " who was everlastingly a thorn in the flesh of the astute Cecil.

The Devise now signed to his satisfaction — or was it Northumberland's? — young Edward died on July 6th,

1553. At the last, Sir Henry Sidney, soon to have a son of his own, held the wasted body in his arms with a tenderness, like everything else about him, utterly unfeigned. It was he who bent to catch the last words of his sweetest prince: " I am faint, Lord: have mercy upon me and receive my spirit." To his final hour Sir Henry cherished that moment. Leaving lamentations to his son-in-law, honest Harry, Northumberland was already busy with more vital matters. To each of the sisters of the little dead king, he sent messages to say that Edward was very ill and wanted her by him. Receiving hers, Mary started in tears, headlong for Greenwich. It was only the insistence of intercepting friends who knew of the trap to gain possession of her person that caused her to turn her horse about and gallop furiously northward to Kenninghall where she might muster her supporters. When Elizabeth received her summons, she needed no warning. Instead of hastening from Hatfield in the heat of early July, she took to her bed, victim of the same ailment which so grievously afflicted Cecil. In after years it was to be remarked that in their mental processes there was frequently similarity.

Meantime the crowning of Jane admitted no delay. She was enjoying the country solitudes of Chelsea just to the west of London. To her at the Manor House there came the Lady Mary Sidney, daughter to Northumberland and Sir Henry's wife. It was no ordinary family visit. " She told me," said the Lady Jane, " that she was sent by the Council to call me to them, and she informed me that I must be that night at Sion House where they were assembled, to receive that which was ordained for me by the King." By river that afternoon, the two young women went together westward to Richmond, past fields sweet with midsummer. At nightfall they came to Sion House. The lords of the Council came as well, to bend the knee to the little queen of sixteen and to swear by their souls to shed blood and lose life in her defense. Lady Jane took their allegiance more seriously than they were later to take it themselves, for she " swooned and lay as dead." Being a young woman of sense, she did not want the crown. But Northumberland had no time for hysteria: she did as she was told.

On the next day, when she was conveyed to her royal residence of the Tower, in the King's own barge, she probably thought better of her new state. From the landing at Tower Stairs, she proceeded to the entrance of the Great Hall, under a gorgeous canopy, with ladies of the blood to hold her train. To make her appear taller before the admiring throngs, she had been " mounted on very high Chopines " which were concealed by her rich robes of green velvet stamped with gold. She wore wide sleeves and a white coif bright with jewels. In the afternoon sunshine her hazel eyes sparkled with excitement and her hair shone like red gold. When she smiled the people saw that her teeth were white and very small. By her side all in white and gold there walked " a very tall strong boy with light hair who paid her much attention." It was young Guildford, caught up as innocently as she in the pitiful pageant of her queening. At six o'clock, the trumpets blew. Heralds appeared on the battlements in all their crimson glory to proclaim to the south, the east and the west, even to the north where Mary mustered her men, that the rule of Queen Jane had begun.

Northumberland lost no time in pressing his son's advantage. When on the morrow, the Marquis of Winchester brought Queen Jane her crown from the jewel house hard by, the Duchess of Northumberland was present to suggest that Guildford's be made ready, too. In earnest of future greatness, some of the crown jewels were actually delivered to the lad. Already his father had sent to the Continent news that Guildford was now king, and Don Diego de Mendoza, minister to Charles V and the boy's godfather,

made the accession of His Majesty matter for a congratu-
latory visit to the English ambassadors in the Low Countries. Somewhat dazed but too diplomatic to admit dismay,
the gentlemen reported the interview to London. It was to
cost Guildford his life. When the news of it came, Mary
had rallied all to her; Jane's power, and with it Guildford's,
had gone for good. So it happened that there never was any
use for the Great Seal which Northumberland's forethought
had provided. Upon it was Jane's name, but the initials
" G. D." appeared under the arched crown, and the royal
arms were in a position less important than that accorded
the bear and the ragged staff which was the cognizance of
the house of Dudley.

For all his planning, the Duke had, in July 1553, chosen
an unfortunate time. Eighteen months before, he might
have had with him some mass of public opinion and at least
one of the great continental powers, Spain or France. But
in aligning himself with the reformed religion and the
French, he had automatically incurred the resentment of
conservative nobles like the Howards who in the main inclined to the older ritual and the cultivation of the friendship of the Emperor. By the same move he had roused the
animosity of the merchants whose lucrative trade was with
Spain and the Low Countries. They blamed upon him the
debasement of the currency and the piracies of the French.
With equal relevance he was held responsible for the mass-
ing in the cities of suffering poor who had been driven from
the great estates which were now converted from tillage to
pasture. In short people were sufficiently uncomfortable
to take a passionate interest in politics and somebody had to
pay the piper. Even so, had the King of France sent over
6000 men to support Jane, as was looked for, Northumberland might have held his own. But France feared the Emperor and did nothing. The Emperor feared France and
did nothing. In the crisis Mary alone was resolute. To her

the people flocked. Mustering men as he might, Northumberland set himself at the head of an army, and with his sons in minor commands, left London on Friday, four days after Jane had been proclaimed.

Of the Duke's army, the chroniclers record that " their feet marched forward, but their minds moved backward." The soldiers scarcely waited for the shelter of hedgerows and ditches in the open country to fall away by scores. On Sunday the 16th, Ridley at Paul's Cross, and John Knox in Buckinghamshire thundered away for Jane. But the prophetic vicar of St. Bartholomew's hard by Smithfield, where heretics were soon to burn, called on his congregation to thank God for the victory of Mary. That night Queen Jane ordered that all the gates of the Tower were to be locked and the keys fetched up to her. It was the pretty gesture of a housewife. It could not stave off rebellion.

By Monday the 17th of July, Northumberland, who had got no farther than Cambridge, was practically a prisoner in the quiet quadrangle of King's College. Guildford had been whisked away by his affectionate mother, and was safe at Sion. Under pretext of securing re-enforcements, on Wednesday July 19th, Jane's Council obtained the permission of the Duke of Suffolk, the Queen's father, to leave the Tower. Promptly they foregathered at Barnard's Castle, the grim fortress-mansion near Blackfriars where Richard III had lived and Henry VIII had dined, and in a happier day Philip Sidney was to spend many hours. With speed, the members of the Council swore allegiance to Mary. To a man they manifested the utmost zeal in causing her to be proclaimed in Cheapside by four trumpeters and the same heralds who nine days before, almost to an hour, had proclaimed Queen Jane. None too soon, either. Every spent messenger brought news of Mary proceeding in triumph to her city of London. The Council summoned Suffolk and told him. In silence he heard them.

Sadly he rode back to the Tower to Jane. The streets were bright now with the bonfires of rejoicing, loud with the hilarity of crowds who had hauled tavern tables into the open to make carousing more sociable. From one parish to another the church bells clanged. The Duke found Jane sitting forlorn under her cloth of estate on the throne in the Great Hall. She was alone. " Come down from that, my child," said Suffolk suddenly gentle. " That is no place for you! " As Jane stepped down to his arms, her words were those of a tired little girl: " Can I go home? "

Next day William Cecil went over her proclamation and other documents that had accumulated during the brief reign. On them he wrote with business-like brevity: " Jana Non Regina." Jane, but no Queen!

By that time Northumberland had begun to drink of his own bitter brew. In the gray mist of early morning, his former colleague, the Earl of Arundel, came to Cambridge to arrest him in the name of Queen Mary. With his red cloak muffled about him, Northumberland himself opened door to the summons. For some time he had been ill, and the excitements of the last days had told heavily on his slender strength. Nevertheless, with his cloak huddled about his shoulders he set out for London, heavily guarded by a motley crew of ill-mounted horsemen and rapscallion foot. All the way he suffered tortures with the gout. Greater, though, were his sufferings of soul. He had brought to the scaffold with him the dear sons for whom he had ventured so high. He had brought ignominy upon children yet un-born of the blood of Dudley. That night the poor wretch slept in a barn. Drearily the troop trailed into London as shopkeepers were taking down their shutters against the day's business. Apprentices bawled at Northumberland the traitor and flung mud on his scarlet tatters. When they brought him to a dungeon in the Beauchamp Tower, he had not one friend save his wife. Eager partner to his venturings, she was fiercely loyal in his disgrace. On her knees, she begged his life of Queen Mary. Begged in vain. Shortly there were lodged with him in the somber Beauchamp Tower, all of his sons: Robert and Ambrose, John, Henry and poor Guildford. If the Dudleys had reached like Lucifer into highest heaven, they were now thrust down to a hell of their own devising.

By the 1st of August they had all been indicted for treason. So, too, Lady Jane whose hope of going home had been rudely shattered. The cruel days dragged on without further action. Meantime little Edward, by whose aided hand all the tragedy had come about, was brought from Greenwich to Whitehall for his burial. It was a " very shabby funeral." Around the small coffin in the Abbey dimness shone the standard of the Seymours, a white dragon on a red ground, and the white greyhound of the Tudors. Cranmer read the plain English service. It was the last time it would be read publicly for five years. It was the last time that Cranmer would officiate. He, too, was bound for the Tower. Affectionate Harry Sidney stood bareheaded at the bier of the monarch whom so many people seemed to have forgotten already. When he stepped out into the thin London sunshine afterward, there was more than sorrow in his heart — the sense of a sinister future.

On the 18th of the month, under the soaring roof of Westminster Hall, Northumberland was condemned to die at the hands of the common hangman as befitted a traitor. Gripping the bar to steady his weakened frame, he heard the ghastly details of the hanging, drawing and quartering. Most dreadful of all, John his eldest son, the Earl of Warwick, was to share his fate. With difficulty the Duke made his formal plea that his " children might be kindly treated." Two days later he found comfort and

strength for the ordeal which was ahead in reconciling himself to the faith of his childhood. At the last, the Queen was
moved to some degree of clemency. John was not to die and
it was to decapitation that Northumberland went forth
on the 22d of August, an emaciated figure in " swan-
coloured damask " walking bravely up Tower Hill. In
his set face a woman brandished a bloody napkin which
she had dipped in the gore of Somerset months before. As
they forced her back into the crowd she shrieked at him
venomously: " Behold the blood which thou didst unjustly
shed does now apparently begin to avenge itself on thee! "
A few moments later, the mob about the scaffold on Tower
Hill was dipping kerchiefs in the life stream of John Dudley. In their eagerness for a souvenir they forgot that he had
died, not for his daring but because he could not grapple to
him a strong party when most he needed it; above all because he had trusted to the magnanimity of the King of
France. Stout fellows tumbled his body into a cart which
forced its way through the crowds down to the Tower.
There a faithful servant by the name of Cocke begged the
Duke's body and gave it burial in the sad church of St.
Peter-in-Chains within the Precincts. By some sardonic in-
spiration, Cocke had him interred beside the Lord Protector
Somerset! The wheel had come full circle.

Shortly after Queen Mary was crowned. The Princess
Elizabeth in pale blue velvet shot with silver, had ridden
beside her through Aldgate into the jubilant streets.
She knelt beside her at Mass in the Abbey, no less con-
formable than the charity children who had sung Calvin-
istic hymns over little Edward and now called down
upon the new Queen the blessings of saints who had returned to fashion. They had had seven weeks in which to
rehearse.

In mid-November the twisted London streets saw another procession. This came on foot from the Tower,

through the Poultry to the Guildhall. In it there walked behind the Lieutenant of the Tower, Lady Jane Dudley. In her close black dress and black hood she looked tinier than ever. There were no chopines to raise her ladyship nearer to Heaven. Only a black prayer book on which she kept her eyes to avoid the curious scrutiny of the hostile crowd lining her way. Behind her came Cranmer, two of her husband's brothers, and Guildford so young and lovely in black velvet with slashings of white satin, that women cried out as he passed, for pity he should go to his trial. When the procession issued from the Guildhall later, people milled around the door to see how the Gentleman Warder carried his ax. A shiver of delicious vicarious horror ran through the streets ahead of the prisoners. The edge of the ax was pointed toward them. They were to die!

Nothing, however, was done about it for three months. Even then, if discretion had possessed Jane's father, Suffolk, instead of an insane fury at the prospect of the Queen's marriage with Philip of Spain, all might have gone well. Well, at least with Guildford. Poor lad, he was not of the blood royal. His death could do Mary no good! Unfortunately, though, when Suffolk was ordered by the Queen to proceed against her rebels in the midlands, he made the cardinal mistake of rousing them instead. Like Wyatt who raised his abortive rebellion at the same time, actuated by the same hatred of Philip, Suffolk and his small force were soon put down. On the very day that her father was brought prisoner to the Tower, February 8th, 1554 Lady Jane and her husband learned that they must die.

Originally the sentence had run that they were to suffer together on Tower Hill. But etiquette, it appeared, must be observed in all things, even in executions. As one of the blood royal, Jane had privileges. She was permitted to lose her head on the Green, inside the Tower Precincts, on the same spot where King Henry's wives had put off mortality.

The occasion was to be graced by a select group of courtiers, invitations being limited to five hundred. Guildford, on the other hand, was but a lord. As such he must die on the common scaffold on Tower Hill, before as many persons as could jam themselves into the open space there, or hang from the masts of ships anchored in the Thames for the show. Before this forest of faces, he made his end manfully. For a moment he stood slim in the black velvet in which he had chosen to die. A chill breeze from the river ruffled the yellow curls about his flushed cheeks. Then he stretched out his graceful length, and in a moment all was over. As Fate would have it, Lady Jane was at the window of her lodgings in the Tower when the cart rattled into the Precincts, with the huddled corpse. Not fifteen minutes before had the poor girl raised to Guildford a gallant hand in farewell. Not unnaturally she was unnerved. She had one more moment of panic when she saw at the head of her own procession the striding figure and swelling calves of the mighty headsman dressed in scarlet. Only for a minute, though, did she clutch at comfortable Mrs. Ellen, her old nurse. Once on the scaffold, she spoke serenely enough to the gentlefolk who had come to see her die, as the wind creaked in the bare trees of February and the rooks wheeled against the sun. After all she had been but a player princess who had neither said nor done more than was set down for her. But she died like a real queen.

With Guildford's going, the Dudleys had not yet made their last blood payment for the brilliant plot which was to have made theirs the reigning house. Kind Sir Harry Sidney drew on all he had in the aid of his wife's family. Invaluable at this juncture were his own connections. Two sisters had been in Mary's service for the better part of their lives and were now among her favorite ladies-in-waiting. His niece was Jane Dormer who as a little girl played cards with the royal Edward and drew from him the infant *bon-*

The Lady Jane Gray whom Sidney's Grandfather made
a Queen.

mot: " Now, Jane, your King is gone. I shall be good enough for you! " She was now the wife of the great Spanish Count de Feria who stood close to Philip himself. From a grateful reference in the will of the Duchess of Northumberland to the help of " Lord Dondagoe Damondesay," we know that Guildford's godfather, the mighty Don Diego, did all in his power as well. One way or another Queen Mary was prevailed upon to release from the Tower the four surviving Dudley sons. This was in October 1554, less than two months before Lady Mary Sidney bore her little boy. John Dudley, who was to have died with his father, but suffered in durance and disease all these months instead, came home to Penshurst. He never saw his nephew. Ten days after his release, and only five weeks before the baby came, he was buried.

After Philip Sidney was famous, people spoke of Penshurst as " a goodli Kentish garden " where

At his great birth were all the Muses met.

But it was no place for gardens or for muses in that chill hour before the dawn on the last day of November, at the end of a cruel year which had brought only death and desolation to all his mother's kin. Honest Sir Harry was to call this eldest son of his, the " light of his line." Robert Dudley, not so honest, but passionately devoted to this Philip, was to see him as the " sun upon the horizon." Surely sun was never more prayerfully yearned for than this which came feebly up as the cold stars paled in a bleak and watery sky.

THE SECOND CHAPTER ENTITLED
THE GOLDEN
BOUGH.

WHEN little Philip was still in his nurse's arms reaching dimpled hands to the marvel of flame leaping from the floor of the Hall at Penshurst, Latimer and Ridley were feeding more sinister fires at Oxford. They were only the greatest of many martyrs under Mary. When he was two, a certain other Philip became the King of Spain, a Philip who had once ridden down through Kent to give a royal name to the little heir of the Sidneys. Before he was three, in November 1558, Catholic Mary died. The Princess Elizabeth came to the throne, to declare herself a Protestant by slow, and safe degrees. In the June of 1559, before he was five, the lovely Mary Stuart made the first of her pretensions to the English crown. That same day, Henri II of France died in a tilt, by the lance of Gabriel de Lorges. That made Mary a queen indeed; but of fair France, as the wife of François II. Sixteen months later he was dead. On his sad demise, the widow wrote an elegy which utterly ignored him, but stressed with a charming pathos the blight on her own " sweet spring." Immediately Charles IX, a sickly child of ten, succeeded to the throne. His mother, Catherine de' Medici, had never liked Queen Mary.

So in the August of 1561, when Philip was not yet seven, the pretty Queen Dowager reluctantly sought her native kingdom in Scotland. To the country of psalm-singing and stern morals, she brought a splendid cargo of French hoods, farthingales, lutes and missals, ruffs, priests and romantic young courtiers like the gallant Chastelard who was so shortly to be fished from under her bed by scandalized ladies-in-waiting. Her galleys put into Leith in a chill fog. There was no one to meet her. Similar had been her welcome to those same bleak shores nineteen years before. For then James V, gazing on his new born daughter, had raised himself from his couch sufficiently to say: " The Devil go with it! "

While young Philip was shooting his first bird bolts into the trees about Penshurst Place, his uncle Robert was aiming even higher at court. He and Elizabeth had been born on the same day and in the same hour. Together they had been prisoners in the Tower. And in their common durance, Dudley had managed to convince Elizabeth of his entire devotion although he was at that very moment doing penance for the plot to steal her crown! He had to do with a lady who at no time in her career was unduly soft, either of heart or head.

Incontestably, Lord Robert had fascinations! Now that the Princess was Queen and " the best match in her parish," Robert showed a continued disposition to share her fortunes, and she to find him fascinating. In the company of her suitors at twenty-five, were Philip of Spain, the Archduke Charles of Austria, Eric of Sweden, the Earl of Arran, even her premier noble, the fussy old Earl of Arundel, who wooed her practically with whole cupboards of costly plate. Of the lot, William Cecil feared Lord Robert as likeliest to succeed. The Queen had made him Master of Horse. " Robin " was consulted about everything. Gossip soon ran that the unconventional daughter of the Tudors visited him " in his chamber day and night." Most dreadful thought: " She wishes to do as her Father did! "

What Elizabeth really wished, it is not easy to get at.

What the Dudleys wished is clearer. They wanted Lord Robert to marry the Queen. Little Philip's mother, who had some of Northumberland's flair for intrigue, helped to the best of her ability. Commissioned by the Queen, she tested out old Bishop Quadra, the Spanish Ambassador, to discover how King Philip would stand affected to the match. The Bishop was wary, but pleased at the prospect of using his master's support to win " these heretics " back to the old faith.

However Cecil was not pleased. Rumor ran on. Lord Robert had a wife. But she was ailing. She would grow worse without doubt. Just watch! The week after she " went," Lord Robert would marry the Queen.

In 1560 when little Philip was six, the scandalous prediction came true. His aunt, Amy Robsart died. "She broke her neck. She must have fallen down a staircase! " said the Queen. But a few days before the catastrophe, the Bishop recorded that Elizabeth returning from the hunt had told him that " Lord Robert's wife was dead, or nearly so " ! It was, perhaps, scarcely surprising that Arundel should order an investigation. Nor that ministers should make a nuisance of themselves by speaking " roundly " from their pulpits. Nor that Sir Henry Sidney should feel it necessary to assure Quadra that the charge against Lord Robert was without basis. Nor that Cecil should discreetly threaten Elizabeth with the growing dissatisfaction of the people. Always sensitive to the popular temperature, Elizabeth summoned the Bishop.

To him she " confessed " with a sweet frankness that " she was no angel, and did not deny that she had some affection for Lord Robert," but she had " not yet decided " to marry him — or anybody else. Her protestations did not prevent Quadra from sending a rare tale to Philip in Spain, soon after. Elizabeth and her Master of Horse were really married after all! It had happened at the Earl of Pembroke's London house of Barnard's Castle. The proof? When they had returned together, the Queen's own waiting-women had asked her " whether they were to kiss Dudley's hand as well as her own." When the Bishop was taken to task for reporting mere rumor, he had blandly replied that " considering the way people were talking, he did not think he would injure the Queen by saying she was married! "

Clearly, the Catholic party was scandalized. Lord Robert could hope for no support from them now. Resourcefully, he tried out the Protestants in France, to find they were not edified either. Therefore Dudley, who inherited his father's flexibility as well as his ambition, settled back to wait. If Elizabeth had not been as fond of Lord Robert as she ever allowed herself to be of anyone, she might well have feared this man. The old leaven was at work in the new loaf.

What, then, of the bannock? Sir Henry probably often wondered how much of the old Duke there was in his young Philip. He was a solemn child, even as a wee lad "never other than man." The terrible travail of sorrow which had torn his mother in the months before his coming had left its mark on a boy whom his parents adjured " to be merry."

We do not know at what stage Philip first heard of the grandfather who had burned his fingers reaching for the sun. If the tale came from his mother, we may be sure it lost little in telling. In that project, as in this later scheme of her brother's, Lady Mary had borne her part. Undoubtedly she passed on to her small son the intense family pride, the sense of the Dudley glory which had sustained her in the bitter days after her father's fall. Now they were serving her anew over years in which, like another Jacob, Lord Robert was serving for a royal Rachel, and people who did not stickle to charge him with adultery and murder were not chary of references to Tower Hill! Years later, when

sensitive Philip had won a rarer poise than his mother ever
knew, he was to write certain ringing words:

*My chiefest honor is to be a Dudley, and truly I am glad
to have cause to set forth the nobility of that blood whereof
I am descended.*

*Our house received such an overthrow. Hath none else
in England done so? I will not seek to wash away the dishonor with honorable tears. But this I may justly and boldly
affirm: let the last fault of the Duke be buried!*

There had been tears, then. If Sidney could write thus of
" dishonor " at thirty, what must have been the poignant
hurt of the child who heard it first? What series of small
victories lay behind the shield of soberness which he bore
with him to Shrewsbury School? There he would meet
sons of both gentlemen and " very common people " who
had read of his grandfather as a traitor in the pages of
Holinshed's *Chronicle.* We may be sure that with his little
rapier he buckled on a mighty resolution to do something
with his life to bring old glories back to the Dudleys.

He rode off to Shrewsbury on his own little nag in October 1564, before he was ten. Already he was a small personage. Undoubtedly he knew it. With him he had as servants a
lad of his own age named Randall Calcott and an older man
named Thomas Marshall.

For four years since 1560, his father had been Lord President of Wales. In 1562 he had gone to France as ambassador in those terrible Wars of Religion, and in the autumn,
the Queen had sent him to Edinburgh. There he had seen the
great preacher, John Knox, and had had audience with
the pretty Queen of Scots in her garden. Philip was justly
proud of his father!

He had cause to be proud of his mother, too, for in 1562,
most devoted of waiting-women, she had nursed the Queen

through smallpox. Mercifully, Elizabeth was unmarred. Philip's mother had caught the cruel disease. Although Sir Harry left her " a full fair lady," to him " at least the fairest," on his return he found her " as foul as small-pox could make her." After that Lady Mary had not gone to court unless summoned. Even at home she wore a mask. Against heartbreak, the gallant soul had needed no veil but pride. But this was a matter of complexion!

Philip was doubtless more than a little sorry to leave his mother and the younger children. Red-headed Mary in wee ruff and trailing gown was already a fascinating witch at three. Robert was not yet a year old. However regrets do not last long on a highroad — not for a boy who has seen it only from park gates! The pangs of parting were doubtless forgot by the time Master Philip proudly led his entourage into the parlor of the first inn, and ordered his beef and small beer with dignity. Dignity sat well on one who had already been inducted into two church benefices, and who had for a full year drawn money for his little holland shirts from a Welsh prebend!

The school at Shrewsbury had been founded by Edward VI in buildings then far from new. It stood just across from the Council House to which on certain days Sir Henry came to administer the business of the stout little Welsh kingdom. Close by was Shrewsbury Castle, " built in such a brave plot that it could have espied a bird flying in every street." The town, ten centuries old, stood on a peninsula of rising ground surrounded by the Severn on all sides but the north. Its streets bore quaint names like Shoplatch, Pride Hill and Dogpole.

Philip soon knew those streets well. In frosty winter he ran along them long before daylight, for the boys who came from a distance were " tabled" by townsmen who were surety for their behavior outside the classroom and

engaged to see that they attended church twice on Sunday.
Philip lived with a Mr. Leigh. He must have broken fast
early to be ready to kneel for prayers in the cold school-
room precisely as the bell tolled six! After that there were
lessons. Marshall's accounts, which despite the ravages of
damp and the Penshurst mice, may still be read, have a
cheerless entry:

> *To wax sises to burne in*
> *the scoole amorninges before daie*   *iiij* d

At eleven the boys were released for dinner. But at quarter before one the bell summoned them from their various
lodgings for further prayers and further lessons till half-
past four in winter and an hour later in summer. The combined vacation time at Christmas, Easter and Whitsuntide
yielded a bare month's holiday!

Featured in the curriculum was the participation in Latin
plays which were acted once a year in an outdoor theater
called the "Quarrel." Diversions officially sanctioned were
chess, wrestling, leaping and that patriotic exercise, shooting with the long bow. Surreptitiously there was attendance
on bull and bearbaitings. But only the utterly "lewd" and
abandoned sank to the level of playing at "fote-ball."

Marshall has one item about the mending of a "glasse
windowe" in Master Philip's "chambre" and another
about

> *an oz. of oile of roses and an other*
> *of camomell to suppell his knee that*
> *he coulde not plie or bende*   *vj* d

which does not sound as if all of his charge's energies went
into conning his Cato. Indeed, the complaint of townsmen
concerning "unreasonable noises, fightings and disorders,"
especially at election time, indicates that most of the young
Salopians were of a lively habit. Little Calcott wore out

several pairs of shoes to Philip's one. However young Sidney's bills for washing were just double Randall's. Activity takes various forms.

While the useful Marshall was making worn doublets over into hose, and Philip was learning to write the clear hand demanded in those unregenerate days, Sir Henry was named Lord Deputy of Ireland. Like everybody else who had once served in that turbulent isle, he showed a marked reluctance to return. In fact, he said he would rather go anywhere else! Yet when the Queen persuaded, Sir Henry accepted the calamitous charge as a painful duty.

He was not disappointed in the pain. Lady Mary insisted on sharing trouble. She was not disappointed, either, for she narrowly escaped abduction by Shan O'Neil at Drogheda! To Philip alone did the prospect hold joy, for he had been granted a special holiday to ride up to Chester with Calcott and Marshall, and make his farewells to his parents.

When Sir Henry and his wife finally took ship at Holyhead, their Irish tribulations had already begun. The vessel containing all Lady Mary's household gear, her plate, her jewels and every stitch of clothes she was taking to Ireland, foundered and sunk. The loss came to £1500. No wonder there were new economies to be practised on Philip's wardrobe, and Marshall set down in apology the need of making him

> a coate to waire with his cape againste
> Christmas not havinge any fitte garments to
> go in.

His lady mother was in like case!

To Dublin Castle Philip sent letters in his newly acquired French and Latin. These productions Sir Henry received, as a father should, " in good part." He wrote in return a letter full of the good advice respectfully received in the sixteenth century. It begins with an exhortation to the use of prayer as " an ordinary act and at an ordinary hour." However, there is a worldliness in the recommendation to be courteous to all men "with a diversity of reverence according to the dignity of the person." Philip is to eat moderately and to drink wine " seldom." But he is told to "accustom " himself to wine, lest " being enforced to drink on a sudden," he may " become inflamed." He shall " use exercise of the body " choosing such as is " without peril to bones and joints " — this is scarcely advice for a bookworm! Always he is to "delight to be cleanly in body " that he may " be grateful in each company," otherwise " loathsome." (Ours are not the only days of plain speaking.)

Sir Henry continues with precepts which do much to explain the aura of perfection which gathered about Philip's head at a Greenwich where even the Queen swore and — shall we say quibbled?

Let never oath be heard to come out of your mouth. . . . Above all things, tell no untruth; no, not in trifles. . . . And let it not satisfy you that for a time the hearer take it for a truth; for after, it will be known as it is, to your shame. For there cannot be a greater reproach . . . than to be accounted a liar. . . .

Tenderly enough, this Polonius recognizes the moral limitations of a twelve-year-old:

Well, my little Philip, this is enough for me, and too much, I fear, for you!

Yet before he has done, he adds to general ethical truths a bit of particularity:

Give yourself to be merry. . . .
Remember, my son, the noble blood you are descended

The Great Hall at Penshurst Place.

of by your mother's side; and think that only by virtuous
life and good action, you may be an ornament to that illus-
trious family.

They both knew the incentive. Rare indeed, in the days of
formal family relationships, was the understanding between
this fine Christian gentleman and his trusty little lad.

In February of the same year, 1566, Philip acquired two
mighty aids to the virtuous life and good action enjoined
by his father. Marshall bought him " a Virgile " and " Cal-
vines chatachisme." The combination is typical of the
Renaissance in England. There, almost from the begin-
nings of humanism at the end of the fifteenth century, the
warm loveliness of ancient art and literature had worn
some moral garb. Beauty in her naked glory was, perhaps
not improperly, thought to be dangerous.

Virgil was always balanced by some Calvin or other.
Not that Virgil was not sufficiently moral of himself when
the good monks who had loved him through the Middle
Ages had done turning him into a Christian allegorist.
Long since he had ceased to sing of a pagan Aeneas, who
fled from Troy to Rome, and was guided through Avernus
by Apollo's Golden Bough. Long before Philip's time, this
Aeneas had become any learned and pious Christian. His
journey now lay from the Hell of this world to the
blessings of Heaven hereafter. He found the true path by
grace of the Bough of Wisdom which he plucked from
God's tree of Virtue.

Probably some time before he came to Shrewsbury after
this Branch of Knowledge which would make him good,
Philip had read the passage in Virgil on that " goldilocks
of boughs " in the new translation of " fairest Phaer ":

When one bough broken is, another springs as fresh in sight
Of gold, and twigs are ever alike, with buds of metall bright,

*Seeke out therefore with speede, and whan thou duely hast
    it spied*
*Lay thou thereon thy hand, for willingly, with ease,
    onwried,*
It selfe it shall release, if destinies thee therto call,
For otherwise, not break if will, for strength nor wepons all.

Now as he conned the Latin, *Si te fata vocant* leapt out at
him from the page. *If Destinies thee call.* Those were
almost the words of the Sidney motto upon his father's
scutcheon! They represented what he was to seek, the
more as he was " mindful of the noble blood " from his
mother's side. His grandfather had not waited on Destiny.
He must. And only by winning this Golden Bough of
Wisdom was he sure of knowing what was Virtue and
what was Fate.

Upon his infant searchings into mighty matters which
have occupied many a lifetime, summons came in early
August 1566, to a different kind of glory. The Queen was
coming to Oxford! Uncle Robert, who was now the great
Earl of Leicester and Chancellor of Oxford University, had
bidden him come with his attendants and fetch Master
Aston, the head of Shrewsbury School.

There had been a great pother about clothes. It appeared that one might not gaze on the Queen in hose thrift-
ily patched up from old doublets! A fine new wardrobe
was packed into the little trunk which bore the bear and
ragged staff before which every beggar louted by the road's
side.

Master Philip himself rode a fettlesome horse, more than
a little hard to manage, which was a gift from Lord Ferrers
of Chartley. Lord Ferrers would soon be Earl of Essex.
Already he was father to a little lass of three named
Penelope and a very new son to be called Robert; with one,
Philip Sidney would yet fall in love, and with the other,

Elizabeth herself. For the nonce, though, Philip's most poignant pang had to do with " two canvas alum bagges " full of school books, which formed part of the luggage. That was the trouble of taking Master Aston, he thought moodily, as his mind shaped the next Latin sentence with which to address the learned gentleman who rode soberly beside him.

And so, away from the blue Welsh hills and the shining Severn, went the impressive cavalcade past green hedge-rows and timbered houses with clustered gables, westward to the gray and ancient city of Oxford.

THE THIRD CHAPTER ENTITLED GLORIANA THE MAGNIFICENT.

HE years of his wooing had made Leicester enemies. That they did him so little mischief is, perhaps, the best proof that Elizabeth loved him. To oust the favorite, " old " nobles like Arundel, Norfolk and Sussex united with the " new " man William Cecil who was now Chief Secretary. They all feared the upstart whom they called " the son of a Duke, the brother of a King, the grandson of an Esquire and the great-grandson of a Carpenter who was the only honest man in the family, and the only one who died in his bed." Clearly, they hoped there would not be two!

The Duke of Norfolk openly remonstrated with Robin. It was not seemly, he said, this bearing about the Queen's bedchamber of " a garment which ought never to be seen in the hands of her Majesty's Master of Horse," this kissing of the Queen " without being invited thereto."

But none dared take Elizabeth to task. She found dis-cretion unnecessary. Perhaps it was. In the royal bedcham-ber with its gilded ceiling and its one small casement, she showed Robin's portrait to the ambassador of Scottish Mary, Sir James Melville. Holding the candle close, he saw she had written upon it in her own hand, " My lord's pic-ture." At Michaelmas 1564, she made of Lord Robert no less than the Earl of Leicester. As he knelt, handsome, be-fore her, she " lovingly tickled his neck " inside the perfumed ruff. " How do you like him? " was the question she put to Melville.

Sir James was not habited to any great decorum in Queens. (In fact at the time he was schooling Mary in Scottish propriety.) Yet he was shocked. So, even, the foul-mouthed Bothwell, who having observed Elizabeth in action, brutally announced that " both queens would not make one honest woman."

What alarmed others gave Leicester hope. In October 1564, he resumed his angling for Spanish support. In the summer of 1565 he entertained the Queen magnificently at the Kenilworth she had given him. Though in August Cecil noted with satisfaction that Elizabeth was " very much offended" with Leicester, she shortly after herself announced that she could " not live without seeing him every day "; he was like her lap-dog, as soon as he was seen anywhere, folk said she was at hand! By December Leicester became insistent. Being lap-dog excluded all other occupation, and was expensive to boot. He wanted his answer by Christmas. The Queen put him off to Candlemas. In February 1566, she was as uncertain as ever. Cecil, however, was certain. He laid before her " Sixe Objeccions " to the marriage! Chief and most telling, was public opposition.

Even at court not every one shared her Highness's delight in Lord Leicester. Arundel had come to fisticuffs with him. In Council meeting Dudley and Sussex had threatened each other, and only six weeks before Elizabeth came to Oxford, she compounded differences between them. However often Leicester and Sussex might strike hands, under constraint, these two uncles of Philip Sidney hated each other with gusto. On his dying bed, the Christian Sussex was to say of Robin: " Beware the gipsy. You do not know the nature of the beast as I do! "

In this August of 1566, Leicester might well have wished himself gipsy, if only to look into the heart of the inscrutable Queen. In one breath she swore she would never marry. In the next she fondly declared that " should she alter her determination, she would chose none other " than him!

Of the hates and loves in these mighty bosoms, our Philip knew little. To him, the Queen was not so much a possible aunt as the glorious bodying forth of his glorious England. And Leicester was a handsome and generous uncle who was providing a particularly delightful holiday.

For the holiday Elizabeth was grateful as well. She needed it. Against terrific odds she was shaping England from confusion and weakness into union and strength. If she performed the miracle by equivocations, by a score of changes of mind to a weather-cock's one, by taking long chances and giving short shrift, it took all the more out of her. Penurious and pinching when it came to pennies, of herself she was a very prodigal.

The most annoying of the troubles that wore her that summer was the coil of Scottish Mary. In the nick of time, Elizabeth had manoeuvered her out of a match with Don Carlos which would have united Scotland and Spain against her little England. Desperately in 1564 she had laid Robin on the altar. If her dear sister must marry, she should have " the best." Why not Leicester? But Mary was shrewd. She wrote back that she looked " on the offer of a person so dear to Elizabeth as proof of good will rather than of good meaning." In short, exceeding good sense . . . less!

Then without consulting Elizabeth at all she had married at Holyrood in late July 1565, the long lad, Henry Stuart, Lord Darnley. Months before Elizabeth had been " scandalized " when Mary had gone to his chamber to nurse the boy through the measles.

Now she had even livelier reason for horror: Darnley's mother, the Countess of Lennox, was Pretender to the English throne! It was small comfort to Elizabeth that the bridegroom had been " stylit kyng " without consent of the Scots Parliament, or that John Knox had infuriated the newly married pair by preaching before them at St. Giles of " Ahab and Jezabel joined in Idolatrye." She had more solace in the scandalous rumors which soon drifted south about Rizzio. On March 9th, 1566 the Italian Secretary had been murdered as he clutched at Queen Mary's skirts. They buried him with Darnley's dagger in his heart, though Darnley had been afraid to thrust it home himself. After that the husband and wife could not be " three days together without a riot." In such peace was James Stuart born in the June of 1566.

A sweated post brought the news to Cecil in Cannon Row. In haste he had come to Greenwich to whisper it in Elizabeth's ear. The dancing and music stopped on a sudden, for she had turned white. The ladies who fluttered about her caught the honest expression of her tortured soul: " The Queen of Scots is the lighter of a fair son; but I am of a barren stock! "

Next morning however Elizabeth was herself. When Melville came with the news officially, she met him " with a merry volt." She rejoiced in her sister's good fortune. She was delighted to be godmother.

Nevertheless she had suffered a shrewd blow. In his small person James united the pretensions of both parents to the English throne. Others saw the point beside Elizabeth. The Pope sent 20,000 crowns to Mary, with the assurance of 4000 a month for such army as she " might need." Philip of Spain renewed to her his promises of help. Most alarming of all, the Catholic nobles in Elizabeth's own bailiwick of North England were just enough disgruntled to make common cause with any invading army that promised to restore the old faith.

Elizabeth's was not merely the cry of the childless woman. This danger of James cut at something more vital than her own concerns, the safety of England itself. Had she not been deterred by the ill augury of an ungrateful Darnley, she might at this stage have given to Leicester the favorable answer which he had bided so long.

But wiser than Mary, Elizabeth saw that her strength was in remaining free. Free to seek (but never to make!) the Protestant marriage, or the Catholic marriage, whichever might for the moment balance forces against which she could not contend. Besides, in a nipping remark of Melville there was real truth. She had a " stately stomach." Had she married, she would have been merely Queen of England. As it was, she could be " king and queen baith! "

Thus in maiden meditation, fancy (but not trouble) free, Elizabeth came to Oxford. She would scarcely have been the daughter of Anne Boleyn and Harry Tudor if she had not eagerly abandoned the political cumber for the prospect of pageants, shows and goodly " bankets."

Philip had been in Oxford more than a week. First they had gone to Kenilworth. For one thing, Master Philip had been troubled with " meriegalles and breking furth through the heat," and needed rest. For another, Marshall wished to " speke with my Lorde of Lecestre for the knowledge of his apparell."

Evidently my Lord thought little enough thereof, for a long list of really proper raiment was ordered from William Whitell, the Earl's own tailor in London. Puritan writers might (and did) point out that the Children of Israel wore " theire Fathers attire fortie yeeres togither in the wildernesse." However, Philip was not faring into the wilderness of Judah, but to the court of the Queen of England. He must be furnished bravely. His uncle's generosity provided him with damask gowns trimmed with velvet; with doublets of " crimosin and green taffety "; with jerkins of blue leather, and of white compassed with parchment lace of gold; hose of carnation color; and shoes of white and green and blue!

While tailors in London worked cross-legged by candlelight to finish all this glory, Philip's little train traveled to an Oxford sweet in the meadows and gardens that swept up to its very walls. At the west gate they entered. Through the north, the Bocardo, the Queen was to come and folk were already preparing. So past the Norman Castle of St. George, they rode softly to Carfax. That queer name, our young scholar knew, was a corruption of *Quadrifurcus,* or the Four Ways. From there he had the sight for which he had waited, the gray beauty of a dozen colleges set in green turf and embowered in flowers!

As they followed the High Street, on the left hand there rose the wonder of Magdalen Tower, delicate and stately. They could see it from the upper windows of the inn where they lodged and Philip tried to read Sallust with Mr. Aston, though his mind was far from the wars of Jugurtha.

However, they were not long for inns. On Sunday, August 25th, they were bidden to Lincoln College. The Rector there was one of Leicester's chaplains, a Mr. Bridgewater. (In Latin conversations Philip had to remember to call him *Magister Aquaepontanus!*) On Thursday, Leicester came on ahead of the court. With him was Cecil who always was fond of Philip and somewhat later would seek him as son-in-law. As they checked over lists together and made sure of all the royal arrangements, Leicester listened to a Latin oration in his honor. Because of the rainstorm, it could not be delivered out-of-doors. He heard it in the commissary's lodgings at Christ's Church, not to upset the ordered Great Hall. In but two days' space, Elizabeth was coming.

Bright and early on Saturday that last day of August, the gray city seethed with activity. There was much for a boy to see. Leicester riding out to escort the Queen from Walvicote. The streets swarming with the " faithful subject " come from every hamlet about, with undergraduates, with the Mayor and Aldermen and burgesses glorious in scarlet who gravely filed out from Bocardo to meet her a mile from the city. Then the University Orator, Roger Marbeck, under his gown the Latin oration in which he would greet Elizabeth. Then mere pushing and shoving for place — and waiting.

At last there were shrill cries from small townsmen precariously perched in the tower of St. Michael's Church which had been watching turret to the city walls in times less peaceful. The Queen was coming! Eager for first glimpse of the Queen, the crowd pressed close around the Bocardo.

First there rode in Clarenceux-king-at-arms who managed all royal processions. Followed three Esquire Bedells carrying golden staves. Then came the Chancellor of the University, looking very splendid and handsome, with the Mayor at his right hand. Thereafter the Queen's chief nobles. Among them rode Philip's uncles, the Earls of Warwick and Huntingdon; Don Guzman de Silva, the Spanish ambassador who was his father's friend; the Earl of Ormonde, who was his enemy; the Earl of Oxford with whom Philip would himself contend in time; and Mr. William Cecil on a gentle nag, for he suffered severely from gout. At last came the royal lictors bearing huge scepters of gold, and, bearing the jeweled sword of state, that "other uncle" of Philip's, the Earl of Sussex.

Then, climactic in glory Elizabeth herself, the " greatest Gloriana " of Spenser. In a litter open on all sides, drawn by mules gay in scarlet and gold, she sat on a high golden seat. Her headdress was of spun gold, her dress of scarlet silk interwoven with gold, partly obscured by a mantle of purple and ermine. Her shrewd eyes shone with an honest delight in the plaudits and the wind stirred her hair, as red as her glorious temper. By her side rode the royal cursitors in coats of cloth-of-gold, and marshals to restrain the loyalty of the crowd which was eager to press as close to the Virgin Queen as it could.

Like minor stars in a firmament already dazzled by the sun, came the ladies-in-waiting, rich in jewels and cloth-of-gold and of silver. After them Spanish jennets in silken trappings and " led " horses with no riders, whose feet made a neat clopped din on the roadway. Last of all, two hundred of the royal guard in gold and scarlet who bore on their shoulders huge bows and iron clubs.

Into the restrained beauty of Oxford, all this glory swept, to halt within the Bocardo where Robert Deale of New College greeted Her Majesty on behalf of the students. The procession then went on. Young scholars in academic garb lined both sides of Northgate Street to Carfax. As the Queen passed, they knelt and cried " *Vivat Regina!* " Graciously Elizabeth gave them her thanks in " *Gratias ago.* "

At Carfax there was a Greek oration to which the Queen replied in kind. Unfortunately her answer was Greek to the mules who drew her litter. Noticeably they were bored. Worse than that they were restless. Though she finished to the admiration of all her other hearers, Elizabeth was obviously annoyed.

Between ranks of bachelors and masters and learned doctors, she passed to the Great Hall of Christ's Church. There the witless mules were dismissed and Gloriana sat under the oaken roof of Wolsey's oldest building to hear a Latin oration by an unfortunate Mr. Kingsmill. When he had done she declared that " it would have been well," if he had had anything to say! And she greeted the Puritan Laurence Humphrey with the tart remark: " Mr. Doctor, that loose gown becomes you well. I wonder your notions should be so narrow! "

Her feelings thus relieved, she proceeded under a golden canopy to the Cathedral. There she knelt as the Dean praised God for her coming. The company now dispersed. Elizabeth went to her lodgings through the garden and ladies-in-waiting whisked in and out of the chambers of Christ's Church recently vacated by the scholars.

Probably some time in the day, the Chancellor presented his nephew to Gloriana. Kissing her truly lovely hands, Philip made his first courtier's speech. Later as he knew her Majesty better, he came to admire her less — and vastly more. Always he was devoted, too devoted to tell her untruths. " No, not in trifles." Though she might rail at his inconvenient ethics Gloriana called him " My Philip." To distinguish him from the King of Spain. A very different person!

On Sunday night there was a Latin play in the hall of Christ Church. The Queen was indisposed and did not attend. Doubtless our Philip saw all the marvels of the stage " set about with stately lights of wax variously wrought," the tiered seats and the empty royal bower fairly decked with tapestries and cloth-of-gold. When Elizabeth heard of the grandeurs she had missed, she was " inconsolable," by which we may gather that Philip, seeing, was greatly impressed.

They both enjoyed *Palamon and Arcite,* a play by Richard Edwards, Master of the Children of the Chapel. The costumes were most gorgeous. Emilia wore apparel once belonging to Elizabeth's sister, Queen Mary. (There was a rare pother later when " one forequarter " of the gown, "a purple vellat " without sleeves, was lost.) In the course of the hunting scene, undergraduates hallooed and barked in the college quadrangle with such rare realism that Gloriana cried out from her box most merrily, " Oh, excellent! These boys in very troth are ready to leap out of the windows to follow the hounds! "

As the performance was actually in English, it was heavily attended by townsfolk who were making all they could of their one opportunity to understand what was going on. So great was the press that the wall of a stone staircase fell with a crash. Three persons were killed. Fortunately (say the accounts) no one of the court, and only one scholar! Elizabeth was " very sorry for the mishappe and forthwith sent her own surgeons." The victims were past all help. The play seems to have continued.

Among the many Latin disputations which her Majesty attended, the one which interested her most was to the effect that *The moon is the Cause of the Ebb and Flow of the Tides.* Mr. Edmund Campion of St. John's was the respondent. He was a protégé of Sir Henry Sidney. Soon after he became a Jesuit. Philip saw him again in Prague eleven years later. In December 1581, he died for his faith, most horribly at Tyburn. Now he was linking the names of Elizabeth and the new Chancellor, just subtly enough to please them both. A much safer occupation.

On Thursday in Saint Mary's Church her Majesty made to the whole university a " very comfortable and eloquent oration " in Latin. As she discoursed, her eye fell on Cecil standing on his lame foot. Halting immediately, she ordered a stool for him, and only after he had been comfortably seated, did she resume her Latinity. When she had finished, the very walls resounded to thunders of loyal (and well-deserved) applause.

On Friday there were long faces. The Queen's departure was imminent. The fronts of St. Mary's, All Souls' and University College were white with the " schedes of verses " which attested the irreparable woe of individual students. After dinner, Mr. Toby Matthew, in the name of the colleges, bade the Queen farewell. His speech took flattering account of her wonderful oration, her accomplishments in Learning (for once not exaggerated), and the mighty honor she had done the place in coming. So deftly eloquent was Mr. Toby as to be nominated Queen's Scholar on the spot.

Now at last, the procession of six days before formed
again. Philip must have been as sorry as any to see the gold
and glitter of it sweep through the High Street, pausing at
the lovely Magdalen Tower to receive the farewells of the
city's representative, where the liberties ended. He may possibly have been allowed to follow after with Mr. Marbeck to
Shotover which marked the bounds of the university. There
with deep feeling, the Orator made his final remarks. The
Queen took her own leave in words which are more rhetorical in English than in the sonorous Latin in which she pro-
nounced them: " Farewell, the worthy university of Oxford; farewell, my dear scholars, and God prosper your
studies; farewell, farewell."

The town to which her " scholars " returned seemed
quiet and empty and a little shabby without her.

Two days later, Philip and Mr. Aston and an erudite
gentleman named Wilson who had written a book on *The
Arte of Rhetorique* left the sweet worn beauty of Oxford
behind them. They rode along wooded roads already sharp
with September on the long journey back to Shrewsbury.

At Chipping Norton they halted. Within the red-cur-
tained inn-parlor Philip had a blind harper play for him.
Later Marshall gave him a shilling, a very splendid gra-
tuity. We can only guess that the tune Philip liked so much
was the *Ballad of Chevy Chase*. If so, he bought it " good
chepe." For many years later he wrote of the nature of
poetry, this youth who was a poet himself. He said then

> *I never heard the old Song of Percy and Douglas that I
> found not my heart moved more than with a trumpet, and
> yet it was sung by some blind crowder with no rougher
> voice than rude style.*

Was this his coal of Isaiah?

On the 9th of September, the party tarried at a town
which to Marshall was " Stratforde upon Havon." There

they needed the services of a smith and a saddler who worked while Master Philip and his two grave guardians had dinner. At a stretcher table in a house on Henley Street not far from the bridgehead inn where they tarried, a child of two was having his pottle of milk and brown country loaf, knowing little and caring less for the heir of the great Earl of Leicester. The tiny lad was William Shakespeare.

Philip, had he known it, was that day, even closer to glory than when he kissed the lovely hands of England's greatest queen.

THE FOURTH CHAPTER
ENTITLED PAN
ON OLIVET.

 HEN Philip next came to Oxford, he was one of the seven hundred scholars which the university gathered about her knees, in the days when boys entered at twelve. To such hopeful infants, Christ Church, at which he enrolled, stood a parable in stone to the perils of mere existence. Wolsey built it from a ravaged priory and named it Cardinal. When he fell, Henry VIII called it King's. Now it was Christ's.

That last was parable too — of the piety of English humanism. Spenser ran true to form when he put his " great God Pan upon Mount Olivet." Let other lands if they chose worship all that the ancients wrote! England admired only the moral. Thus Philip might read Petronius and Juvenal, but solely in " selections." He was taught that the Latin of Ovid was pure in *Metamorphoses,* not so pure in the *Art of Love.* Horace passed muster. But the sultry Catullus? Never! In that time of burgeoning beauty when the New Learning arrived in Oxford, less than a century before, her greatest figure had been Erasmus, the moral. There the austere Dutch scholar felt himself absolutely at home. He found even the climate " pleasant," perhaps because it was " wholesome."

No one so great as Erasmus was teaching in Philip's day. The old time lived on, but chiefly in the curriculum. That went back to the Middle Ages. Officially Philip made banquet on grammar, rhetoric and logic. Mathematics he supped on lightly and music ended the feast. The greater part of his training was in Latin disputations. Latin was justified as the magic carpet which bore him into the company of the learned in every nation in Europe. It enabled him to hold converse with William of Orange, without any Dutch. It made him at home in Frankfurt, without a word of German. And resolutely Oxford refused to teach any modern language. Nor, though the face of Europe might change overnight, any modern history. Nor, though new worlds were still being charted, any geography. Philosophy still meant Aristotle. More complete isolation from contact with reality could scarcely have been achieved — except in a vacuum. Youth was still trained for the cloister. At the end of four years, or of three if the scholars were nobles (here, at least, touch of this earth!) they were loosed on a dangerous world.

Fortunately, even then, boys resisted their education. They learned much from each other drifting on the narrow streams about Oxford while they discussed every topic there was; reading the *Hundred Merry Tales* of Boccaccio and the love poetry of Petrarch, another " modern." They told tales on their tutors and punned on their names. Philip's was Nathaniel Baxter. But Philip called him *Tergaster* and thought well of himself, for *terga* meant *backs* in Latin! Providently these scholars kept up a rapier practice which would serve them better than Plato in the dark alleys of London. Sedulously they cherished a pretty taste in doublets. That and a " sweet breast " for the lute would win a lady sooner than any amount of Hebrew. Back of Bocardo, they held mock disputations on *Which was the elder: the " stirrops " of Alexander the Great or the Dutch butter at dinner?* Joyously they harried the watch, were " unthrifte of their credite " at inns, sang jovial tunes on their walks, like *Hunt's Up* and *Lusty Gallant.* Or wakened wistful echoes in Christ Church meadow with the haunting refrain of Anne Boleyn's song in her prison.

> *None hath power, o'er an hour*
> *Of his life bereaving.*

From them a silent Philip learned of comradeship under tall Tudor chimney-pieces rich with oaken carvings and plaster scrolls. Came to love Virgil anew as his own delight was warmed by that of his fellows. Came to love all literature, not merely the sacred classics but the simple ballad and story that in his own fine phrase " holdeth children from play and old men from the chimney corner."

His mates were a brilliant crew. There was the old companion of Shrewsbury days, Fulke Greville. In time he played Robin Goodfellow to Elizabeth's waiting maids, and gallantly took on himself the blame for their sweet mischief. Poor soul, he died by the stab of a servant. But first he wrote Philip's *Life,* and gave direction for a tombstone on which, confident of glory, he inscribed himself " The Friend of Sir Philip Sidney." There was William Camden already grave in his ruff who turned antiquarian later and wrote *The History of Elizabeth.* Richard Hooker who was destined to chronicle her *Ecclesiastical Polity.* George Peele and John Lyly who brought a lovely grace to the masques and plays of her court. Lyly who would shape the very speech in her courtiers' mouths when he wrote his *Euphues.* Thomas Bodley who afterwards became merchant prince, leaving his coffers and name to dower the noblest of libraries in Oxford. Richard Stanihurst who translated the classics, leading the unlearned Briton to Virgil over even rougher seas than those traveled by Aeneas.

Walter Raleigh, handsome dark youth, spoke the broad speech of Devon. He joined a love of ribbands to a passion for the sea. He would yet spread a cloak at Gloriana's feet; with a gesture as gallant, lay before her, too, a whole new land in the western world to be called for her " Virginia." He would sail for gold to Guinea, write *The History of the World* from his lodging in the Tower, and come to his death on the block. In the times ahead, Walter and Philip would plan on a voyage together. Westward ho! for the finding of gold, and " garboiling " of Spain. This Walter was a man to mount. His hair was ruffled as by sea-breezes. Even when he tamed it, Elizabeth called him her " Ocean." Already he was full of tall tales. Few folk in Devon but kept a swift pinnace for a bit of pious piracy on the Spanish ships they might " meet " — enterprises strictly private, not to embarrass Gloriana (and to obviate sharing with her!). Fit chronicler for such adventures was sober Richard Hakluyt. Later he dedicated to Philip his *Divers Voyages* which told in ringing prose the prowess of English seamen.

There were two others, eager and subtle of mind, and so far, of Elizabeth's flock. Shortly they owned a new Shepherd, the Pope. Campion was Fellow of St. John's but he sought greater honor as martyr. Robert Parsons was Master of Balliol. Soon, now, he would be at Rheims, the head of the great Jesuit offensive against Gloriana and all her works. For years he kept her busy, matching intrigue with intrigue, but never catching him. Rumor would hold him responsible for the libelous book on Leicester known as " Parsons' Green Coat " from the verdant edge of its leaves. Loyal, furious Philip writing masterly trouncing reply, would challenge him to fight, in " any place in Europe! "

If this Oxford still slept with the centuries, there was drama enough slept with her.

Slept at Whitehall, too, for a conspiracy more immediate than any of Parsons was there secretly shaping itself under the noble Roman nose of Gloriana herself. As had hap-

pened before, and would after, Mary Stuart, so appealing
in widow's weeds, was at the bottom of it.

Mary was now twice a widow. Following close on her
passion for Bothwell, early in February 1567, she had toled
Darnley to a monastic ruin just outside the walls of Edinburgh, Kirk o' Field. There she had left him ill while she
went " for the night " to a wedding. First, with a strong
Scotch thrift that functioned even in a crisis, she removed
a costly bed. That night the house was blown to pieces, but
Darnley was strangled first. A month later, in mourning,
Mary married her Bothwell. Though strangely enough, she
was wedded by reformed rites, her people were not placated.
Furious rather, in June 1567, they shut her in Lochleven,
and a week later, forced her to abdicate in favor of infant
James.

For the next twelvemonth, Mary employed all her wits
and fascinations to get out of her island prison. Her third
attempt succeeded. She escaped May 2nd, 1568. Eleven
days later her army was defeated at Langsyde. On May
16th, she fled to Cumberland. She was safe on English soil,
yet her troubles were only beginning. Gloriana announced
she was sorry, but she could not bring her immaculate
Majesty to receive even a sister over whom there hung
charges of murder — and, here she shuddered, adultery!

Thoughtfully, though, she provided lodging in Bolton
Castle where Mary was virtually a prisoner. Better meet
charges for board, grumbled the thrifty Gloriana, than to
have Mary the fêted darling of English lords in Carlisle!
The expenditure was wise. Already Mary was plotting.
She had won over Thomas Howard, Duke of Norfolk
and Leicester's old enemy. Norfolk was Elizabeth's cousin,
powerful, thirty-three; handsome, weak and ambitious.
Mary's dish exactly.

Her plot was bold and simple: to rouse the Catholic
nobles and to get the help of Spain; to depose Elizabeth

and set herself on the throne. If Norfolk could compass this, she would make him her fourth husband and King Thomas of Catholic England. The scheme found ready supporters.

Early in 1569 while Philip Sidney was roaming Oxford meadows golden with gorse and prankish spring breezes were taking his ruff for the small sail it was, Mary wrote blithely from prison that before the year was out, she would be Queen of England! That her plan miscarried was the merest accident. Perhaps two accidents. One was due to Philip's precious uncle Leicester. The other to those pious pirates that Walter Raleigh told of.

The matching of Norfolk and Mary was more or less open secret. Even Elizabeth knew. Inviting Norfolk to dine at her own table, she gave him a friendly "nip." He had better, she said, " take good heed to his pillow." (Considering Kirk o' Field, she could hardly have done less!)

But Leicester urged the marriage. He hoped it would take Thomas to Scotland. Besides, he quite approved a part of the scheme (which Gloriana knew nothing of) which involved the " removal " of Cecil and Sussex. To him the whole plan was a pleasant arrangement which swept from his path the trio that opposed his espousals with Bess. Robin never despaired of that wedding.

But even Leicester did not know of the change of religion which the Norfolk marriage involved; nor of the danger to Elizabeth. Not until some time in July 1569!

Leicester might complain of "some spice or show of hysterick fitts " in his mistress, but to give the devil his due, this lover of hers was loyal. There was some real affection at the bottom of such pretty informal scenes as Norfolk himself had witnessed when he

came unaware into the Queen's privy chamber and found her Majesty sitting on the threshold of the door, listening with one ear to a little child who was singing and playing the lute to her, and with the other to Leicester who was kneeling by her side.

Just as soon as he saw that the plot threatened the Queen, Robin determined to tell her. Even his own selfish share.

Accordingly he took to his bed at Tichfield on July 27th, 1569 and sent her a mournful message. He was ill and like to die. First he must have her forgiveness. The ruse brought his doting mistress in a fine haste to his bedside.

White against his bolster, Leicester revealed the plot in the thin voice of one *in extremis*. With tears he confessed to writing to Scottish Mary to urge the match with Norfolk. What Elizabeth Tudor said doubtless had point and vigor. She may even have fetched Robin a box on the ear, despite his grievous illness.

Nevertheless she forgave him — Had he not done it for her sake? She bound him to secrecy. Then she sent Philip's uncle Huntingdon, to guard Scottish Mary more strictly, and bided her time.

The warning came none too soon. While Philip was hunting in the autumn woods about Oxford, Queen Mary was the whipper-in, who set her hounds after a royal quarry. But, just as all was ready for spur and hallooing, Elizabeth wound her horn from Windsor. Thither she summoned Norfolk.

He protested that he was ill. " Fever or no fever," he must come, was the stern order. On the instant! The guilty Norfolk fled. In short order he was arrested and clapped into the Tower.

Thereupon the Catholic lords of the North " rose " against Gloriana. Riding hard to Durham, on November 14th, 1569 they entered the mighty Cathedral, pillaged its Protestant altars, tore up Elizabeth's Prayer-book. After hearing Mass, they issued their ultimatum. They wanted

Robert Dudley Earl of Leicester, an Uncle out of Machiavelli.

Sussex and Cecil removed from Elizabeth's Council, Norfolk released, and above all, the old faith back. Swiftly Elizabeth ordered that Sussex march north with an army. By mid-December, he had the rebels beaten and in retreat. There was bloody business of " hangings," two hundred to a town. Young Yorkshire scholars at Oxford blanched as they sighted the post. " Not ten gentlemen" in that county but favored the old faith.

Then came merrier tidings. The rising had failed for lack of munitions and money which Philip of Spain had promised. He had sent them, too. But Elizabeth's pirates had stolen them in transit!

While the young cockerels were still crowing over this latest sally of Fortune, news came through that was no laughing matter. The Pope's Bull against the Queen duly translated in English was posted on the Bishop of London's palace gates in St. Paul's, of a morning in May 1570. Not only did it excommunicate her Majesty. It absolved from obedience to her all of her Catholic subjects! Bitter indeed was the choice which Catholics must now make in the little island they loved as home, for whatever course they took, they failed either Queen or Pope. That night, little lads of Christ Church who had kin of the old faith tossed on restless beds, in the buildings that Henry and Wolsey had ravaged from the monks.

Norfolk was released in June 1570, on his bond not to deal further with Mary " in that course of marriage " nor " with any cause belonging to her." If he did not " resume " conspiring, it was because he had never stopped. Even in prison, he had steadily heard from Mary. Once free he went at her work in earnest.

This time his " practice " amounted to high treason. Letters in cipher were shortly passing from Norfolk to the Pope, from the Pope to Spanish Philip, thence to Alva who was Philip's general in Flanders and so back to England.

They spoke of something as " it " and "the principal execution." By word of mouth, and behind closed doors, Ridolfi the trusted agent explained: as the first step in this new rebellion, the Queen herself must be " captured or killed " !

While cautious, deliberate Philip of Spain was being manoeuvered into giving consent to Elizabeth's murder (Rome was reported to have agreed), one of Mary's envoys was seized as he disembarked at Dover in April 1571. His capture told Cecil something, even though in the castle at Dover, his letters were spirited out of the way, and a dummy sent on in their stead. It was then only a matter of watching.

In August 1571, one of Norfolk's servants was laid by the heels, with £600 on him representing the contribution of Catherine de' Medici, Queen Mother of France, to the expense of dispatching Queen Bess.

Thus it appeared that, unknown to Spain, Mary was wangling money from France. She had even tried to wheedle funds from the thrifty Presbyterians in Scotland by promising that, under her, England would still be Protestant! Clearly Norfolk and Mary were guilty. Yet only Norfolk went to the Tower. Gloriana reverenced queens.

The news of this latest conspiracy burst on an Oxford already rudely jounced from its pleasant sleep by the first. As the London post reined his spent and foaming steed in the High Street, the scholars flocked about him, their academic gowns flapping about their long slim legs as they raced in the August twilight to get the pamphlets they had ordered from London. Those printers in Paul's Churchyard had the news within a week after it happened! With all sorts of new details!

Disputations went by the board, outmoded as Aristotle. They gave place to arguments in racy excited English. Into the night, young politicians explained what Cecil should do, about spies, and ships. They told Elizabeth what she should do (it was safe enough at that distance), about Norfolk and Mary, about Catholics in general.

At Oxford, as elsewhere in England, the mass of reaction was loyal. Philip of Spain and Mary were to be thanked at least for this: they had helped to weld England to oneness. Partly the welding was fear (alack for the Northern gibbets!). Partly it was discovery. The land was no appanage, either of Spain or the Pope. England was England for English!

This all focused attention on Sidney. His one uncle had disclosed the first plot. His other had fought the lords. A third had guarded Mary. Attention was not pleasing to Philip. He was sensitive and shy. At seventeen he had not yet mastered the taut nerves he had of his mother. Just now he was suffering acutely.

In the black looks bent on Norfolk, the denunciations of preachers, the loyal prayers in the Cathedral, he knew what had come to his own grandfather not twenty years before. Through his serious young life Philip had blushed for that treason, without really understanding. He had realized, of course, that the Duke had aimed high for his sons, a kind of selfless sinning. Now he saw in that very aiming, a " plot." He saw that in any case, treason meant stealing. Stealing the public safety. Underhand! He saw it and felt ashamed. They had bred him so fiercely loyal. Following the first disclosures about Norfolk, Philip had fallen ill, ill enough to have license from the Archbishop of Canterbury for the eating of meat in Lent. His uncle Robert had got it. Poor Philip! The ghost of old treason had ridden into Oxford with every news of the new.

He took no degree. But before his university days were ended, he spent some time at Cambridge. " For the time of his continuance," he was "reputed the best scholar " there, despite many " rare yong plantes of learning."

Easily the flower of them all, was the poet Edmund Spen-

ser. Probably he was twenty to Philip's seventeen, and as a
wee child had seen the Marian fires of Smithfield. He had
come from the Merchant Taylors' School famous for its
scholars and trouncings. He had lived no country life like
sheltered Philip Sidney, but knew his Bankside and Strand.
Even so they were kindred souls. It would be pleasant to
think of their heads together over Marot and Ariosto, poets
taught at Cambridge no more than they were at Oxford,
but loved by these poets-to-be. Edmund's maiden book he
dedicated to Philip. When Sidney left Cambridge, Spenser
was going to Irish service with Sir Henry. Probably Philip
secured him the post, for constantly all his life he dispensed
a princely assistance to those he loved and admired.

Later the two would meet at Uncle Robert's, at Leicester
House hard by the garden wall of the Temple " which on
Thames broad aged backe doth ride." And not once but
many times, Spenser's verse bewailed the passing of Philip
in Flanders. Through the horrors of an existence that lost
him wife and child when the "wild Irish" burned Kilcol-
man, Spenser cherished his *Faerie Queene.* Life for both
was a wild and joyous beauty chastened by duty and depri-
vation, Pan on Olivet in spirit and in truth.

In the early spring of 1572, as primroses were paling on
the level lands about Cambridge, Philip came to London to
prepare for his journey abroad. Gravely (but not without interest) he was choosing sarcenets at the silkwomen's shops
in Ludgate, bright buttons in Bucklersbury. Buying a good
dagger! Gloriana had given him leave to travel to " parts
beyond the sea " for " attaining of foreign languages." But
Philip was eighteen and frankly hoped for excitement. His
uncle Robert was writing to Walsingham in Paris about
him as " young and raw " and like to find foreigners
" strange." In short — young, shy — and English!

Perhaps for the sake of the *savoir faire,* and certainly for
safety, Philip was not traveling alone. He was attached to

the suite of the Earl of Lincoln who was going to Paris to sign a treaty of " perpetual peace " between England and France. Tagging this gorgeous train, like the tiny tail on a kite, Philip followed the Dover road, with his small company of three servants and four horses. To take ship at the foot of great white cliffs, like luminous pearl in the mist. To hear as the stout little craft weighed anchor, that Norfolk had lost his head. To hear but to forget as he felt under his feet the tremor and swell of the Channel. To be bound for Boulogne with a fair wind behind. Ahead lay two years of exciting travel—at least " if the world be quiet," his uncle had said. Quiet, quotha! With Bartholomew in the offing?

THE FIFTH CHAPTER ENTITLED
A MARRIAGE AND
A MASSACRE.

 OWEVER well-founded the proverb may be in the twentieth century, in the sixteenth the Devil did not take the hindmost. That was the lot of religion. This was nowhere more true than in France. Since the first of the Wars of Religion, in 1562, thanks to Catholic and Huguenot alike, the land had known only rapine and burning. The very altars had been desecrated. Both parties had pillaged them out of the purest piety, in the name of the Prince of Peace. One outrage avenged another, or better yet, anticipated it! Such thoroughly hellish hatred as existed between Rome and Geneva would have been inconceivable in any cause but Heaven's. Christianity had well nigh vanished in chicanery and carnage.

On the heavy seas which were whipped by such horrid winds Catherine de' Medici sailed as best she could, and thanked God for this new art of tacking. For thirteen years, since 1559, she had been a lone widow, with three quarreling sickly sons who never agreed among themselves and were too weak to do anything about it, even if they had. Inevitably she was the captain of the ship of the house of Valois. To save it she veered with the wind: toward the Catholic Guises when she had to; toward the Huguenots when she must; took a halfway course when she could.

Now she was trustfully planning to sew both winds in a

sack and enjoy a continuous calm. She was marrying her daughter Margot, a princess lovely to look at, and a most devoted Catholic, to Henry of Navarre, the Huguenot and son of that Arch-Huguenot, Jeanne d'Albret. It was a credulous age. People still believed that marriage wrought miracles.

In May 1572, after months of unholy haggling, the form of the nuptial ceremony was at last decided. But there had been a small War of Religion over every single detail. Should the wedding take place in Catholic Paris? or in some "neutral" city, supposing such could be found? Should there be Mass or Huguenot *prêches?* In Cathedral or Calvinist *temple?* Finally Charles IX, the brother of the bride, and now a youth of twenty-two, constituted himself arbiter. He decided in favor of Paris. He yielded to Jeanne d'Albret by arranging for the ceremony, not within Notre Dame, but on a scaffolding outside. To his sister he conceded a nuptial Mass to follow, from which Henry might be excused. The matter of celebrant he settled rather subtly: the Cardinal of Bourbon should officiate, but not as priest — as prince of the royal house! Not all of this suited the inflexible Jeanne d'Albret. In her perplexity she turned in March 1572, to Francis Walsingham, Elizabeth's ambassador in Paris and himself a devoted follower of the reformed religion. Since he advised compromise as the only possible basis for a *mariage mixte,* Jeanne reluctantly consented to the royal arrangements.

On June 4th, 1572 Queen Jeanne of Navarre was busy. The etiquette of the French court enjoined that the bridegroom's mother should buy the bride's trousseau. Jeanne was worn out with bickerings. Undeniably, she was ill. A woman of less heroic mould would have kept to her bed. Jeanne was bustling about the cobbled streets of Paris all day. In and out of the *boutiques* she went, buying gloves of pinked leather scented with civet, perfumed ruffs, fans and jeweled girdles — a score of trinkets for the pink-and-white princess Margot. At the end of the day she looked into the fashionable shop of Maître René, the court perfumer. Then, utterly fagged, she returned to the Hôtel de Condé in the Rue de Grenelles, Saint Honoré. In the *foyer* she collapsed from sheer exhaustion. Three hours after she had been put to bed, the news ran through Paris like wildfire. The Queen of Navarre had been poisoned!

With every new group of Huguenots which arrived at the gates of Paris, come to see the royal wedding, the sinister news spread. The Queen Mother had poisoned Jeanne! Catholic protests were bootless.

If Philip Sidney, riding in Lincoln's train on the long white roads from Boulogne to Paris, did not hear it by the way, it was one of the first bits of news he got when he reached the city. That was on June 7th, the third day of Jeanne's illness. The Earl of Lincoln's suite was lodged in " a Chasteau of the King called the Louver," in the great unfinished palace begun by François I, the " king of gentlemen " and the uncle of poor Jeanne d'Albret. Philip may have accompanied Lincoln. More likely he parted with the gallant party in the Faubourg-Saint-Germain, about a mile from the city. There stood the house of Francis Walsingham. Philip was to live with him, during his stay in Paris.

Two days later Jeanne d'Albret died, on June 9th. By then there were three stories going. All were authentic. All were vouched for by the most " absolute " Huguenot witness. One, that the King's elder brother, the Duke of Anjou, had given her a " doctored " drink. Another, that she died from a poisoned ruff. A third, that Maître René, by especial request from the Queen Mother (Jezebel was her pet name among the Huguenots), had " prepared " a pair of gloves. It was the version about the gloves which was put on the stage in London.

Though poisoning was common, and rumors about

it even commoner, Charles IX was annoyed. He ordered an autopsy to be performed in the presence of the Huguenot physicians. Inflammation of the lungs was then shown to have been poor Jeanne's affliction. Undaunted, the Huguenots stubbornly clung to " poisoning," even contending that the drug used had been so subtle that every trace had disappeared. Besides, they pointed out, the head had not been " opened."

The court went into mourning. Princess Margot was frail but rosy in black. " Such a pretty creature! " poor Jeanne had written her son after she saw the girl at Blois in February, four months before. Henry of Navarre's small sister Catherine thought Margot was lovely, too. In a charming little postcript to her mother's letter, she set down her reason — Margot gave her a puppy!

Elle m'a donné un bau petit chien que jeme bien . . .

Poets of Huguenot France were now addressing scores of elegiac verse on the passing of Jeanne d'Albret to this same little " Madame la Princesse Catherine de Navarre." As she struggled through the sheaf of them (omitting those in Latin, Greek and Hebrew, and all the really " big " words in French), we hope that the little dog she loved so had his nose on her arm, in comfort.

Jeanne d'Albret lay in state for five days in the Hôtel de Condé. She was one of the greatest — and most inflexible — folk of her time. Philip was doubtless taken by Walsingham to gaze on the chiseled strength of her face, with its fighter's nose and mouth. She was of no common mold, this woman who as her son Henry was born, had chanted a canticle! This woman who donned a steel casque to harangue her soldiers, before the battle of Jarnac. This woman who dragooned François La Noue into having his arm amputated after Saint Gemme in the June of 1570; had held it while the surgeons sawed, in those hardy days be-

fore anaesthetics; had ordered an iron arm with which he
could guide his horse, this terrible *Bras-de-fer*. Europe still
rung with the retort she had made in 1562, when the Queen
Mother had urged her to compromise with her husband,
by attending Mass — at least, sometimes. " I had rather,"
proclaimed this Jeanne, " rather than go to Mass, throw
my only son in the sea! " She had meant every word, too.

In the interests of the reformed faith, Jeanne had lost her
husband (if Antoine de Bourbon could be counted a loss),
her kingdom, most of her revenues. In the coffers of Philip
Sidney's English Queen there even now reposed the crown
jewels of Navarre and Béarn. In exchange for funds to feed
her armies, Jeanne had gladly placed them in pledge. Elizabeth had the gems appraised at about half of what they were
worth. Later she tried to sell them back to Henry of
Navarre — for a great deal more than their value. Canny
Gloriana!

Perhaps Philip had heard of the letter which Jeanne had
written Elizabeth in 1568. In it, she said in all simplicity:
"We queens should be nurse to religion." Gloriana knew a
trick which she thought was worth two of that: Make
policy nurse to religion!

So far, however, Philip Sidney had not seen all the
" streams of sweet Sovereign humours " in Gloriana's
breast. He stood grave and handsome, with his high
crowned hat, long feathered, in his hand. Sunshine
streamed into the bare high room in the Hôtel de Condé.
Honest himself, he that moment honored honesty, and
with it vigor. Doubtless he thought as he looked, that here
was the other great Protestant princess, the only peer of his
queen. Walsingham, however, knew them for very different stuff. Jeanne was like a heavy iron sword, built for
cracking skulls, for hacking where hacking served. Elizabeth was like a rapier of flexible polished steel, made for
fencing and shrewd wicked thrusts. Perhaps, as they went

out into the twisted streets of old Paris, Walsingham was thinking that a tempered steel lasts longer. It would take Philip Sidney some time to come to that conclusion.

Margot, the pretty Valois princess had stood in the tall room too. She disliked the austerity, the absence of cross, of candle, of priest. She had come with Monsieur le Cardinal de Lorraine (Mary Stuart's uncle), Madame la Guise, and the sister-in-law of the dead queen, Madame de Nevers. Of all the women in this world Madame de Nevers hated Jeanne most cordially. The company had stood silent, ill at ease in a death chamber, so bare and so bright. At last Madame de Nevers advanced toward the bed. Before the dead woman she swept a deep curtsey, a curtsey studied as insult. With cryptic twisted smile she moved even closer. Then she kissed the dead hand, in the tribute of mockery. With another deep obeisance, she turned and left the room. The cold hatred of the business affected little Margot. At that she had never liked Jeanne herself and was not easily shocked.

The funeral baked meats did not furnish forth the marriage tables, but they followed as close upon them as decency permitted. Jeanne was buried in the middle of June. The wedding was postponed, but only to the middle of August.

Meantime Philip was meeting a brilliant group in Paris. With some of the Huguenots, his period of friendship was brief, bounded by Bartholomew. So, his contact with Coligny, Admiral of France and brave old leader of the Protestant party. So, with Petrus Ramus whose interpretation of Aristotle had made him famous all over Europe (though it had yet to penetrate Oxford!). The English lad of eighteen and the French philosopher of fifty-seven became warm friends. Philip mourned him with " tenderest love."

The esteem in which young Sidney was held by older men of distinction, was something more than the polite interest in a precocious boy with powerful family connections. Something it owed, no doubt, to an engaging personality, but only in the first instance. What held the friendship of such a fine and critical soul as Languet was something more rare: a certain clarity of spirit, a simple and unaffected love of all good things, a warm loyalty, the more grateful for being surprised out of shyness; and most delightful of all, an enthusiastic admiration, the more charming for its utter sincerity.

Hubert Languet was fifty-four in this summer of 1572 when he met Philip in Paris. At the time he was in the service of the Elector of Saxony, but he had been everywhere in Europe. He had lived in the Cimbrical Chersonese, as people still called Denmark (because the ancients had done so). He had lived in Lapland. Though he had been born in Burgundy, this Languet was a citizen of the world. Both as a scholar and as a statesman, he had accustomed himself to weigh men, as assayers test metals, to see what they are worth. In Philip he saw a store of purest gold. After the fashion of elders, he set himself to smelt out the dross. Precious indeed were the things he sought in its stead: a wise worldliness without either dishonesty or disillusionment in a time richly productive of both; and above all, self-discipline. Philip loved him devotedly, enough to endure all the good advice. And never was the mind of a youth shaped by pressures of greater dignity.

Sidney must have taken a fine assortment of exciting new ideas to bed with him through those nights in July and August. He was probably encountering the Augustan poise of Michel de l'Hôpital, the equable chancellor whose serene mind, alone in all France, comprehended the difficulties of Catholic and Huguenot alike. Small wonder that so understanding, in an age of ardent appraisals, he should not be understood. Philip was too good a Protestant not to be puzzled by such exemplary fairness, but he caught the chancellor's quality when he wrote that never was " a more accomplished judgment more firmly founded on Virtue." This Philip was no ordinary young man! With a mind as open, he was hearing François Hotman enunciate certain thoughts with regard to free governments which would find an echo in a French Revolution centuries later. He was hearing Philippe de Mornay voice ideas on tyrants which would annoy Stuarts yet unborn, thanks to a pernicious theory to the effect that if a monarch did not behave himself, he might be eliminated, with propriety. In fact, had Gloriana known on what meat young Philip fed, she would have thought Master Walsingham was a great deal at fault, not to look to him better.

Probably at the house of Walsingham, Philip met the unforgettable Gabriel de Montgomerie, Lord of Lorges. He was a picturesque combination of Scotch and French, of the sober convictions of kirk and a swashbuckler's addiction to danger. In his twenty-third year, back in 1543, he had gone to Scotland — " in case of a ruffle." And with gusto he had ruffled it ever since. In the fateful tourney of 1559, his lance had accidentally pierced the eye of Henry II, and killed him. Since then, Gabriel found it salutary to avoid Catherine de' Medici, the widow. Rarely was he in Paris. Sometimes he performed bloody marvels with the Huguenot armies. When things grew too hot even for that, he took a vacation in England. He had a gift for raising storms, and escaping to raise others. Philip who had doubtless heard tales of him at school, viewed with undisguised elation the pious, trouncing reality. It was an adventure to be in the same room with Montgomerie, or to see him riding like mad through the Faubourg-Saint-Germain where he was now living, reining his horse to glower at some naughty *gamin* who swore. By grace of Heaven and just such another swift steed he escaped at Saint Bartholomew. Catherine's regret was great because she was thereby forced to make a separate job of him, later. Within a twelvemonth after, she got him at last, this luckless lucky regicide who was such a godly romantic.

Godly, so far (thanks to his mother Queen Jeanne!), and romantic always, most certainly also with a gift for raising storms, was Henry of Navarre. The new king, and coming bridegroom, was just Philip's age, eighteen. The two youths probably met soon after Henry came to Paris. Early in July he had ridden in with eight hundred men in his train, *Bras-de-fer* riding beside him. All were silent and sad. All wore long cloaks of black. The Parisian crowds usually gay and vocal, stood and watched, also in silence. Except for the erect figure, the masterful nose and chin, there was nothing to show that here rode Henry the Great of France, perhaps her greatest king.

Philip was also at court. There, one of his friends told Spenser in Ireland later, " the graver sort of courtiers " were " very joyful " when they " could at any time have him in their company and conversations." No less delighted were they " with his ready and witty answers than astonished to hear him speak the French language so well and aptly, having been so short a while in the country."

On August 9th, a signal honor came to him. He was made a gentleman of the King's bedchamber, with the title Baron de Sidenay. There, through the royal nuptials, Baron Philip respectfully held the slashed shoes as King Charles thrust thin shanks into primrose-colored stockings. Or gravely proffered the cape encrusted with jewels which His Majesty would don next, inadvertently noting the while how shrunk was the kingly waist before his valet buttoned the padded jerkin which hinted at robustness. Seeing how pale the cheeks, how bright the eye, how nervous the twitch with which His Highness jammed his velvet hat far down over one Valois ear. Observing how ill-controlled was the royal impatience when Henry the Duke

The so-called Zucchero Portrait of Philip Sidney.

of Guise walked in upon the robing. Guise might as well be King of Paris, said his petulant Majesty: he had the town in his pocket! Soberly, not without awe, Philip looked at this Duke of Guise. The Huguenots hated him fiercely. Yet his greatest enemies would never have credited Guise with the horror he had in hand — with the massacre of Saint Bartholomew.

While gay preparations were being made for the wedding, there were also certain precautions. On July 5th, the day Navarre came to Paris, Charles IX had forbidden the use of swords and firearms. He had even provided for the inevitable gallant complications which arose between gentlemen. All affairs of honor would be arbitrated either by the Duke of Anjou or by the Lieutenant General. Like another Canute poor Charles sought to stem the tides of hatred: his edict forbade the people " to recall the past to give occasion to new quarrels." Nevertheless something sinister was shaping. This person and that had letters in cipher, warning in vague terms of a " general conspiracy," urging departure from Paris. Even Coligny received such a secret message. However he stood his ground. He had faith, he said, in the King. The King had promised that the Huguenots should be safe.

The wedding which was to heal all wounds and wipe tears from off all faces, took place on Monday August 18th. Since dawn the space before Notre Dame had been jammed by an eager mob. The people had crowded themselves closest about the scaffolding which was hung with arras of gold, blazing richly in the sun. According to ancient custom the bridal pair were met at the door of the church. There in his vestments Cardinal de Bourbon greeted them. Thence with the greatest difficulty the party pushed to the platform, and mounted its crimson carpeted stairs.

On that height the tall figure of Henry of Navarre ap-

peared to fine advantage in the rich garments which had
replaced his mourning. He towered over the frail young
king, who was weighed down by robes of massy gold. The
little bride chronicled her own sartorial glories with care in
her *Mémoires,* setting down with satisfaction that she was
dressed *à la royalle.* She gloried in a queenly crown! She
had a mantle of ermine, ermine with tails! Her train of
blue satin was four ells long, and it took three princesses,
no less, to bear it. It was well that the poor child's clothes
consoled her.

For little Margot loved the Duke of Guise, although she
was marrying Henry of Navarre! In the time to come, she
would not stickle at cherishing both lover and husband.
Yet now, when the moment came for her to accept Henry
as her wedded lord, some native honesty kept the poor girl
silent. It was her resourceful brother, the king, who saved
the situation. He put his hand on her head, and firmly
pushed it down. That was Margot's consent.

After the new Queen had swept into the church in her
comforting ermine, to find what balm she might for her
spirit in the Mass, the bridegroom walked outside " with
certain of his religion." Was Sidney of those certain?

Through the open doors of the ancient Church of Our
Lady, Henry and his train heard the solemn swell of the
organ, the thinner sound of chanting. Within they saw a
forest of candles, with little leaping leaves of light that
flickered against the gray. It was four o'clock when Margot
came forth in her glory, Margot Queen of Navarre!

Gayly the court set itself to enjoy tournaments, ballets,
balls. In her native Italy, the Queen Mother had acquired a
taste for extravagant pageants. In France she had bettered
the lesson. Philip may not even have seen the naïve entertainments of the thriftier Gloriana. At all events he admired all this Medicean magnificence.

After the wedding supper on Monday night, there had

been a ball by torchlight, in the Grand Salon of the Louvre.
The dancing was brief. At a sudden signal, the court lined
the walls of the lofty room, leaving the center vacant.
Drawn in giant chariots came musicians, clothed in silver.
One, shimmering in the light of a hundred tapers, was
Étienne le Roy, the loveliest singer of his time. He sang of
the beauty and bravery which were now united in Hymen.
His dulcet voice was itself a marvel of shimmer and silver.
When he had done there was courteous applause.

Nothing like the torrent of noise let loose by those
elegant people as the first of seven " mounts " was borne
into the apartment. For there enthroned beside Neptune,
the king of the sea, on a rock that shone with iridescent
shells, sat Charles himself, the mighty monarch who condescended to share his sovereignty, but only with a god!
Upon a second chariot, almost, but not quite so richly dight,
sat the Duke of Anjou who within two years would be king
of both France and Poland. On a third rode his Majesty's
younger brother, a pockmarked swarthy boy with prominent eyes who was the Duke of Alençon. Later he wooed
Gloriana herself and she called him her darling " Frog."
Now he fitted exactly into the grotesque glory of this
aquatic pageant. When the " mounts " had circled the salon
and the princes three had descended, the king of Navarre
led out Margot. Dancing went on till dawn.

Indeed King Charles " so earnestly bent to these festivities that he had no leysure, not onely for waightie affaires,
but also not so much as to take his naturall sleepe." Presumably his new English gentleman of the Bedchamber
did not get much more. Tuesday, the 19th, the Duke
of Anjou gave a banquet and entertainment. And on
Wednesday the 20th, the " devices " were not only more
elaborate but fraught with what time and Bartholomew
were to turn to a dreadful allegory.

The court assembled in the hall of the " Petit Bourbon,"

a palace built two centuries before by Louis, the second duke
of the line to which the bridegroom himself belonged. To
the right was a representation of the Abode of the Blessed.
There twelve lovely nymphs disported themselves in an
orchard, combining gallantry and holiness in a concept
truly French. To the left was Tartarus. Whereas the Elysian
Fields had been lit by stars, by the planets, even by the
twelve signs of the Zodiac, hell was illumined by sulphur-
ous flames which started the ladies to sneezing. Between the
heavenly and the hellish regions there ran a stream of real
water. In it a great number of little devils merrily disported
themselves when they were not turning the great wheel of
Ixion (decorated with hundreds of little bells which never
came out of the description in Virgil). Upon the scene there
now came several knights riding, at their head Henry of
Navarre. They were eager to storm the heavenly ladies.
But they were repulsed and driven back into Tartarus!

The Huguenots never forgot this particular passage, nor
that they had been driven to hell by the king and his two
princely brothers.

At this stage (and time enough!) came Mercury mounted
on a cock. The hautboys and viols de gamba played
loudly to cover the creaking of the very substantial ma-
chinery thanks to which not only Mercury but a good solid
Cupid as well, descended from the ceiling. Mercury was
Étienne le Roy. Once he had safely dismounted he sang the
praises of the three Valois princelings. Then he climbed his
cock and was laboriously hauled back by windlass to the
regions whence he came. Nervous ladies in his immediate
path were doubtless much relieved! Young Sidney probably
enjoyed this grand " effect " more than he did the ballet
of Elysian nymphs which followed — and lasted a full hour.
At length the entertainment came to an end, as in answer
to the supplications of all the court, the bridegroom and
his attendants were at last let out of hell. (It was easier

to escape from than the murderous inferno of the following Sunday!)

On Thursday the 21st, Philip saw his first French tournament. The lists were prepared in the grand square of the Louvre. Before the Queen Mother and Margot in their boxes hung with tapestry, paraded King Charles who led the challengers. He had garbed his knights like Amazons, with the hair of their tawny wigs streaming out behind them. At the head of the defenders rode Navarre. His troupe was no less gorgeous, though perhaps a bit more plausible as Turks in flowing robes of gold, with turbans on their heads. After both companies had made the circuit of the tilt-yard, they retired to their tents, whence they shortly issued in full mail and fought each other in deadly earnest. Eagerly Philip watched. Eagerly watched the ladies, the Queen Mother still with an effort, remembering another tournament under the shadow of the Bastille. . . . Tilts were dangerous. Often knights were unseated, or picked up by their pages " as men dazed," to be hastily drawn from the reach of flying hoofs. Success was indeed a matter of skill. One of the reasons why Leicester sent Philip abroad was that he might " study " with Pugliano, the Emperor's Master of Horse, who trained his young knights in Vienna to " run " in " thick capps " till by practice he made them " good men of the tourney."

Although the tilt was continued the next day, an event in the morning robbed it both of excitement and interest. As Coligny was walking through the streets on his way from the Louvre, Maureval, an assassin hired by the Duke of Guise, shot at him from a window. Fortunately at that very moment, the Admiral had stopped to adjust an overshoe. To that he owed his life. The ball took only two fingers and lodged in his arm. Quietly he pointed to the house whence the shot had come. Then he went home and sent for the King.

Poor Charles was nearly distracted when he arrived with his surgeons. After Coligny was comfortable, the King sen everyone from the room and sat beside the bed. They talked long and seriously. When at last he left, the frightened prince promised to exact such vengeance as the murderer would never forget.

Meantime the fury of the Huguenots rose to fever pitch Many, without doubt, rashly urged reprisals. All through the night, thirty or forty of Navarre's closest friends vigor ously debated the subject with him. And Queen Margo who lay beside her husband in the great curtained bed heard so much heated talk that next day she had a headache By the time the Protestant partisans at last took their de parture, it was already day. Characteristically, the lady re corded that in all the rumpus, she had not had a wink of sleep!

Neither had Walsingham, for Gabriel de Montgomerie returning late to the Faubourg-Saint-Germain from a num ber of such councils, stopped in to report. He had found he said, a general faith in the King's sincerity and a belief that he would take vengeance for the hurt sustained by Coligny. At the same time he brought the disquieting news that a number of Huguenots were determined to protest to the Duke of Guise directly. It appeared also that the Vidâme of Chartres had renewed his appeals to the Admi ral to leave Paris.

The English ambassador was too shrewd a judge of men and situations not to have been appalled by the prospect Philip Sidney had come to Europe, partly to study political problems at first hand. Besides, he was a steady trusty youth. It is therefore likely that before Walsingham sat down to write home to the Council that night, he explained some thing of the business to Philip. There in a room shuttered for safety, they talked with a candle between them. Sidney was getting his first lesson in statecraft from the first states-

nan in Europe. It was hardly a beginner's assignment.
Even Walsingham did not guess that Bartholomew was
brewing.

The reasons for that dreadful massacre were, even so,
easier for Walsingham to get at, than they are for us. He
had only to gauge the incredible hatreds and fears of the
Wars of Religion which lay behind. For us, the way to
truth is blocked further, not only by the carnage itself but
by the fierce passions which that carnage still inspires.
We can only fall back on the contentions of the parties involved. They are highly contradictory. The Huguenots said
that they were lured to Paris expressly to be exterminated,
and that the Guises began upon the Admiral. The Catholics, on the other hand, maintained that they acted in self
defense, and only to forestall the vengeance which the
Protestants were preparing for the attempt against
Coligny.

So far as an arrant weakling can be sincere about anything, Charles had been sincere in his promises to the Admiral. But the King was as clay in his mother's hands. She
told him that the Huguenots held him responsible for the
Admiral's attempted murder. She said they were everywhere arming against him. She persuaded him that his
throne, even his life, depended on this brilliant counter-
stroke conceived by the Guises, this scheme to kill the Protestants off *en masse.* Yet she was careful not to tell Charles
all this until the last moment, just in time to secure his
necessary consent, but too late for revelations had he been
minded to make them.

How far the Queen Mother believed her own arguments
we cannot tell. Certainly she loved the Guises no more than
she did the Huguenots, and as recently as June 1572, she
had cast her lot with the Protestant queen of England in a
league of " perpetual peace." Now, less than three months
later she was shifting back to the Catholics! Was the change

due, perhaps, to the discovery that Elizabeth played her own shrewd game, that she could not be relied on? That was true enough. Did Catherine know it? On the other hand, the Guises offered support she was sure of. Both the Duke and the Cardinal of Lorraine his brother, had enormous power. Behind them hovered Spain, even the Pope himself. Singly she could not fight such strength as they combined. She had her sons to look out for. She espoused the cause of the Guises.

It was two hours after midnight on the morning of Sunday, August 24th. Shortly, with dawn, would come the feast of Saint Bartholomew. Suddenly the great bell of Saint Germain l'Auxerrois began to toll. Soon every steeple in Paris had taken up the sound. The air was ashiver with brazen banging — the signal for the massacre!

Out of the darkness, candles blazed up at casements. The streets must be light, lest the Huguenots escape, lest Catholics be slain. To guard against that, the murderers wore white crosses on their hats, and on their arms white kerchiefs. Already they swarmed the streets. They were armed to the teeth. They had bludgeons to beat in the doors of the houses that sheltered Huguenots. They were pounding on wooden shutters, shouting to " heretics " to open.

Roused from their beds by the clangor, Protestants rushed to their windows. As they peered out, they were shot at. Before they could dress or arm, or hide their wives and children, the doors below had been shattered. Down the steep stairs they were hauled to be slain in the streets. Many of them murdered before they could leave their beds, and their bodies tossed out of the windows.

In the forefront of the assassins was the Duke of Guise. Hastening to the Admiral's dwelling, he ordered his servant to go in and kill Coligny. When the fellow threw down the corpse, the Duke turned it over with his foot. He wanted no mistake this time! Then, satisfied as to his own vengeance, he went on to wholesale public slaughters.

Even the royal palace was drenched with gore. From room to room the soldiers pursued their victims, cut their throats, sent them hurtling into the courtyard. Drunk with excitement, King Charles joined in the sport crying out *Voilà un Huguenot!* and firing his harquebus. Like hounds in full cry, the courtiers followed the chase, harrying the wretched heretics till they drove them into the streets for other hunters to slay.

In the streets the gutters were choked. The cobbles shone with blood. Women clutched cloaks about them, scuttled from shadow to shadow, escaped one ruffian to fall before another. Aged people fell, fell and could not get up, were shortly buried in corpses. Children toddling into the brightness of those streets whimpered at shots, shrilled at the flash of swords, were run through and pitched into the river. "Here is a Huguenot!" — "It's better to catch 'em small!"

A mile out of the city in the Faubourg-Saint-Germain, the tocsin was not heard. The sounds of the fray were faint. While Paris was reeling in carnage, the household of Walsingham slept. The ambassador, busy into the night with her Majesty's affairs, was not even disturbed. But as the dull day dawned, the noise of confused shots, of cries, of church bells ringing at unaccountable times caused Walsingham to send a servant to Montgomerie, to discover what was happening. The word which came back was reassuring. Although there had been serious disorders in the city, the King had now suppressed them and set guards about the house of Coligny. The news was good, but old. Coligny was four hours dead.

By afternoon Philip knew the gallant old Admiral's fate. Some one had found the body and known it for his by the chain and medal about the neck. Philip had seen that

medal which was one of a dozen that Jeanne of Navarre
caused to be struck for her chieftains. He recalled the motto:
Complete Victory, Assured Peace, or an Honest Death.
Those were her aims for the Huguenots. Alas for Coligny,
despite his patient efforts, he achieved not even the last!

With bitterness Philip now thought of his service in
the royal bedchamber of the Louvre. Once he had counted
it honor. Fiercely he resolved that never again, so long as he
lived, would he use the hated title of Baron de Sidenay! And
though he waited for more than ten years before he was
" Sir " Philip, he kept the vow of that moment.

Before evening Walsingham's house was crowded with
English refugees. Some were young nobles who had made
their way on horseback, using the back streets, and guided
by Huguenot servants. Some, like Timothy Bright, were
clergymen. (Torn were their parsons' cloaks, their parsons'
peace torn with them.) Some were merchants who had
seen their shops looted before their eyes, and now without
livelihood, were still thankful for life. All were terrified.
Each group had its tale of atrocities: of women hung up by
the hair; of dogs lapping blood in the streets as they sniffed
about the corpses; of bodies bobbing in the Seine. The
carnage was going on, unabated. It was merely shifting
ground.

Now it moved into the suburbs. Closer at hand Philip
heard those banging bells. The shouts and shots grew louder.
With clattering of hoofs and cries to clear the way in the
name of the King, the royal guard came thundering to Walsingham's door. Charles had sent it for the protection of the
English embassy. Yet there was little assurance in that.
Coligny had had a guard!

By now there were many dead in the lanes and gardens
of the Faubourg-Saint-Germain. The tumult was clearly
increasing. Even through shuttered panes, the roar of it
came in to the Englishmen of all sorts and conditions who

found asylum with the ambassador. They filled the passages and the rooms. They sat on the staircase. They huddled against the doors. There were handsome boys like Philip, young nobles in sullied satins; there were sober Scots of the kirk with a vengeance culled out of Scripture; frightened women hugging the comfort of *sauvegardes* even in those warm rooms.

Night came. Outside the roar continued. Within they lit candles. What with the little flames and the breath of frightened human beings, the air grew hot. No one dared to risk opening a casement.

Then like the cool shadow of Heaven's benediction on that close and sultry air came the voice of a minister:

The sacrifices of God are a broken spirit: a broken and contrite heart. . . .

Inside the house there was silence. Suddenly people remembered that the hell from which they had escaped had fallen on a Sunday. This was the Lord's Day. Safe at home in England, in the twilight, their relatives and friends were gathered in parish churches to hear this same service of Evening Prayer. Philip thought of Sir Henry and his lady mother, of his uncle Robert.

The voice was strangely strong in the little house. Against the murmurs of murder, it came to them firm and clear. It compelled with a new conviction. It was pregnant with new need. The minister was reading from Elizabeth's Protestant Prayer-book, the Lesson for the feast of Saint Bartholomew:

Now late on the Sabbath day, as it began to dawn toward the first day of the week, came Mary Magdalene and the other Mary. . . .

Philip knew the passage, the twenty-eighth chapter of Matthew. The story of watchers who " quaked " by the

Tomb, who " became as dead men," who were " afeared
before the guard come out from the city. . . ."

To those who had recently companied with Death, who
had quaked indeed as they saw it, who even now were
affrighted by the guard that stood at the door, this was no
tale of what happened fifteen centuries past and more.
It was the authentic voice of the moment. An authentic
comfort lived in the closing verses:

I am with you always even to the end of the world. . . .

Philip never forgot that Lesson.

THE SIXTH CHAPTER
ENTITLED
STRANGE COUNTRY.

OME time in September 1572, Sidney left Paris for Frankfurt. His travels were to continue, but not because the world was " quiet." On the contrary, France was so unsettled that Walsingham's messenger had trouble getting out, although he carried no letters. When he finally reached the English court with his verbal account of terrors, Philip's parents became prey to the cruelest anxiety. The result was an order from the Privy Council itself. Walsingham was to secure the boy's safe-conduct and send him home at once! Fortunately for Philip, the letters did not arrive until he was well on his way to Germany.

He was a very different Philip to the ingenuous lad who had cantered so blithely out of Boulogne three months before. He had savored the refinements of the grandest court in Europe and sickened, viewing its perfidy. He had companied with the good and great, only to see them snuffed out like candles. Some of his friends, like De Mornay and Languet had escaped by a miracle. But others, like Ramus, were dead. If stable older men wrote, years after, of that " bloudy massacre of Paris " as a horror still " fresh in memorie," we can imagine its impression on a delicate high-strung boy. For our Philip, the bitterness of his first encounter with triumphant Evil, was the more poignant because he was himself loyal, forthright, of an honesty almost aggressive. Moreover, Bartholomew cut where he felt most keenly: at the reformed religion which since the Pope's Bull against Elizabeth, involved for him patriotism as well.

It was not therefore extraordinary that in the heart of the youth who was finding new pleasure in the fresh autumn air, who was feeling a new joy in the horse under him, there should be, as he rode toward Germany, a passionate hatred for the King of Spain. His godfather had just approved the Massacre as the greatest of blessings vouchsafed by God to a sinful world! Nor was it remarkable that Sidney should years later write to Gloriana that Catherine de' Medici was the " Jezabel of our age " and pay his respects to her sons as scoundrels who " made oblation of their own sister's marriage, the easier to make massacres of both sexes." However terribly he was affected by Bartholomew otherwise, Philip came out of it as honest as he went in.

The same may be said of Gloriana. But she wore her honesty with a difference. Although the news from France might goad her people to fury, Gloriana preserved a queenly and open mind. With all London flouting Fénelon, the French ambassador, she could scarcely do less than delay his reception for a day or two, and when she finally gave him audience to drape both the room and the courtiers in deepest black. As concession to public prejudice, also, she began by speaking coldly of the " accident " in the dominions of her dear brother Charles whom " she loved honored and confided in of all the world." But before she had done, she abandoned the business of being horrified to her Protestant clergy. (They certainly did nobly with it!) She herself was not one to let a mere massacre invalidate the " perpetual peace and amitie " between England and France. Least of all when she was still at odds with Spain over the Norfolk business! Shortly, therefore, she was making it clear that it was her " infinite jealousy " for the

French king's " honour " which actuated her distress. Not for a moment did she believe that it was " according to his disposition nor from any premeditation of his own that these murders had happened." Then just before she dismissed the flustered Fénelon, she coyly drew forth a letter from the mourning dress which she wore for the dead Huguenots. It was a love-letter to the ugly little Frog Prince of the pageant at the Louvre! She had no intention of letting Bartholomew interfere with the farce of a courtship which, like her present complaisance, was dictated by policy.

For his further disillusionment, it was well that Philip knew nothing of these royal duplicities. He was making his way through hilly country, past vineyards purple with grapes, to the mighty Vosges mountains. To the north, beyond the great Rhine with its castles, itself on the lovely river Main, lay the ancient town of Frankfurt. There he was to meet Languet.

In the hundred odd years since printing had been invented, some of the most beautiful books in the world had issued from Frankfurt presses. Fittingly enough, while Philip remained there, he and Languet resided with the printer Andreas Wechel, a fine old humanist in his sixties. Like them, he had escaped Bartholomew. He had known Philip's honored friend, Ramus, in Paris where he printed all his works.

Wechel's shop was low-studded. Its very air was pleasantly acrid with the smell of new inks, fragrant with fair strong paper which would outlast the centuries. There Philip turned the pages of great folios. As men do still, he admired their noble illustrations. Some had been done from engraved copper plates by a process which was already producing lovely maps. Some pictures were still made from the wood-blocks which had first suggested the idea of printing. At once vigorous and detailed were the full-page portraits which Wechel achieved with his wood-blocks.

Proudly the bearded craftsman showed them to this English lad who loved the varied types, whose eye warmed to the delicate spider's tracery of Greek characters, to the peasant strength of black-letter, to well poised italics. Most glorious, Philip observed the marvel of printing presses at work! He heard the tale of Jeanne d'Albret's visit to the shop of Henri Étienne most scholarly of French printers. There she had been so moved by this " singular art " of printing that she composed four extempore verses upon the miracle. Étienne, who was as good a courtier as he was a printer, had had her lines set up before her very eyes, and struck off on cartels for her to carry home!

Scholars from all over the world came to Wechel's shop. As other men met at inns to drink and gloat over the day's adventures, scholars foregathered here. To be sure Erasmus had once poked fun at their mighty undertakings:

What a joy if they can discover some little word unknown to common people, or dig up somewhere a piece of old rock with worn out letters! By Jove, what triumphs, what glorifications, as if they had conquered Africa or taken Babylon!

But then, as now, all the new lore of this world came out of ancient books! A studious Sidney, reading long hours with Languet daily, treading with delight the strange country which opened up with each fresh tome, regarded these men with reverence. To the talk by Wechel's fire, he brought the questioning quiet mind that marked him out to them as the stuff of which scholars are made. Happy in his books, he was finding a resource in the past, a balm for Bartholomew.

But Languet knew well enough that the great Earl of Leicester's nephew would never be permitted to sink so low as a scholar! On the other hand, Philip had too good a mind for a courtier. Diplomat himself, Languet hoped to see this

Sidney of his a statesman. In the conduct of embassies and
the delicate business of negotiations, Philip would need his
scholar's training in accurate appraisal, his scholar's experience with the tangles of the past. Under the tutelage of
Languet, the boy was already learning to use his eyes to
arrive at shrewd conclusions. In March 1573, he wrote to
his uncle Robert:

*I was upon Thursday with Count Louis the Prince of
Orange's second brother. I found one Shambourg a Ger-
man with him, a gentleman whom I knew at the Court of
France, always very affectionate to the King's service. I
doubt not but he assayeth to draw the Count to serve the
King, but I hope he laboureth in vain. . . .*

Utterly without assistance, Philip was developing his
native Dudley gift for spending money. Like young men
since, he was finding the higher education expensive. Yet
even by modern standards, eighteen hundred dollars was
a tidy sum to be owing to one man at the end of a mere
six months. No wonder Sidney piously headed the statement of his indebtedness, " Glory be to God! "

Early in the summer of 1573, Languet was summoned to
the imperial court at Vienna. Eagerly he pressed Philip to
avail himself of the valuable contacts which a visit there
would afford. It was settled that Sidney should join him,
but first the youth was to take a leisurely journey alone
through the humanistic centers scattered along the way.

Chief of them was Heidelberg where there had been a
university since 1386. However, many noble young tourists
contented themselves with seeing the Great Tun and sam-
pling its contents with gusto.

Philip found intoxication more heady, for in Heidelberg
he met Henri Étienne. With his father Robert, who was
also a printer and scholar, Henri had spread the New Learning through all France. His own work had begun with the

first Renaissance edition of Anacreon which he published
in the year that Philip was born. His printing of French
Bibles earned him a place on Pope Paul's *Index Expurga-
torius* before Sidney was five.

Étienne was now in his mid-forties, temperamental and
restless. He was still as eager a traveler into strange lands,
those on the map and those on the printed page, as if he
had been nineteen, like Philip. Recently he had produced
two utterly different works, both with enormous appeal.
One, out since 1572, was the mighty *Thesaurus of the Greek
Language* which has never been superseded. The other, just
off the press, he found it safer not to claim. It was a naughty
Huguenot *Life of Catherine de' Medici!* With unscholarly
gusto he listed her murders. Behold, Jeanne d'Albret's
name led all the rest! Inevitably he compared Catherine
to Jezebel, rudely concluding his compliments with a
rhyme as rough and ruthless as a school-boy's:

> *The dogs devoured Jezebel*
> *The Bible doth that story tell.*
> *Such fitting vengeance divine*
> *Will never come to Catherine.*
> *For dogs who on vile carrion sup,*
> *Will sniff at her, and pass her up!*

Henri Étienne took a great fancy to Philip. Later he
journeyed to Strassburg, especially to give him a volume of
Greek maxims which he had copied out in his own hand.
Among the treasures which young Sidney bore in his bags
to Basle, was Étienne's famous edition of Plato in three
volumes. That was also a present. Étienne dedicated to
Philip twice: in 1576 a notable issue of the *New Testament*
in the original Greek, and in 1581 the *Histories* of Herodian
and Zozimus. In both prefaces there is the eulogy befitting
a great earl's nephew; but there is more besides, real affection and solid admiration.

Basle, Sidney found full of printers who delighted in
" purging the classics, as Hercules in clearing the Augean
stables." Under a roof of blue, yellow and red tiles arranged
in checker work and " visible afarr off," the Cathedral
sheltered the famous theological school which had cradled
the great German reformers. Upon its walls, Philip read
painted testimonies to the great leaders in " religion " who
had been taught there. Thorough Oxonian that he was, he
stood piously before the tomb of Erasmus. It was a " flat
stone with beside it a pillar of red marble three yards high
and two feet thick at the top." A bust surmounted it with
the legend *Terminus*. The device signified that Death
is the end of all. However, it had no blighting effect on
Philip who was tasting the joys of freedom and did not
arrive at Vienna till September 1573.

Then, to the uneasiness of Languet, the impetuous boy
showed a dangerous " disposition." He wanted to go to
Italy with his young friends! Pious Protestants regarded
Italy as the corrupter of all manners and morals. Languet
was no exception. In his affection for Philip, he sorrowed
the more. Before the boy secured his consent, he was forced
to promise that he would keep away from Rome. Alas for
poor Philip, Rome was of all cities the one he wished most
to see. Like a most exemplary lad, he gave (and kept!) the
promise. When he finally took leave of Languet in his long
furred gown, Philip carried south with him many injunc-
tions and warnings. He must take care of what he ate, and
drank. He must write regularly. Above all, he must not
return the " Italianate Englishman," who was the very devil
incarnate, wearing ruffs of immoral cut, swearing strange
oaths, and practising " foreign " vices. Thus bludgeoned
with instruction, young Sidney at last made his escape to
Italy.

Before he had gone very far in the lovely land of vineyards, of olive and orange trees, young Philip had reason

to shake his English head in horror. An inn-keeper collected his bill twice, once from Sidney and once from the friend Coningsby who was with him! Unfortunately we have cause to shake our heads, too. In sad horror, also, for before he thought of investigating, this hot-headed Philip, furious at finding the common purse short, accused his friend point-blank of taking the money! And when the incident was explained, he does not seem to have been particularly apologetic. The defensive pride which Philip had built up in himself kept him both tense and self-centered. More, his sense of his own importance had not been mitigated by the attention of the mighty. And before he had it in hand, the ruthlessness of old Northumberland lived in him too much. For many years, despite the loving labors of Languet, he continued over-impulsive. It is tribute to his charm and generous affection that people forgave him such passages as this, with promptness and completeness — even when he did not understand that forgiveness was in order!

At Venice, doubtless to Languet's relief, Philip met the Count of Hanau. Together they got the news of the Rialto, and saw the " magnificent magnificences of the magnificoes." To outward appearance, Venice still held the gorgeous East in fee. Actually, both commercially and politically her power was on the wane. In a last access of glory she had risen to defend Famagusta in 1571, and a few months later in the same year had fought the Turk at Lepanto and defeated him. But as soon as Rome and Spain, who had been parties to the victory, abandoned her, Venice was forced to cede Cyprus to the Turk, and to pay indemnity besides.

Yet other glories were upon the proud Adriatic city of canals and time-touched palaces. Tintoretto and Veronese were producing their great masterpieces. Churches were radiant with the color of Bellini and Carpaccio. Here were precious cargoes like none else in the world. Silks and rare wines, books from the presses of Aldus and Sessa, maps by Zoppino and Bordone which charted the New World were heaped high in this the most auspicious port of the old.

Few of Sidney's letters have been preserved. Did he see the church of the " Grecians," like Coryat thirty years after? Did he hear the " delectable rare and superexcellent " ravishment of vocal music and sagbuts which swept other tourists " up with St. Paul into the third heaven " ? Was he, like them, also " rapt " by lovely ladies in white and yellow veils? (Fat widows in black ones would naturally not have engaged him!) Did he, too, watch the *donzelle* who sat on balconies in broad-rimmed crownless hats which enabled them to apply the " oiles and drogges " which kept their locks so golden? Did he see the sirens of this modern Gomorrah who curled their hair with " frishing pins " while they conned Greek epigrams at their windows? Old Languet would indeed have been full of fears had he known how mysterious Philip found gondolas by torchlight, how glamorous to his law-abiding English mind were the tales of huddled murders and open poisonings!

On February 26th, 1574 Philip sat for his portrait to Paolo Veronese. He probably wore the black velvet affected by Italian nobles. Surely he was a figure for an artist as the light beat warmly upon him in Veronese's studio: the gold of his hair, his grave affectionate mouth, his trim waist and slim horseman's legs — a very sober young man, of fine mind, fine manners, fine family, taking himself and the moment with a very fine seriousness! The painting occupied three days. Languet, at least, found in the portrait no masterpiece. " It seems," he wrote, " to represent some one like you rather than you. At first I thought it was your brother! " Afterward he conceded that the likeness " grew." He had it copied because it was " elegant " — above all, his Philip had sat for it.

In April 1574, the Council of Ten in Venice solemnly debated whether to give Sidney license to carry arms, or no. As the ayes carried the motion, he had his permission. Yet there was one " neutral," presumably a conservative voter who thought that foreigners would bear watching!

With June 1574, came the " new king " of France, Henry III who was passing through Venice on his way to Poland. Languet pressed Sidney to renew acquaintance with him. " It would be useful to you," he urged, " if you ever went to the French court again." Thus adjured the stiff-necked Philip bowed to social exigency. He also met Pibrac who was in Henry's suite and had issued the official " apology " for Bartholomew. When downright Philip " despised " him, Languet was stern. He pointed out that Sidney must not dismiss a man as a scoundrel simply because he made one mistake. Pibrac was a gentleman and a scholar!

From Venice Philip went to Genoa and to Florence. Languet disapproved. To weight his arguments he listed the sins of Etruscans and Savoyards since the beginning of time. Florence meant much to Sidney, for there until 1492 the great Lorenzo de' Medici had nursed the New Learning.

Greek scholars had brought it to him, men who barely saved their lives, and more precious, their manuscripts, after the fall of Constantinople in 1453. Into his great Laurentian Library, this magnificent de' Medici had gathered all their treasures. Philip had heard of its wonders from Étienne who spoke glowingly of illuminated parchments, bright as jewels and as heavily set in gold. There the Renaissance had been cradled in richness, not in spareness and bleak sacrifice, like the Reformation in Basle.

A second humanistic shrine was the garden of Lorenzo's villa overhanging Florence. Its loveliness was unmatched, even in Greece and Rome. In it the scholars Landino and Politian debated with Lorenzo on Goodness and Beauty in

Plato. Below lay the beautiful belfries and palaces of the ornate luxurious city; beyond the walls lay pastures and mountains bright in shimmering Italian air. Philip loved the sunny beauty which spread there, the burgeoning richness of Florence, and the Arno yellow as Tiber. The Tiber he might not see.

Padua had cooler attractions. Languet had attended the university to which scholars flocked from all over Europe. A number of Englishmen were regularly in residence — not always peaceably, for soon after Sidney left several were badly hurt in a *fracas*. There Philip took a house, to pursue his studies in quiet. Astronomy and geometry he wanted most, with music. Greek, too, he had longed for. But Languet thought German more useful, and docilely Philip began. Probably he did not make much progress for he wrote to Languet in those charming Latin letters which have fortunately survived: " Concerning this German language I flatly despair, dear Hubert! " In February 1574, Philip reported with querulousness that some of his friends had left town without coming to say farewell. Languet replied firmly: Philip must not take himself so seriously; at this rate he would spend his entire life quarreling! Yet shortly it appeared that the boy was more than oversensitive. He was ill. In haste Languet called him back to Vienna and nursed him with loving care.

In November 1574, though not " in good estate of body " Philip made a journey to Poland. The winter was otherwise spent at Vienna. Time passed quickly what with Languet to direct his studies, and to train him for tilt, Pugliano, the Emperor's esquire of the stable. In this tournament practice Edward Wotton, the English Resident, joined. Philip afterward wrote of Pugliano's eloquence, with regard to the military profession, that he called soldiers " the noblest of mankind, and horsemen the noblest of soldiers "; he said they were " maisters of warre " and the " ornaments of peace." Clearly Philip had begun to consider the possibilities of this glorious military " estate," as close second to Languet's diplomatic program.

Sidney's leave, which had already been extended, was now fast running out. In early March of 1575, he took his homeward way as far as Dresden. Thence he passed to Frankfurt where happily Languet could join him. About the middle of May, the scholarly old legate was recalled to Prague. The parting of the two friends was tender and tearful. Those were the days when brave men did not disdain " gracious drops " of feeling. Very soon after, Philip traveled to Heidelberg. On the last day of May he was in Antwerp, awaiting the ship for home, his bags full of the books and maps he had bought from the famous Plantin.

When he left England in 1572, Sidney had been " young and raw." Now he was returning at twenty, with the polish of foreign courts and universities upon him. He had survived the greatest cataclysm of his time. He had been honored by the attention of the world's greatest scholars and thinkers. He had made his lifetime's friend in the good and gracious Languet. As he braced himself on the deck of the caravel which carried him over the Channel, he could not have told you whether most he wished to be ambassador or general! Perhaps it was just as well. Uncle Robert would make him a courtier, a creature of charm and beauty, of perfume and pretty speeches. In short, a very " Primerose of Nobilitie."

THE SEVENTH CHAPTER
ENTITLED A PRIMROSE
OF NOBILITY.

HILIP joined his family at the London mansion across from Paul's Wharf, with its view of the misty Thames and its democratic juxtaposition to the fragrances of the Blue Boar cook-house. He found the Sidney fortunes, on the whole, more favorable than when he left.

To be sure, his mother had a long list of grievances against the Earl of Sussex who as Lord Chamberlain was in charge of living arrangements at court. He denied her " linnen hangings." He placed her in lodgings both chill and " wide " which had never before been used for any but servants! Possibly Lady Sidney was magnifying unintentional slights. Possibly Sussex was venting his pique at the continued importance of his rival Leicester.

Undoubtedly, Robin was in high favor. He would shortly entertain the Queen and court at Kenilworth. Already rumors flew about that the diversions there would eclipse in magnificence any ever prepared for the gorgeous Gloriana. Perhaps the news had leaked out through Elizabeth's new maid-of-honor, Mistress Mary Sidney, Philip's lovely auburn-haired sister just fourteen, an age then judged of as suited to royal " service " and the fluttering of courtiers' hearts.

When Sir Henry Sidney left Ireland, in March 1571, anarchy closed in behind him. Though the Queen had made his tenure there just as trying as she could, at bottom, she knew that no one could handle Irish affairs more adeptly. Now she had persuaded him into resuming his difficult charge. This time, however, Sir Henry was to go back more or less on his own terms. At least he thought so! The details were to be discussed during the Progress to Kenilworth.

Philip found that he, too, was to accompany the Queen. Leicester considered his placing at court a matter of prime and immediate importance. Everything hung on his pleasing Elizabeth. Without her permission he might not even marry. Through her favor alone could he hope for title, or his share of the plundered estates sequestered from wretched Catholics. Through her alone might he achieve the business of state he craved, or participate in " any good Warres " that were to be had in Europe.

On June 12th, 1575 Philip wrote of Elizabeth to his friend the Count of Hanau. The Queen was forty-two. Sidney described her as " somewhat advanced in years " though " hitherto vigorous," and the " frail thread " on which the public safety depended! In an age of extravagant flattery the frankness of this is unmatched. Closest to it comes a remark credited to that mad wag, the Earl of Oxford. Once (and in his cups at that), he rose to the boldness of saying that the Queen " had the worst voice and did everything with the worst grace that ever woman did! " Upon the mere rumor, he was put in close " restraint."

Leicester knew that his royal mistress was only annoyed by frankness. Accordingly with the zeal of a proselyte who had himself won a good seat in heaven, he sought to drive out of Philip Sidney such offending candor as this. If he did not entirely succeed, we may be sure that under his tutelage the handsome nephew bowed deeply before his Queen, and spoke of Youth and Beauty with sincerity quite sufficient. Perhaps in memory of his lesson, Philip wrote later of a princess in his *Arcadia:* " She was a Queen, and therefore beautiful ! "

So Uncle Robert taught him to be a courtier. Philip went in before the breakfasting covers were placed. He bared his head as the Queen came forth from her chamber. He knelt as she passed and cried " God save Your Majesty ! " Then, as royal cupbearer, he knelt to proffer her drink from a vessel of Venice crystal or goblet of purest gold. He marked if she praised his jerkin. If she said " 'Tis well enough cut ! " or the color liked her well, he hastened to order another of just that cut and color. (Her Grace had once " misliked " of a certain " fringed cloth " and gracelessly spat upon it !)

Philip was doubtless restive. But young men of his time knew their " duty." Leicester was architect of all the Sidney fortunes. Besides, as he " waited " all day, and danced the better part of the night, Philip made observations of his own. Not every courtier won Gloriana's favor, yet of those men who had it — Hatton and Edward Dyer, and above all his uncle of Leicester — all were accomplished courtiers. They studied the moods of their mercurial mistress devoutly. They met them with resource and a superhuman patience. They knew when to be bold, when to be stricken and silent. Most important, they knew the right use of flattery, that holy-water of court.

In this same month of June, Elizabeth came to Grafton on her Progress. There Philip witnessed one of the " jars " of her unpredictable temper on a " marvellous hot day," when the Queen came in from hunting, and called for her golden cup to quench her royal thirst. Then, to the horror of everyone from Robin himself down to the smallest scullion, it was discovered that the ale had worked. In the entire place ' there was not a drop of good drink ! " The Queen loosed a Tudor tempest. Solicitous courtiers tasted every keg in town, all to no avail. The drink was all " too strong " for any man to stomach. The royal storm continued. Post-haste, Hatton sent up to London after wine. Post-post-haste, Leicester ordered ale to be fetched from Kenilworth. Then the courtiers bowed their heads and waited. At last good drink arrived! In pious relief, Leicester wrote of the business to Burleigh: " God be thanked she is very merry and well disposed, *now.*" His letter closed with fervent prayer that his " dearest Dread " would like of Kenilworth better.

As a matter of fact, he invoked the aid of Providence in no small matter. Coming to Kenilworth with the Queen, were all her waiting-maids in their shining white and silver, his little niece among them. There would be forty nobles of the very first rank as well, and some seventy " principal lords." They would all bring attendants. As his lordship knew, there might well be " jars " in the twelve days of the " visit."

On July 9th at eight o'clock in the evening, Elizabeth came to Kenilworth. On the way she had seen a famous " fat boy," and a sheep of Leicestershire breed which was also enormous. She had tasted of a banquet in a fair tent. Above all, she had enjoyed " good pastime in hunting." She was, God be thanked, in excellent humor!

At the park gates, she graciously accepted a " proper poesie in rhyme and meter " which was delivered by a sibyl. She listened to the harmonious blasting of six trumpeters " every one an eight foot tall." Finally she received with kindness the Lady of the Lake who approached by torchlight, and recounted all the mighty glories of Kenilworth from the time of King Arthur. Her speech concluded with lines in which, obviously enough, Leicester renewed the respectful tender of his heart:

Pass on, madame, you need no longer stand
The lake, the lodge, the lord are yours for to command!

Elizabeth was quick with her parry. " We had thought," he said, " the lake had been ours, and do you call it yours! "

Beyond the base court were other pageants. Full welcome after the heat was the sight of " great livery pots of silver filled with claret and white wine." Then, most delicate of compliments, just as Elizabeth passed to the inner court, every clock in the castle stopped. Time itself should stand still during the royal sojourn!

Leading the Queen to her chamber, Mistress Mary and her sister attendants began to unpack the gorgeous multitude of Gloriana's dresses. As they were shaking out waistcoats of silver and smocks of Milan work, the thunder of fireworks sent them running to the casements. For two hours the show continued. By the light of the rockets, they counted the gold tassels and jeweled silver aglets which had been " lost from her Majesty's back " during that strenuous day. Eliza wore her raiment with a free Tudor grace!

July 10th fell on a Sunday. In the morning the Queen and court attended Divine service. But the afternoon was noisy with music and dancing. The Puritans were not yet in command, and the English sabbath was joyously pagan. Indeed, the " junkettings " ended, as on the preceding night, with fireworks. This time the tumult was so terrific that the humbler sort were " vengeably afeared." Perhaps they remembered that at Warwick two years before, such a " play " had burned two houses!

The days passed in hunting and in " ambrosial feasts." There was bear-baiting and morris dancing. The court laughed itself into stitches over a rustic " bride-ale," all because the bride was ugly! (Philip enjoyed the joke and saving the poor woman up in his mind he put her into his *Arcadia,* as Mopsa, whose mouth was " heavenly wide.")

There was running at quintain, a jolly kind of tilt in which a bag of flour burst over the head of the elegant youth who failed to turn his horse in time. While the victim coughed and sneezed and shook his ruff and his ears, the court rocked in innocent mirth. There were tournaments, not so amusing but infinitely more dangerous, in which Pugliano's pupil doubtless took part as well.

The loveliness of the water-pageant reminded Philip of the gracious shows in the Louvre. The Lady of the Lake appeared on her torch-lit isle with a mermaid in attendance, and a dolphin who actually swam although he was more than twenty-four feet long. Upon him rode Arion. Yet even in these refinements there was a sturdy English touch, for Arion had visited my lord of Leicester's cellar. As a result he was unsure of the speech George Gascoigne had written him. He had conned it, and it was poetical. But when the time came for it at last, Arion whisked off his mask, amiably announcing that " he was none of Arion, not he, but honest Harry Goldingham! " Gloriana was delighted.

Not so poor Gascoigne, who like other dramatists, was discovering that something always happened to his best speeches. He wrote one for a Wild Man, all dressed in leaves, who brandished an uprooted tree, and hailed Gloriana with verses as she came in from hunting. Elizabeth was bored. To get rid of him, she gave her horse the spur, to no avail, for he followed her fleetly, reciting as he ran! Between vexation and laughter, she finally stopped her steed to hear the fellow out. Whereupon with real gallantry, the panting actor made her compliment of his own, saying he had " rather run as Her Majesty's footman on earth, than be a god on horseback in heaven! "

Somewhat later the Wild Man had ill success with another scene. Leicester staged it with care, making sure by prearrangement that Elizabeth was within earshot. Lustily, then, the Wild Man shouted:

Who gave all these gifts? I pray thee, Echo, say,
Was it not he who (but of late) this building here did lay?

Echo, thus adjured, answered very audibly (and with a pun) " Dudley! " The Wild Man continued:

O Dudley! So methought: he gave himself and all
A worthy gift to be received, and so I trust it shall —

Whereupon Echo, echoing Robin's hopes, boldly answered, " It shall! "

Perhaps it was the Queen's lack of response to the Lady of the Lake's hint and to Echo's that led Leicester to countermand the performance of the *Masque of Zabeta.* Under the transparent disguise of the nymph Zabeta, Elizabeth Regina was to have heard a public plea for her marriage, with one who had shared her " afflictions." In short, with Leicester who had also endured the Tower. Though the troupe all " prepared and ready (every Actor in his garment) two or three days together," the mask was never called for. Leicester knew when to stop.

On July 27th, Gloriana mounted her palfrey to depart. Philip and all the court were ready to go with her, and sumpter mules with the luggage were champing in the base and inner courts. But even at the end there were gallantries. From his uncomfortable stance in a holly bush, an actor dolefully announced himself as Deep Desire. (Was his other name Dudley?) Once he had loved a Queen. For his mad presumption he had been turned into a tree. Temporarily he had power of speech vouchsafed him, because when his " deare delight went by," he expected to die of woe. The effect of pathos was marred. For, unlucky to the last, the Wild Man brandished his tree in what was intended as rustic gesture of farewell. Perhaps Elizabeth's palfrey thought it meant another hour of his verses! At all events, the royal steed shied and reared with such violence that Deep Desire and the Wild Man were struck dumb with apprehension. Gloriana quieted the horse. " No hurt, no hurt! " she said.

The court rode on to Lichfield. Nevertheless the
" princely pleasures of Kenilworth " had significant results.
One of the Dudley retainers, a friend of Philip's, named
Edmund Spenser, found in the speech about King Arthur
a hint for his *Faerie Queene.* A neighboring " rustic," a
lad of eleven called Shakespeare, would remember a mermaid later, a dolphin and a Queen who like a votaress
passed on, " in maiden meditation fancy free." Most important of all, for Philip and Uncle Robert, the votaress
had at last declared herself. Whatever else might happen,
Leicester knew he would not be king.

As a matter of fact, Robin was even then accompanying
his sovereign to Chartley where the mistress — Lettice Devereux, Countess of Essex — was fated to console him.
While Philip Sidney walked among the knotted beds of the
Countess's garden, he, too, unknowing, saw his sweetheart,
Penelope Devereux, the daughter of the house and a lass of
twelve. Before the year was out she and Philip had plighted
their troth. Soon, though, for lack of money, this elegant
poor young Philip was destined to lose her, finding, alas
too late, that he loved her with passion! By stranger caprice
of Fortune, the lady he finally wedded became when he
died, the wife of Penelope's brother, Robert. Happily for
the present, all this lay ahead! Now a Robin of nine was
spinning his top on the well head, innocent of the future.
Even so, Gloriana was a gracious guest, serenely unaware of
the turmoil and pain that both her Robins would cost her.
She even smiled on Lettice.

On August 12th, 1575 Philip and his father kissed Elizabeth's hands and took their leave devoutly, as befitted pil-
grims quitting a shrine. Sir Henry was bound for Ireland,
and Philip was permitted to go with him to the coast. They
had almost a month together before Sir Henry sailed, time
to arrange about a will. (It was always safer to make one
before venturing to Ireland!) As they passed through

Shrewsbury, the devoted Corporation tendered hospitality to the Lord President and his son. The " wine, cakes and other things " with which they were regaled cost all of seven shillings. By September 8th, Sir Henry was in Ireland. Before the year was out, Philip would be there with him.

Now, however, he returned to London, whither the Queen would soon come, too. There he settled with Richard Rodway, of the Worshipful Company of Merchant Taylors for the clothes he had bought for the Progress. In modern money, the bill came to over a thousand dollars! Also, somewhat tardily, he caught up with his correspondence. He had treated Languet badly, since upon December 2d, 1575 the old scholar received the first letter in six months. Those were not the days when elders suffered neglect with patience. Languet wrote sharply: Philip might have satisfied him " abundantly," had he " sacrificed but one dance a month! "

During the winter of 1575–1576, Sidney's practical interest in English politics began. His experience at Bartholomew gave his thinking the strongest Protestant bias. From the start, he was convinced that the safety of England was tied up with the safety of the Huguenots in France and the Protestants in Flanders who had risen against Spain in 1567. He wanted England to join them in a definite policy of open defense — if not of open aggression — against the Catholic powers and chiefly the King of Spain.

But Gloriana had no intention of tying herself to anybody or anything, least of all to a definite policy. She never planned ahead. She acted when she had to, and never one way long. She rarely took a straight tack when a by-course was in sight. By masterly indirections she found directions out. Consequently when William of Orange sent St. Aldegonde to England in the autumn of 1575, to offer her the Sovereignty of the Low Countries, to Philip Sidney's disappointment she refused. She might aid the Dutch " underhand " (at a high rate of interest), but she wanted to be free to express to Philip of Spain the liveliest horror at his wicked rebels!

To Sidney's direct and very impatient mind, all this was duplicity, nothing else. It was duplicity, true, yet it was something more. England had no money to fight Spain alone, to say nothing of Spain allied to the Catholic Guises. The Protestants did not agree among themselves, either in England or in the other countries; they would give no solid support. Moreover, the King of Spain was a cautious soul of an infinite vacillation, Elizabeth chose to fight him with his own weapons. They were hers as well. She knew their use to a miracle!

Sidney was already proving a restless lap-dog. However charmingly he might lead corantos at court, or assist at fashionable christenings in Westminster Abbey " with a fair linnen towel on his left shoulder," he yearned for action.

When the Duke of Alençon, now posing as chief of the Huguenot party, invited Philip to serve under him in France, he was most enthusiastic. All that winter he hoped to go. He wanted to study affairs in France as he had in Austria and Poland. He wished to serve " religion." He sought a man's outlet for his energies, in camp or field of battle.

Unhappily, the scheme miscarried. It was the first in a chain of disappointments to his thrusting ambitious spirit. Possibly Elizabeth refused her permission then as she did later, on the ground that his presence among the Protestants would seem to commit her to an anti-Spanish plan. Possibly he had already decided on going to Ireland.

However we may judge of Walter Devereux, Earl of Essex, and the Lady Penelope's father, there is no doubt that he loved and admired Philip. Sir Henry had been known to take God to witness that he, at least, could not " abide "

the man! Yet Philip found him charming when the two
met at court in this winter of 1575–1576. The Earl had
just returned from Ireland, a place newly appealing to
Philip. Their friendship so flourished that when Essex was
made Earl Marshal in May and sailed for Ireland on
July 22d, 1576 Philip Sidney was with him.

As soon as they landed, Philip joined his father. Sir
Henry was in Connaught repressing some " stirs." It was,
in fact, a poor week in which he hadn't such occupation.
The English Deputy led a rousing life. Philip was to see
the action he wanted, and without delay.

Just now it was the young Burkes who had broken their
parole. Shearing their English raiment to ribbons, by way
of paying respect to law, order and Elizabeth, they crossed
the Shannon to rouse as much of the West country as they
could in so short a time. They succeeded very nicely. For six
weeks there was wild work in wild country, and break-
neck riding on the swift little Irish horses. Laboriously
Sir Henry and Philip followed up false clues, to the de-
risive delight of tribes temporarily too quelled to join in
the open revolt, but not so far lost to decency that they
would co-operate with the English!

Edmund Campion who was priest among them wrote
of this Irish people that they were " religious, ireful, sufferable of pains infinite, very glorious, with many sorcer-
ers." He went on to say that they were " great givers of their
own laws." He might have added that they gave them
more cheerfully than they took even those of their making.
The hated English law they flouted with ardor and resource.

To men like Spenser, Sir Henry, and Philip, who regarded Gloriana's laws as the " best in the world, the most
just and agreeable," this attitude continued incomprehen-
sible to the last. They were sent to enforce order. When they
caught their rebels, they strung them up sixty at a time.
They impaled the head of Shan O'Neil on a pole before

Dublin Castle. During the period over which any single policy was allowed to continue, they managed to impress a people who were "sufferable of pains infinite." At that, Sir Henry pitied their misery — as much as became an Englishman — and wrote to the Queen that a Christian could not behold it with dry eyes. He had tales aplenty for Philip as they scoured the hills and "marishy" lowlands together.

At night they were glad of the shelter of rude huts, where by fires of peat or sea-coal, young Sidney met some of the "tale-tellers" that "brought their lords asleep" with stories "vain and frivolous." One which amused Father Campion was about a bogus priest. This man told his congregation that St. Patrick and St. Peter had just come to blows over whether or not to admit an Irish soldier to heaven. "In the argument" the candidate over whom they contended suffered a broken head. The folk of that pitiful parish were so touched that they took up a sizeable collection for the relief of the lad with the bloody coxcomb!

Like Spenser before him, Philip was interested in a "certain kind of people called Bards" which the Irish had "instead of Poets." They set forth "the praises and dispraises of men in their poems and rimes," and were in "so high request and estimation" that no one dared to displease them "for fear of running into reproach" and being made "infamous in the mouths of all men." Both Sidney and Spenser doubtless smiled at such a naïve and barbarous arrangement. In civilized London, the Queen through the Stationers' Company held bards in proper subjection! Witness certain amputations both of limb and fortune by grace of the royal censor, which Philip would see in August 1579.

One colorful passage has come to us, thanks to a letter which Sir Henry wrote years after:

There came to me also a most famous feminine sea-captain, called Granny O'Malley and offered her services unto me wheresoever I would command her, with three galleys and two hundred fighting men, either in Ireland or Scotland. She brought with her her husband, for she was by sea as by land, more than master's mate with him. He was of the nether Burkes and called by the nickname ' Richard in Iron.' This was a notorious woman in all the coast of Ireland. This woman did Sir Philip see and speak with: he can more at large inform you of her.

Although Philip's account of the visit is lost, we learn from other sources that Granny could and did swear " most horrible." She was indeed " very glorious " about her exploits, this female pirate with the meek husband who bore a terrible nickname but trailed in her wonderful wake!

Philip and his father continued very busy, thanks to the " hollow hearts of the inhabitants and the secret lurking of the rebels." They were at Athlone on September 4th, 1576. They reached Galway a week or ten days later. There, on the 20th, Philip left his father to travel in haste towards Dublin. Word had come of the illness of the Earl of Essex who had been stricken on August 20th with such suddenness as to produce the inevitable rumor of poison. He wanted passionately to see " son Philip " before he died.

By the time young Sidney reached Dublin the Earl had already gone. His disease was dysentery. He died on September 22d, leaving a special message for Philip:

Tell him I send him nothing, but I wish him well, and so well that if God do move their hearts, I wish that he might match with my daughter. I call him son; he is so wise, so virtuous and godly; and if he go on in the course he hath begun, he will be as famous and worthy a gentleman as ever England bred.

The affectionate boy was deeply moved by the praise of the handsome Earl whom he loved. With a heavy heart this Philip whose quality Essex had caught so soon, prepared to take him home. Edward Waterhouse, who was in the Irish service, went back to England as well.

As soon as they landed Sidney sent on to Lord Burleigh letters from his father, reserving till later, an exhaustive verbal account of the Irish situation. Then with a new gravity on him, he traveled bleak November roads to Carmarthen where the Earl was to be buried.

After the funeral Waterhouse wrote to Sir Henry that people were wondering at court what would become of " the treaty between Mr. Philip and my Lady Penelope." He went on to remark:

Truly my Lord, I must say to your Lordship as I have said to my Lord of Leicester and Mr. Philip, the breaking off from this match, if the default be on your parts will turn to more dishonor than can be repaired with any match in England.

Sadly enough, Walter Devereux was the second man in England to call Philip son, without cause. The first had been Lord Burleigh. As early as 1568 he betrothed his daughter, Anne Cecil, to Philip Sidney, probably in the hope that the boy would prove to be Leicester's heir as well as his father's. Three years later however, he married his child to a wealthy erratic peer, the Earl of Oxford, with whom she was utterly miserable. In the case of Mistress Penelope who looked so staid and sweet in her mourning blacks and comforted her mother as a great lass of thirteen should, exactly the same thing happened.

When the estate of Essex was settled, it was found that like most courtiers he was sinfully in debt. Lady Penelope had £100 a year, hardly enough to keep her in ruffs of real lace to say nothing of gloves and pantoffles! And alack and alas, Philip Sidney was poor. Both as Lord Deputy of Ireland and Lord President of Wales, Sir Henry expended far more than the stipends that came to him from Elizabeth. From a slender purse his son supported the courtier's expensive trade. And shortly, even his prospects as the Earl of Leicester's heir would vanish to nothing!

THE EIGHTH CHAPTER ENTITLED
ISLANDS OF PURE
GOLD.

"T O BEAUTIFY their Walls, Parlers, Chambers, Galeries, Studies or Libraries" wrote John Dee in 1570, " there are few but liketh, loveth, getteth, and useth, Maps, Charts and Geographical Globes." Philip Sidney was not one of the few.

It was only natural that his eager mind and thrusting spirit, confined as they were to the narrow bounds of court attendance, should find fascination in wide horizons and new worlds. Particularly when, as everybody knew, one had only to sail west long enough, to come upon store of gold and silver, pearls as large as pears, and rubies so luminous that one could find them in the dark! Comfortable doctrine, this, for a young man who had already more bills than rose nobles with which to pay them. No wonder that Philip took shares in the voyages of Martin Frobisher from 1576 to 1578. Frobisher was searching out golden isles which lay along the North-west passage!

" Venturing " ran in the Dudley blood. The Duke of Northumberland had promoted Sebastian Cabot's voyage to Cathay by the Northeast route in 1551. He had wanted to raid Peru! Philip's uncle John studied cosmography with the learned Dr. Dee who knew more about it than any man in England. His uncle Robert's passion for schemes to fetch bullion out of America, Muscovy, the Le-

vant, and this same Cathay (as people called China) was
notorious. Though Philip's other uncle, Ambrose Earl of
Warwick, was Frobisher's patron in the present enterprises,
Leicester took shares amounting to £150. Out of his own
slender coffer, Philip invested £25.

At the time of his first voyage to find the North-west
passage in 1576, Martin Frobisher was verging on forty.
Before he was fifteen he had shipped for Africa after gold
and ivory. Since then he had done a bit both in trade and
piracy. There was a pretty story of his capturing an
Andalusian vessel called the *Flying Spirit* and spirit-
ing away her cargo of cochineal! That was in 1565.
The King of Spain had complained to the Privy Council.
Frobisher was "sent for." Oddly enough, there was
similar trouble in 1569, for Frobisher was no man to be
discouraged.

As the nephew of the lord patron of the expedition,
Philip was doubtless more welcome while the ships were
fitting than the average courtier would have been. He found
Frobisher a huge sun-burned giant of a man with a choleric
blue eye and a very business-like way of stowing an harquebus. His hairy arms had enough strength in them to heave
a sailor over the side, or fish him back from the maw of the
sea as need might arise. He towered over the brawny crew
on the *Michael* and the *Gabriel,* stout little boats of twenty-
four tons apiece. As he directed the business of "new taking and rigging" the third boat, a "pynnasse" of only
six tons, he checked the "drogges" for the voyage. There
was rhubarb, spikenard, tumerick, cardamon seed, borax,
camphor and lapis lazuli. Plenty, too, of that seaman's specific of all time, *aquavitae,* or brandy!

In the cabin of the *Gabriel,* Philip found the ship's library, comprising just seven books on geography and navigation, being all there were in English. One, he saw, had
been dedicated to his father. A second had come out under

Leicester's auspices. A third was the *Travels* of gullible
John Mandeville!

But there were plenty of maps, " hover " glasses, " cartes "
of navigation, and some wonderful instruments. Philip
had studied enough mathematics at Padua to appreciate
them. For himself, Frobisher would cheerfully have swept
the whole lot over the side — equinoctial dials, holometers,
meridian compasses and balastettas! They had been in-
stalled by Dr. Dee whom Philip knew as an astrologer of
parts and one of the greatest mathematicians in the world.
Frobisher had heard Dee was a sorcerer and talked with
the Devil. Just now he would rather buy a fair wind of the
man, as one would of any witch, than pretend that he understood the use of all those instruments!

But Frobisher had something more important than
knowledge of " toys " like projections and astrolabes. He
knew his seas. He knew them heaving in sunshine. He
knew them alive with wind, tumbling, turquoise and jade.
He knew them black and mountainous from the dim little
deck at night. He knew them yeasty, and yellow as mustard, sinister in storm. On the best of them, his boats made
but four knots an hour! Still, he wanted to sail the northern
ocean of swirling snows, where fogs blotted the path ahead,
and closed in on the wake. He wanted to find what no one
had found yet, the North-west passage which was a short
cut to the riches of Cathay.

By the first week in June 1576, all was ready for the
start. On the 7th as the court was assembled at Greenwich, a
shot of ordnance shattered the air along the river front.
The Queen herself ran to the palace windows. So did Mistress Mary Sidney and her grave brother. So did the rest
of the court which one way or another had contributed the
bulk of the £900 for Frobisher's venture.

They saw a brave sight. In gallant procession came the
Gabriel, the *Michael* and the little pinnace, making as fine

a show as possible, all flags flying, all hands on deck, the
trumpeter blowing away for all he was worth! Heads over
all, on the deck of the second ship, was the " General "
himself, bowing to the Queen. Gloriana graciously " shook
her hand " out of the window, to him and to the crew that
threw their caps in the air and shouted " Huzza " ! Then,
with the trend of her thinking undisturbed, she went back
to political chess. By the time the boats were at Blackwall,
even the restive Philip was again engulfed in the court.

He probably did not think of them again for a good six
weeks. But as he and the Earl of Essex took ship at Holyhead for Ireland on July 22d, he remembered the adventurers to the Northern void and wondered how they had
fared. He would certainly have been excited had he known
that two days before, on July 20th, at the end of a perilous
voyage, they had sighted land. They christened it Queen
Elizabeth's Foreland. (Although it was actually a part of
Baffin Land, they thought it was Cathay!) What a " stir "
this Sidney would have been in, too, had he realized that
only the day before, on July 21st, the General had found
to the north of this same Foreland, what he took for the
North-west passage and was calling Frobisher's Straits!

When Philip got back to London in November 1576, he
found the town a-gog with excitement. The expedition had
returned the month before. At court where he was " greatly
embraced," Frobisher told of finding the great *Meta Incognita* or Unknown Bound of which he had taken possession
in the name of Queen Elizabeth. In the streets he was " joy-
fully received " with " great admiration," especially when
he had with him the " native of Cathay " whom he had
brought back as a souvenir.

People told with gusto of the " pretty policy " which
had ensnared the guileless savage. Frobisher had rung a
low-toned bell to draw him to the *Gabriel*. Then, as soon as
the eskimo brought his native craft up with intent to snatch

the treasure and make off, the General had reached over the side and " brought him aboard," boat and all!

Londoners were never tired of inspecting the poor creature. Delightedly they pointed out to one another his " very brode face," the fullness and fatness of his body, his hair " cole blacke and hangynge," his eyes " lyttle and blacke," and his outlandish beard. Before long, this hardy inhabitant of bleak lands to the north of Labrador, caught cold in London, and promptly succumbed to the climate.

Even after the Cataian had died, the excitement continued, for gold had been found in some of the ore brought back. There were mountains of it to be had for the mining — whole islands of gold! Philip wrote to his dearest Hubert how the marvel had come about:

By chance a young man, one of the ship's company, picked up a piece of earth which he saw glittering on the ground and showed it to Frobisher; but he being busy with other matters and not believing that precious metals were produced in a region so far to the north considered it of no value. Well, they sailed homewards at the beginning of the arctic winter; and this young man kept his earth by him as a memorial of his experience (for he had no thought of anything else) till his return to London. And when one of his friends saw it shining in an extraordinary way, he tested it, and found that it was pure gold, unalloyed with any other metal.

As a matter of fact, George Best, who went on the voyage himself, had another version. " It fortuned," he said, " that a gentlewoman, one of the adventurers' wives had a piece of the ore

which by chance she threw and burned in the fire so long that at length being taken forth and quenched in a little vinegar, it glittered with bright marquisite of gold.

One tale was as good as another.

Both were infinitely more alluring than the truth, which was that two reputable " gold-finers " of London found the ore to be nothing but pyrites. Undaunted by their report, the promoters finally sought out an alchemist named Giovanni Baptista Agnello. He obligingly found " powder of gold," explaining that " Nature sometimes needs a little coaxing." Human nature needed none at all! The glad rumor took hold of court and ran like wild-fire through the city. To hear was to believe, even for Philip Sidney.

As a result, no sooner was the Cathay Company organized in March 1577, than contributions began to pour in for the second expedition. The fact that new shareholders were charged a levy of £30 on admission proved to be no deterrent. Even the thrifty Queen felt sure enough of fabulous returns, to invest £500 and equip the *Aid* with sixty-five sailors and twenty-five soldiers. Philip himself ventured £50, and Mistress Mary £25. This time Frobisher had orders to fetch back as much of the precious ore as the bottoms would hold, and to look over the ground with a view to planting a colony there later. Literally deluged with poetical " farewells " and laudatory pamphlets, he got off at last on May 30th, 1577. The Queen herself gave him audience at parting.

Philip had wanted to go along! Early in 1577 he wrote Languet a letter, now lost, in which the shrewd old scholar descried " a longing to undertake the enterprise." Sidney was doubtless prevented from making definite plans for the northern voyage, by learning in February that he was to head an embassy to the Continent. But before this occupation offered, he had come to a rare pitch of restlessness which demanded an active outlet.

The routine of philandering and flattery at Greenwich palled upon him more than ever after his return from eventful Ireland in November of 1576. Court life was rapidly becoming impossible. Not only was it expensive, but so far, it had not been productive of the benefits in offices and fees which Leicester's success had doubtless led them both to expect. To be sure, the honor of bearing the golden cup carried with it a stipend of £30 a year, but Philip's clothes cost at least ten times that sum. It was small wonder that the youth was looking forward greedily to the honest labor of loading ore in the Arctic twilight, even at a churl's hire!

When Sidney wrote to Languet on October 10th, 1577 Frobisher had just returned from " the sea which, as he thinks, washes the north point of America." From an island which he found " so productive in metals as to far surpass Peru," he had brought back two hundred tons of valuable ore, as yet unloaded. Philip went on to tell of " six other islands which seem very little inferiour! " It was indeed a " marvellous history! " He begged Languet's opinion on how the precious mines might be guarded from the Spanish and the Danes, " the former as claiming all the Western world by right from the Pope," the latter as nearer to the treasure than the English. He concluded by asking information on " the most convenient method of working these ores." (Evidently there was nothing which the learned were not expected to know!)

Remember so to write as that you may answer to the reputation in which you are held here; for unless you forbid it, I shall show your letter to the Queen!

While the Queen was awaiting Languet's disquisition on smelting, the ore was locked up safely in Bristol castle and the Tower of London. Meantime new tests began. Jonas Schutz, a " gold-finer " who had been with the expedition, said that with larger furnaces, he could get as much as £40 of gold from every ton. Shortly plans were begun for the erection of proper " works " at Dartford. All this took time.

Meanwhile Sidney was getting " marvellous histories "

from the " gentlemen sharers " whom he had wished to join. In *Meta Incognita* they had worked twenty hours a day getting ore into the ships what time it had been so cold that ice formed around the boats; they had been lucky to get away before the winter set in. The landmarks of which they spoke became as familiar to him as the names of London streets: Mount Warwick, the Countess of Warwick's Sound, and Leicester's Inlet. He heard of the tide in Frobisher's Straits which " roared like the Waterfall of London Bridge."

As eagerly as any, he inspected the unicorn's horn which was found on Smith's Island. It was " wreathed and straight, fashioned like a taper of wax," and so precious that it was " reserved as a jewel by the Queen's Majesty's commandment, in her Wardrobe of Robes " at Windsor. Being two yards long it must have been a proper trinket for a lady! From all over the world people came to view it, for everybody knew that the horn of the mystic unicorn both dispelled poison and guarded a body's chastity. No wonder Gloriana cherished it!

Philip also saw the woman and baby which Frobisher brought home together with another man. There had been a rare " coil " getting the woman, for the natives were wary of bells. Finally the sailors had shot this poor creature with arrows. One pierced the arm of the babe which she carried as she ran. When she stopped " to lick the wound with her tongue, not much unlike our dogs," they caught her easily enough. On the voyage back she showed a barbarian obstinacy in refusing " our good chirugion's salves." But she cured the infant's sore by her own " naturall method! "

They could both be seen about London, babe and woman equally helpless in the noise and squalor of civilization. Apprentices pushed through the cramped streets to gape at them. The fishwives in Billingsgate called Heaven to witness that the woman was a filthy slut who did not even know the use of Christian ale, but spat it out on the cobbles!

At last, reports on the ore came in to the Cathay Company. As before, reputable assayers failed to find any gold at all. Yet Agnello continued sanguine, and Dr. Burchard, an expert retained by Mr. Secretary Walsingham, stood ready to wager " lands, goods and life " that the ore would yield precious metal in quantity. Of all this news, only the good got out. The general public, including Philip and Gloriana, fondly believed that Frobisher had found the authentic mines from which Solomon drew the riches which built his temple!

Consequently people subscribed to the third expedition as hopefully as to the second. Sidney increased his stake to £67. 10s. His sister brought hers up to £33. 15s. Lord Oxford dramatically purchased shares amounting to £1000. Fifteen ships were fitted up to fetch back two thousand tons of the ore. It was also planned that " a certain number of chosen soldiers and discreet men " to the number of one hundred were to go along to inhabit the new land for the space of a year. Among them were miners and assayers, carpenters, bakers and " all necessary persons." For their protection against " the danger of the snow and cold air " as well as the " offence " of the Eskimos, the General was taking along a ready-built house which had been " made here at home and cunningly devised by a notable learned man." Such was the scheme for the first English colony on the " main " of America.

On May 21st, 1578 the expedition was ready. Frobisher went to Greenwich to " kiss hands " and came away with a gold chain which Gloriana had put around his neck herself. This time the voyage was not semi-official. It was under the direct supervision of the Crown!

When Frobisher came back dejected in the autumn, the

" colony " came back with him. The west and north sides
of the " fort " had gone down in the *Dennis* which had
been sunk by an iceberg, two other boats had been badly
battered, the ice had set in early. He found the court un-
moved by these sorry details of his failure. It was apathetic,
too, about his valuable explorations around the bay later
called for Hudson; his finding Hatton's Headland, and
christening another spot Charing Cross, " for the simili-
tude." (One wonders what it was.)

There was cause for this lack of concern. While Frobisher
was away, the ore had been declared utterly useless. When
Michael Lok, the treasurer of the Cathay Company offered
to pay £5 a ton for the ore out of his own pocket, no one
took him up! That was just as well, for Lok had fifteen
children, and shortly the ore was being " cast forth to mend
the roadways." The Cathay Company went into bank-
ruptcy. Some of the investors blamed Frobisher. Some
blamed Lok. Lok and Frobisher blamed each other, in
private, and before the Privy Council, with a most unlovely vehemence. At last, perhaps merely because a scape-
goat was demanded, Michael Lok was sent to the Fleet.

During the next two years, in his own phrase, Lok " saw
the inside of every prison in London except Newgate." Perhaps Newgate was full. Yet whatever the rights of his case,
he had two friends. One was Dr. Dee who consented to
receive one of the many young Loks as his apprentice. The
other was Master Philip Sidney, whose kindly heart was
touched, if not by Lok's virtues, at least by his heavy need.

When the treasurer emerged from his prisons in 1582,
he made a *Map of the Western World* which he dedicated
to Sidney. Its delightful inaccuracy suggests what may have
been wrong with Lok's accounts. There is something pa-
thetic in the pride which this man of shattered reputation
and fallen fortunes took in the little island which Frobisher
named for him. On his map it loomed as large as Canada;

half of the " Apalchen " Mountains could be fitted into it! But the man had his honesties. Unlike many map-makers of his time, he knew that he knew nothing of the western coast of America. So he left it out altogether. His America stretches to Limbo, instead of to California.

For his own vanished pounds and pence, Philip found what consolation he could in a letter which Languet had written in the autumn of 1577 when all had looked so hopeful:

Beware I do beseech you and never let the cursed hunger after gold of which the poet speaks, creep over that spirit of yours into which nothing hath hitherto been admitted save the love of goodness and the desire of earning the good will of men.

Possibly, the chief loss to Sidney lay in disappointed hopes, for in 1579 his name was on a list of those who had not yet paid up their subscriptions.

Though his interest in Frobisher's voyages had begun frankly enough with what Languet called his " mountains of gold," that had held for the first venture only. It is most significant that Philip's letter of October 10th, 1577 written when London was wild with excitement over monetary returns, should end with the quiet statement:

The thing is really very important because it may at some time be of use to professors of true religion.

Already at twenty-three, he was thinking of a Protestant haven for the " fortune-bound " of religion, in the New World. The second voyage he had wished to take, partly because it looked toward a colony later. The third, which was to have been the " planting," he planned upon as well. For on March 10, 1578 he wrote Languet in gloriously spacious phrase that he was " meditating some Indian

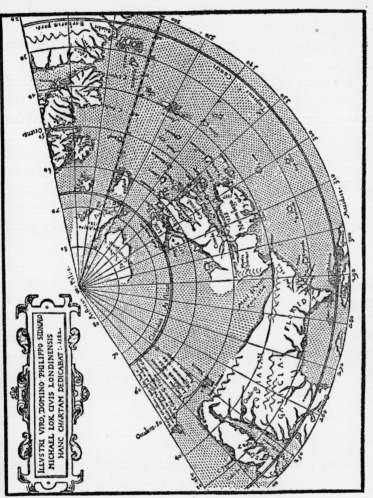

Michael Lok Map showing the Golden Isles of *Meta Incognita* and Frobisher's Straits.

project." And pertinently he added, " I see our Cause withering away."

In the autumn of 1576, then, he wanted his islands — all gold. In the spring of 1577, he saw them as outlet to action. By the fall of 1577, he dreamed of them as the site of a Protestant colony. Something lay back of the shift beside warning against " cursed hunger " ! That something was the embassy to the Protestant princes of Europe, in behalf of a Protestant League.

THE NINTH CHAPTER
ENTITLED
THE QUEEN'S AMBASSADOR.

N FEBRUARY 4th, 1577 Sir Henry Sidney wrote from Ireland to the Earl of Leicester: *Good my Lord, send Philip to me. There was never father had more need of his son, than I have of him. Once again, good my Lord, let me have him!*

When Sir Henry was in trouble, he instinctively turned to the son whose judgment he had come to value, even as he recognized that the uncle had prior rights. Leicester was not arbiter of the family fortunes for nothing.

It was he who " arranged " the marriage of Mistress Mary. She was now sixteen. The husband he selected was Henry Herbert, the Earl of Pembroke, a wealthy widower verging on forty. Sir Henry was delighted and wrote to Leicester in the liveliest gratitude " protesting before the Almighty God that if he and all the powers of earth " were to give him the pick of all possible husbands for her, he " would choose the Earl of Pembroke." It never occurred to anybody to ask Mistress Mary what she thought of the match!

There was rare scratching to collect the £3000 for her portion. Despite the friendly offices of Walsingham, the Queen could not be persuaded to pay her Lord Deputy one penny of the £4600 she owed him, and the poor man was forced to borrow. At last the bulk of the money was scraped together (the rest was to come in instalments!), and on April 22d, 1577 Philip's little sister was married. Fortunately for her, she was happy. The two mansions of which she was henceforth mistress, Wilton House and Barnard's Castle in London, became his havens of refuge.

In appearance, the Countess was much like her brother. Her pretty face was a " sharp oval," and her hair was " reddish yellow." They were almost twins in spirit and mind, with her merry disposition as a cheerful balance to his melancholy. She was his sprightly confidante both in the pangs of love, and in the ardors of creation. Though he was chiefly at Wilton over trying periods when he was " somewhat overmastered " — by Gloriana's anger, or by his passion for " Stella " — Philip was happier there than anywhere else on earth. No man was closer to him than this sister.

It must have been a great disappointment to them both that Philip could not see her married. Neither could he go to Ireland to help his father. For, at long last, his lap-dog's patience was being rewarded. He was going as Elizabeth's ambassador to the imperial court of Austria.

On February 7th, 1577 he received his final instructions. Ostensibly, he was " to condole the death " of Maximilian II. Upon the way to Vienna he was to wait on " the brethren Palatine," Prince Casimir and Prince Lodowick, to express the Queen's sorrow on the recent decease of their father, the Elector of the Rhine. So much, for show. In reality, he was to study the new incumbents of thrones, to observe conditions in Germany and the Empire, and to report on the prospects of a league among the Protestant princes of Europe.

Philip, also, owed his good fortune to Leicester. And at that his appointment had been most suitable. Like the princes whom he was sent to inspect, Sidney was young.

His marked Protestant bias ensured his most favorable
reception in Germany. At the imperial court too, he already
had many friends and some unusual sources of information,
thanks to Languet's assiduity in contriving contacts for him
in Vienna two years before.

Certainly it was not accidental that his suite should in-
clude his two closest friends, Edward Dyer and Fulke
Greville! In lines as innocent and loving as the posy on a
ring, he celebrated his affection for these two, whose initials
he entwined with his own in the margin:

> *Welcome my two, to me*   E.D.   F.G.   P.S.
> *The number best beloved*
> *Within my heart you be*
> *In friendship unremoved!*

A number of Elizabeth's most practised diplomats
swelled his splendid train, since she believed in im-
pressing the neighbors, especially when she could do so
for mere " board wages " and horse hire. As fine as money
(and credit) could make him, Philip went forth in all the
magnificence due to his magnificent mistress and his quite
as magnificent uncle. At last Lady Fortune stood auspicious.
(He had made sure of that by consulting Dr. Dee at Mortlake, in company with Edward Dyer and Leicester on January 16th!) Behind him he was leaving a court of petty in-
trigues. Before him lay an opportunity which spoke to both
mind and spirit. Since Bartholomew he had burned to serve
" religion." More than he realized himself, he longed to
see old Languet.

The party proceeded directly to Brussels. There the English Resident, Dr. Thomas Wilson, had taken lodgings
for them. The night of his arrival, Philip slept in a house
which bore a splendid scutcheon. Its inscription proclaimed to the world in Latin that here resided

The Most Illustrious and Noble Gentleman
Philip Sidney of England
The Son of the Viceroy of Ireland
Nephew to the great Earls of Leicester and Warwick
and Imperial Ambassador
of
Her Serene Majesty of England
Queen Elizabeth

A few days later, on March 5th, 1577, this exalted young personage rode over to Louvain. He was attracted neither by the lovely Cathedral, nor by the ancient University where Dr. Dee had studied under Gemma Phrysius. He was going to see Don John of Austria!

Philip II's handsome bastard brother was at this time his Viceroy in the Low Countries. Since his sensational exploits at the Battle of Lepanto six years before, Don John was the idol of Catholic Europe. Traditionally intrepid, he was crowning all now, as he verged on fifty, for he proposed to marry the Queen of Scots! There was a preamble to the match which we may be sure he did not discuss with visitors like Sidney, a little matter of launching an army on London and poisoning Queen Bess. Had his brother provided the troops, he would have led England a dance. And that despite the army which the watchful Walsingham was even now mustering while he spread rumors of forces more than twice as big! This Don John was the greatest general in Europe. No wonder Philip Sidney wanted to have a look at him.

Sidney's impressions of Don John have not come down to us. But he must have been stirred by the sight of this man who at Lepanto had traveled from galley to galley in a tiny frigate, standing in the prow in light armor with a crucifix in his hand, heartening his Christian hordes against the terrible Turk; this man who proved a Providence at his right hand not only by prodigies of valor, but by bringing his generals and colonels out of the battle " of one mind and satisfied with each other " !

However, Fulke Greville recorded the interview in his own astonishing style, top-heavy with circumlocutions and scrambled figures:

That gallant Prince, Don John de Austria, *when this Gentleman in his Embassage to the Emperor came to kiss his hand, though at the first, in his Spanish haughture, he gave him access as by descent to a youth, of grace as to a stranger, and in particular competition (as he conceived) to an enemy; yet after a while that he had taken his just altitude, he found himself so stricken with this extraordinary Planet, that the beholders wondered to see what ingenious tribute that brave and high-minded Prince paid to his worth; giving more honour and respect to this hopefull young Gentleman, than to the Embassadours of mighty Princes.*

By all of which, one gathers that once the ice was broken, Don John forgot that Sidney was an enemy and was more than usually cordial! Greville's tribute to him as a " brave and high-minded Prince " may be an echo of Philip's.

About a fortnight later, on March 22d, 1577 Sidney reported to Walsingham from Heidelberg that he had just heard there " of a meaning Don John should have to marry the Queen of Scots and so stir troubles in England." Since he does not say whether it was news to him or not, it is possible that he had been made privy to the Don's romance before he left England, and had sought him out under Walsingham's orders. However, like many others who had to do with the procrastinations of the Spanish king, Don John died before Philip made up his mind. Again Mary Queen of Scots was a widow, this time, even before she was wed!

It was something more than engaging manners and an attractive person which commended Sidney to the " haughture " of Don John and, once his embassy formally began, won him golden opinions from everyone else. Wherein that quality or qualities lay, we can now only conjecture from the evidence of the people whom he impressed. Walsingham, who knew all the difficulties of such a mission, wrote glowingly to Sir Henry of the " most sweet savour and grateful remembrance " which Philip left behind him " in all those parts " to which he went. Even the Prince of Orange, the shrewdest strategist on the Continent (incidentally the last man to capitulate to mere charm!) told Greville that Sidney was " one of the ripest and greatest Counsellors of Estate that at this day lived in Europe."

Without doubt his transparent honesty was a factor in the approval. At the time when Sir Henry Wotton made his famous pun, defining an ambassador as one " sent to lye [lodge] abroade for his countrie," that was the last thing looked for in a diplomat. Particularly in one who came from Elizabeth! Perhaps old Languet had intended the boy for negotiations with a full realization of the deadly spell which this crystal clarity would cast upon the Macchiavellian " practises " of the day. At all events Philip's frankness of manner was as rare as it was lovely.

Another element in his charm was his understanding approach. His own sensitiveness taught him sympathy. His official report shows that in April 1577, he handled the interview with Maximilian's widow, the Empress Maria, with consideration and tact:

Of the Emperor deceased I used but few words because in truth I saw it bred some trouble in her to hear him mentioned in that kind.

That is, in the past tense!

Such delicate awareness of the feelings of others prepared

him to deal with prejudice when he encountered it. On May 1st, 1577 he had a conference with Prince Lodowick, the new Elector of the Rhine. Bad feeling between this brother who was a Lutheran and Casimir who like the dead father was a Calvinist, threatened an immediate rupture. When Sidney saw him, Lodowick was industriously uprooting Calvinism. Philip's task was to bring him " to unity," without touching on the theological factors which were responsible for the trouble. Wisely enough, he eschewed argument in favor of an appeal to filial feelings:

I desired him in her Majesty's name to have merciful consideration to the church of the religion [Calvinism] so notably established by his father as in all Germany there is not such a number of excellent learned men, and truly anyone would rue to see the desolation of them. I laid before him as well as I could the dangers of the mightiest princes of Christendom by entering into violent changes, the wrong he should do his worthy father utterly to abolish what he had instituted, and so as it were to condemn him, besides the example he should give his posterity to handle the like.

He was invoking other emotions as well, the Elector's pride in the German learning, and even more potent, his fears for his throne. To the order of the points, it was a masterly piece of persuasion.

He did this sort of thing the more surely for an understanding of character. (He had seen a good deal of it at Greenwich!) As his apt appraisals of the sons of the Emperor show, he took stock not only of accomplishment, but of inherent capacity and the motivations of circumstance. Of the new Emperor, Rudolf II, he wrote to Walsingham on May 3d, 1577 that he was

wholly by his inclination given to the wars, few in words, sullen in disposition, very secret [secretive] and resolute,

*nothing of the manner his father had of winning men in
his behaviour, but yet constant in keeping them. And such a
one as though he promise not much outwardly, hath, as the
Latins say, somewhat in reserve.*

The brother, the Archduke Ernest, he found

*very much like him in disposition, but that he is more frank
and forward, which perchance the necessity of his fortune
drives him to. Both extremely Spaniolated.*

Sidney had learned, too, to distinguish honest conviction
from plausible expression, showing that however scrupu-
lous he might be himself, he was no babe in the woods. Of
Casimir he reported that he spoke " in good terms and with
a countenance well witnessing " that his words " came from
his heart." If he slightly overestimated the ability of the
young German prince, he was no more sanguine about
it than Walsingham. Shrewd Elizabeth went so far as to
consider lending him money, which for her was going very
far indeed!

However excellent his work, Sidney himself was deeply
disappointed with the results as they concerned the Protestant League. Perhaps he was not surprised when Lodowick turned a deaf ear to his carefully calculated appeal,
and with polite excuses went off " to the bathes." (One
could not expect much from a Lutheran anyhow!) But as
he passed from court to petty court, only to find suspicion
and dissension within the ranks of the faithful everywhere,
he was constrained to write home that his hopes grew every
day less and less:

*There is none of the Princes like to enter into any League
(and that rather as it were to serve the Queen than any way
else), but the Prince Casimir, the Landgrave [William of
Hesse] and the Duke of Brunswick.*

Yet if he was not returning with the Protestant League in his pocket, he had deftly opened the way for further negotiations. So well had he performed this task that even a captious mistress accorded to his service " great good acceptation " and admitted that he had evinced " great judgment and discretion."

Languet had been with him for almost all the time. Their companionship brought to the older man what he described as " incredible satisfaction." To Sidney it meant no less. At last he could unbosom himself to this wise good friend on many matters which both safety and good taste had forbidden his putting to paper. Such, for instance, as his unhappiness under the constraint of constant compliment, and his desire for more strenuous occupation than kneeling, even before the greatest and loveliest Luminary in the world. Money matters, too, might now be discussed with dignity. Languet, who knew Philip's exacting pride and his sensitiveness under expectation, doubtless set down these complaints to the restiveness of a young man who expected too much, too soon. He therefore counseled patience and waiting — but he also set wheels in motion to get what the dear boy wanted!

Just as he was about to leave toward the end of May, Sidney received orders in Antwerp to visit the Prince of Orange. Delightedly he turned about to Gertruidenberg where the Prince and Princess were staying. Ever since he had been in Europe, Sidney had " burned to be presented " to this man who was a hero after his own heart.

In describing William of Orange, even the flowery Fulke Greville was betrayed into something like simplicity:

His uppermost garment was a gown, yet such as (I dare confidently affirm) a mean-born student, in our Inns of Court, would not have been well-pleased to walk the streets in. Unbuttoned his doublet was, and of like precious matter [*material*] *and form to the other. His waist-coat (which showed itself under it) not unlike the best sort of those wollen knit ones, which our ordinary watermen row us in. His Company about him, the Burgesses of that beer-brewing Town: and he so fellow-like encompassed with them, as (had I not known his face), no exterior sign of degree, or reservedness could have discovered the inequality of his worth or Estate from that Multitude. Notwithstanding I no sooner came to his presence, but it pleased him to take knowledge of me. And even upon that (as if it had been a signal to make a change), his respect of a stranger instantly begat respect to himself in all about him. . . .*

Between this plain man with the decisive sober face who was the power behind the Dutch rebels, and Elizabeth's handsome and beautifully appointed young envoy there was no superficial resemblance. Yet the same tenacity, the same gift for inspiring leadership, the same fierce devotion to " religion " was in them both. For something like a week, Sidney remained with the Prince and his beautiful Huguenot wife, Charlotte de Bourbon-Montpensier. He stood godfather to their second daughter who was named Elizabeth, doubtless in compliment to the English Queen. Later a boy was to be called for Philip.

So happily did the elegant young Englishman fit into the simple household of William the Silent that when he departed the Princess gave him a chain of gold with a fair jewel. For his own part, the Prince had formed the judgment of Sidney which he imparted to Fulke Greville, evidently with intent that it should be passed on to the Queen. Philip, being consulted, demurred — and with very good sense. If Gloriana who had him by her constantly did not know of his abilities, she would take it very ill that " forrain Powers " presumed to instruct her!

As Sidney took his way home early in June of 1577, his

mind was busy afresh with a proposal which had come to him some time before in Frankfurt. It coincided so closely with Philip's dearest desires that one suspects Languet of setting the business afoot. But ostensibly at any rate, he spoke at the instance of Orange. What he suggested was that Sidney should marry the Prince's sister, and return to Europe for good, to assist in the task of making the Low Countries free and Protestant. The compliment inherent in the offer was tremendous. Now that he had observed Orange for himself, Philip's eagerness was greater than ever. Still he had returned a wise answer to this Languet the marriage broker. He said " he was not his own master " — young men of three and twenty spoke so then! — He must consult his father, his uncle and the Queen. Whether he had even seen the lady we do not know. He was doubtless leaving that part of the business to his elders who would in any case attend to it for him. His protest of " unworthiness " may be set down to mere gallantry. What really attracted him was the prospect of serving " religion."

His comprehension of the problems of Faith had been sharpened by a conversation which he had with Campion in Prague where having completed his novitiate, he was now professor of rhetoric in the Jesuit college. Sidney heard him preach before the Empress at court, and later gave him alms. On the strength of their talk the good father entertained hopes for the conversion of " this young man, so wonderfully beloved and admired by his countrymen " which he promptly passed on to his fellows. Actually there was no chance of Sidney's becoming a Catholic, though it was not the last time that an attempt was made to " water the plant."

What Campion took for ductility was doubtless the tolerance which Philip had all his life for his Catholic friends. The dynastic claims of Catholicism he was bound as an Englishman to decry, but he deplored the individual's suffering. Like his father, he made great efforts to relieve it. Even when, in his need, he sought profit from sequestered lands, he had the grace to be ashamed. And he never joined in the hateful business of persecution.

In the present instance, he was deeply moved by the quiet exaltation of this man he had known at Oxford. Shining in the vivid face above the priest's frock, he saw the ecstasy which would carry Campion home, to save the souls of Englishmen in a kind of patriotic piety which they would curse for heresy and treason! Did Sidney in some divining moment, even in that time of hate, sense that this devotion was identical with that which animated his hero, the Prince of Orange? Probably not. For however his kindly heart may have pitied this protégé of his father's, he wrote like a true child of his time, of the " ignorant obstinacy " of the Papists!

By June 10th, 1577 Sidney was home. Delightedly Walsingham wrote to Sir Henry that " there hath not been any gentleman these many years that hath gone through so honourable a charge with as great commendations." And Waterhouse passed on details more homely: " God so blessed him that neither man, boy, or horse failed him or was sick in this journey; only Fulke Greville had an ague in his return to Rochester." (In short, they were all well — until they returned to England!)

Almost immediately Philip discovered that he must abandon Europe to its fate, postpone as well all thought of his match with the house of Nassau. Sir Henry was in serious trouble. There had been plenty behind that urgent message, " Send Philip to me." It was now full six months old!

At first the boy planned on a trip to Ireland to discuss the situation with his father. Then as the weeks wore on, it became clear that Philip was needed at court even more. There he might anticipate the malicious rumors of Sir

Henry's misgovernment as they came in. Then, as now, a dozen truths scarcely sufficed to oust one lie which got in ahead. Being at hand, Philip knew what fiction was likeliest and could give the Queen actual facts. Theoretically this should have cleared the air in a trice. But it presupposed that Gloriana wanted facts. Actually she believed whatever was convenient. To make matters the worse, the fountain-head of the charges against Sir Henry was his old enemy the Earl of Ormonde, Her Majesty's own close cousin and her very great favorite!

Defending his father's reputation against the insinuations of Ormonde and the receptive royal mind, was like fencing in the dark. It got on Philip's nerves. For like the honest hot-head he was, he preferred to fight in the open. If he failed to force his foe to a public contest, at least he did his best!

While the court was at Oatlands in September 1577, Waterhouse wrote to Sir Henry of " little occasions of discourtesies " between the Earl and Mr. Philip. When his Grace " lately spoke to him," he " answered not, but was in dead silence of purpose " ! That unfortunately got him nowhere, for:

The Earl of Ormonde saith he will accept no quarrels from a gentleman that is bound by nature to defend his father's cause, and who is otherwise furnished with so many virtues as he knows Mr. Philip to be; and so, on the other side, Mr. Philip hath gone so far, and showed as much magnanimity as is convenient, unless he could charge him with any particularities which I perceive he cannot.

To this contest of generosities, Philip would have infinitely preferred his duel! For Ormonde knew court tricks altogether too well to provide him with " any particularities."

Still if he might not use one weapon, Sidney had another. He was shortly presenting to the Queen at Windsor his

Discourse on Irish Affairs. In it he justified his father's rule, under seven neat heads, in a bit of swift analysis. Though his first formal writing, its clean-cut effectiveness merited the enthusiastic judgment of Waterhouse that no man could " compare with Mr. Philip's pen."

However, it left Elizabeth cold. She also chose to ignore the tribute of the Irish who, dear knows, were not easy to satisfy in an English deputy. They said that if Sir Henry could but " sit in his chair " he would yet " do more good than others with all their limbs " ! But Gloriana reasoned thus: Ireland was costing her money. Sir Henry was in Ireland. *Ergo,* the " charges " were all along of him. Besides, the man thought too well of himself anyhow. Had he not come to Hampton Court with such a mighty train that, viewing it from the window, she had asked what prince was this?

Philip had observed his father in Ireland, constantly in a " tub of business ": fighting days, writing into the night, racking his brains for ways to keep up an army without paying it, performing impossible feats of bravery and patience. And now he observed the fruits of those heavy labors: steady abuse (in lieu of wages!), and criticism so harsh that Walsingham apologized as he passed it on.

While noble Sir Henry was under a cloud, men like Ormonde were petted. They basked in Gloriana's favor. Such court " reptilia " as he crept to the royal Sun through the mud of dubious gallantries, extravagant adulation and lying sufficiently shrewd. A flattered Gloriana requited their pains — not in money, but benefices, fee farms, monopolies in sweet wines. They might not even be loyal.

Small wonder that, seeing where he would fetch by honest service at home, this impetuous Philip should dream of his Unknown Bound. There in America, a man might climb with honor. Labor brought solid returns, all gold! There in the words of Ronsard who first sang of human nature transmogrified to glory by the open spaces of the West, " men lived in the Golden Age." They were free alike of tyrants, of doctors and lawyers! In such a heaven, the faithful religious might " plant."

Small wonder, indeed, that Sidney was " meditating some Indian project " in March of 1578. The " Cause was withering away " on the Continent. His house was not flourishing at home. Of course he wanted to sail with that " colony " of Frobisher's, two months later, in May!

THE TENTH CHAPTER ENTITLED
OUR UNBELIEVED
CASSANDRA.

HE fact is that Sidney at twenty-three had a definite political program. It was destined to disturb him more than it did anybody else. Under a queen of less godlike powers, he might have proved a nuisance. But Gloriana did not allow people with aims and ideals to annoy her. That sort of cerebration, she had discovered long ago, carried its own pains. However, even so, she may have regretted sending Philip on that embassy.

He had left England, with his mind firmly committed to the need of an alliance with other Protestant powers. Discovering barriers to a League in Germany, merely sharpened his conviction that England must make common cause with the Huguenots and the Dutch.

At Louvain he had seen the strength of Spain. It was the mightier for being allied to the genius of Don John and backed by the wealth of the Indies. It was the more sinister for its connivance with Mary Queen of Scots. Its danger was the more deadly, because, in her behalf at any moment, it could draw to itself her uncles the Guises. Its peril cut home because English Catholics who had helped in the Norfolk plots, would rally to Mary again. And to Spain and the Catholic Guises. Campion had shown him the brilliance and fervor which would direct conspiracies in future. Out of such a " fearfull Almanack," says Greville, " this wake-

full Patriot," Philip, looking ahead to the " masked tri-
plicity between Spain and Rome and the Sovereign Jesuits
of France," saw but one remedy. English aid. For the
Huguenots, to keep the Guises too busy for mischief abroad
For the Dutch, to occupy Spain, that pivotal point for
alarm.

Thus, continues Greville, " our unbelieved Cassandra "
recognized the " limitless ambition " of Spain which cast a
" particular aspect of danger upon his native Countrey."
His prophetic gray eyes saw through to the coming Armada, to the " great and hidden treason." Sidney was too
young to be a patient Seer. He had Dudley pride and ambition. With their visions of Troy in flames, Cassandras are
never happy. But to be Cassandra, and Dudley to boot!

For the two years following his return in July 1577, he
found England a prison, too narrow for his mind. The
everlasting vacillations of Elizabeth who feared an open
breach with Spain as much as he desired it, marked the
doom of his own high ambitions to serve " religion " in the
Low Countries. What was more, they struck at the very
life of the cause. Both ways he suffered.

In October 1577, there came a proposal from the Prince
of Orange himself. He wanted Leicester and his nephew
to take command under him. The Queen refused to let her
Robin go. Philip himself was sorely needed at court on
his father's Irish business. Nothing came of that. Nothing,
either, of the plan for Philip's marriage with the Prince's
sister. After Elizabeth had dawdled with the proposal for
upwards of a year, during which she drove poor Languet
to distraction concocting excuses to the Prince, she at last
gave Sidney to understand that the suit must be dropped.

Then in April 1578, just before the third Frobisher expedition set out, there was a second invitation to Flanders
which probably explains why Philip gave over going with
the " colony." This time it was Prince Casimir who wrote.

The young German was now serving in the Low Countries, at Elizabeth's express suggestion and with her promise of financial support. He wanted Sidney to share his command. Philip was tremendously eager for the chance. So much so that when Gloriana refused to part with Leicester, the Earl exercised all his power to save the boy from similar disappointment. Toward the end of July, young Sidney waited on the Queen to take his leave and receive her messages.

What happened we learn from his uncle's ironic letter of August 1578:

When my nephew was to receive his dispatch, among other small comforts he should have brought to [the] Prince [of Orange] he was specifically commanded by her Majesty to tell Duke Casimir that she marvelled not a little and was offended with him for giving out that his coming [into the Low Countries] was by her means, and that she misliked any such speeches, and prayed her name might not be so abused, since she did not command him to come, but the Dutch had entertained [invited] him and they should maintain his coming; with other such small encouragement to that prince whose cause of coming you and I and almost all men know! Yet this earnestly has she commanded Philip to say to him, writing such a letter besides of cold comfort that when I heard of both, I did all I could to stay him at home, and with much ado I think I shall, seeing I know not what he should do there, but bring discouragement to all her best friends. For my part I had rather he perished in the sea than that he should be the instrument.

Poor Philip! He must have been goaded to desperation, by his father's troubles, and by his own driving impatience, to warrant that "much ado," in view of the import of the message. About the Queen, he was so far as guileless as Casimir, who could not comprehend why if he had her support, he (or she) should pretend he hadn't! Even under favorable auspices, Her Highness was likely to balk at bills or chitter at complications. When she augured ill, it was high time to cry " 'Ware, storms! " Fortunately for Philip and his poor friends of " religion," Uncle Robert's judgment prevailed.

If the Queen served the Dutch in this scurvy fashion, she was no more dainty with the Huguenots. In April 1577, Sidney's friend, Philippe de Mornay appeared in their behalf. He wanted 100,000 crowns, a loan of course, and was willing to pay good interest. The Queen delayed answer for months. Then she whittled him down to 80,000. At the very end " between the promise and the performance the whole negotiation was upset " wrote Madame de Mornay. When her husband left London in the early winter of 1578, he took back no loan at all!

His stay had brought to Sidney companionship for over a year. He needed the warmth of it sadly. On June 1st, 1578 he had stood godfather to the Frenchman's little daughter Elizabeth. The two men had much in common in their devotion for Languet, their love of learning, their ideas on politics. Philip began a translation of De Mornay's book on the *Trewnesse of the Christian Religion*. Many an evening during the Huguenot's stay did the two Philips, Walsingham, Paulet and Davison, stout Protestants all, debate the affairs of Europe. In such discussions and the books which Languet sent him, a chafing Sidney was to find all the foreign contacts which Fate and Gloriana intended to vouchsafe him withal.

Such stimulus only served to increase his old restlessness a hundred fold. In March 1578, he poured out his woes to Languet:

The use of the pen, as you may perceive, has plainly gone from me, and my mind itself, if it ever was active in any-

thing, is now beginning, by reason of my indolent ease, imperceptibly to lose its strength, and to relax without any reluctance. For to what purpose should our thoughts be directed to various kinds of knowledge unless room be afforded for putting it into practice so that public advantage may be the result, which in a corrupt age we cannot hope for. . . . Do you not see that I am cleverly playing the Stoic? Yea and I shall be a cynic, too, unless you reclaim me!

This youth who was finding the times so sadly out of joint was no Stoic! Acceptance was a mood of which he as yet knew nothing. In his very kicking against the pricks, he showed himself all Dudley. But he was more than Dudley in aspirations for the " public advantage." If this was unrest, at least it was noble!

As a matter of fact, out of his fineness he suffered, out of that and his affections. For his father's troubles continued. Despite all efforts to prevent Sir Henry's recall, in February 1578 the Queen gave Philip to understand that his father must leave as soon as he could make arrangements. To avoid appearance of compulsion friends advised delay. Meantime Lord Burleigh and Walsingham were vainly urging Her Highness, to take the sting from her unjust treatment of the Lord Deputy by an offer of nobilitation which would recognize his unusual service. Through that entire spring the son was busy in his behalf, making use of Lady Sidney's subtle Dudley mind in the blind battle against Ormonde, and writing his father that he " had only light from her " in a business in which none proceeded " either so thoroughly or so wisely."

Then suddenly, it became evident that someone was overlooking the correspondence between Philip and Sir Henry. The first hint came in the boy's letter of April 25th, 1578:

Truly sir, I must needs impute it to some great dishonesty of some about you that there is little written to you or from you that is not perfectly known to your professed enemies.

He concluded with righteous gusto: " This much I am very willing they should know — that I do write it to you! "

Nothing but young Sidney's highly emotional state excused the letter which he sent about a month later to his father's utterly loyal secretary and faithful friend, Edmund Molyneux. Jumping to the conclusion that it was he who betrayed Sir Henry's plans, Philip wrote in peremptory fury:

Mr. Molyneux:

Few words are best. My letters to my father have come to the eyes of some. Neither can I condemn any but you for it. If it be so, you have played the knave with me; and so I will make you know if I have good proof of it. But that, for so much as is past. For that is to come, I assure you before God, that if I ever know you do so much as read a letter I write to my father, without his commandment or my consent, I will thrust my dagger into you! And trust to it, for I speak it in earnest. In the meantime, farewell. From Court, this last of May 1578.

By me

Philip Sidney

Here is temper indeed, and in naughty working order. One almost suspects that Edmund was lucky to be in Ireland, and so to be warned! And yet on his own admission, the hot-head lacked " good proof " and was constrained to " if it be so! " There is some extenuation (though not much) in the number of spies who in those dangerous times served two, and sometimes three masters, with absolute success; in the fact that treason was rarely disclosed save in the most unlikely places. (Not always then. Sir

James Croft, the Comptroller of the Royal Household and highly respected, was for years in the pay of Spain without any of his compatriots knowing a thing about it.)

Molyneux had known Philip from a child. Being completely in Sir Henry's confidence, he knew the shrewd hurts the boy had sustained in recurring disappointments, and in his father's hard fortunes. Taking into account his sensitiveness and suffering, he sent on to Philip an answer notable for its dignified defense — and mollification. Later letters which sign themselves " Your loving Frend, Philipp Sidney " show that this unlovely passage did not interrupt the cordial relations between the two. And the final estimate of Sidney's life and work which Molyneux wrote for Holinshed's *Chronicle* ten years later is all appreciative appraisal and the warmest eulogy.

As the months wore on in 1578, Philip needed every tittle of his slender stock of patience and philosophy. Conditions in the Low Countries which he regarded as so essential to the safety of England were going from bad to worse. It was small satisfaction to him to realize that his Queen was largely responsible. Some time before she had promised the Dutch rebels £100,000 on which they had trustfully begun to borrow. Now there appeared to be little chance of their ever securing the principal! On October 2d, Don John died of the plague. But his successor the Prince of Parma proved, if anything, more formidable. Religious dissensions developed in the ranks of the rebels themselves. They had a further affliction in the two " friendly " foreign armies. One, representing 10,000 German mercenaries headed by Casimir, was on the verge of mutiny because Elizabeth refused to pay them. A second was under the command of Catherine de' Medici's unlovely youngest son, François, whom the English called " Monsieur." And to cap the climax, neither of these " allies " would take orders from William of Orange!

Monsieur had worked his way into the Low Countries by a process of elimination. He had already to his credit a traitorous attempt to seize his brother's throne while Henri was in Poland, and a temporary alliance with the Huguenots whom he cozened egregriously before he finally left them in the lurch. Even now he deserved the encomium of his sister Margot that " if all infidelity were banished from the earth, he alone could supply the void." Additionally he was petulant and skittish. Ever since Gloriana had failed William of Orange, he had been constrained to look upon Alençon as his greatest dependency. To such a pitch had the rebels' fortunes declined.

In December 1578, Orange patched up a truce with Casimir. Immediately after he sent him across the Channel to make a last attempt to pin Elizabeth down to providing some definite financial assistance. Sidney hailed his coming with joy, not because it had any prospect of success, but because Languet was in Casimir's train. They arrived in London on January 22d, 1579.

Sir Henry's pleasure was as great as Philip's. He was deeply grateful to the old scholar who had done so much for his fine eldest son and shortly would undertake the education of the second boy, Robert. He presented him with a gold chain which cost close on a thousand dollars. He took him and Casimir to see the bear-baiting at Paris Gardens on the Bankside, just across the river from Paul's Wharf. To Philip's friend, Prince Casimir, he gave a rich illuminated book on the Knights of the Garter which was bound and " gilden " to order and tied up with strings of " blew ribband."

Meantime Languet and Philip were snatching what moments together they might in the course of the many entertainments which were being lavished on Casimir. Because Elizabeth had no intention whatever of providing the " open aid " which the young prince wanted, she had him feasted to the full — chiefly by other people. Sir Thomas Gresham, the founder of the great Royal Exchange, and mightiest of merchants, made him welcome with flutes and torchlight at his mansion in Bishopsgate. The Duchess of Suffolk entertained him at her house in the Barbican. Gloriana herself invited him to Westminster. For his delight the martial young nobles like Philip Sidney put themselves to the expense of a lavish tournament. He was promised the Order of the Garter. He was given a gold chain. If he wanted to pay his poor men seriously enough to sell it and the plate worth 2000 crowns which the citizens of London bestowed on him, that was his affair. But he received no money!

Pitiably little time was vouchsafed to Philip and Languet after all these festivities were done with. At the end matters were hurried and muddled almost past belief so that they did not even say good-bye. Philip was to remember that often, for he never saw Languet again. The day he landed at Flushing, February 14th, the old man wrote back to the boy:

I am sorry that I could not let you see even tears and sighs as pledges of my great regard for you; but it is not my fault, for our party was hastening away as if they were taking leave of enemies, not of friends, and I should have given great offence if I alone had behaved with common sense instead of being mad with the rest. As it was I did not make such speed but that before I crossed the river . . . all the horses which were to have conveyed us were gone; and had not Sir Hales had compassion on me, and lent me his servant's horse, I must have returned to the town.

The more shame to the parsimony of a princess who to save the hire of a single nag, put an honored guest in the sixties to such an ignoble shift!

However, even in three short weeks, Languet had seen

enough of his young friend's problem to change the trend
of his counsel. Whereas hitherto his advice had always been
on the side of resignation and waiting patiently at home
for the worthy opportunity which would surely open there,
he now wrote:

*The habits of your court seem to me somewhat less
manly than I could have wished. Most of your noblemen
appeared to me to seek for a reputation more by a kind of
affected courtesy than by those virtues which are wholesome to the State and which are becoming to noble spirits
and men of high birth. I am sorry, therefore, and so were
other friends of yours, to see you wasting the flower of
your life on such things. I fear lest that noble nature of
yours may be dulled, and lest from habit you may be
brought to take pleasure in pursuits which only enervate
the mind.*

Small comfort to Philip that he agreed with every word!
Small marvel that he was trying his best for outlet.

Elizabeth's most recent move was ill-calculated to make
her court more congenial or auspicious for a serious young
Protestant. For, advised by Burleigh and Sidney's uncle,
Sussex, she had, to the consternation of Walsingham, revived the negotiations for marriage with Monsieur. Alençon was sending over a representative named Simier, to
go into the details. Her political intent was clearly to avoid
the possibility of alliance between the Low Countries and
France which might grow out of Alençon's committing
himself to the cause of the rebels. Such a combination would
leave her bare against Spain. Facing Spain alone meant
annihilation. Rather than that she toyed with the thought
of wooing (and if it came to the worst, wedding!) a Catholic prince who was twenty-five to her forty-six. To such a
pass had she brought herself rather than give the Dutch

states the open support which would have cost her a little money!

Simier's presence at court soon involved a personal danger for the unbelieved Cassandra who had foreseen calamity, though hardly just this. For danger to Leicester was danger to all the Dudley clan. Shortly the swart insinuating little Frenchman whom Elizabeth fondled in public and called her " dearest monkey," was in a fair way to supplant the handsome Robin.

Alençon's envoy was, in the words of Camden, " a most choice courtier exquisitely skilled in love-toys, pleasant conceits and dalliance," just the sort of person whose gallant protestations fell on her ear like music when she pretended to scoff at herself for an " old woman " who was long past thought of marriage. As the Monkey's graces continued to endear him, and Gloriana held conferences with physicians on her hopes of issue, Leicester became seriously alarmed. By March he was frankly opposing the marriage, not only in the sacred name of Protestantism but in that of his personal safety. He was fighting his old enemy Sussex. He was fighting his new enemy Simier. He was fighting the mass of the people who in every age are reconciled to anything the person in power wants.

In the crisis, Leicester joined forces with his former rival, Christopher Hatton, with Walsingham his colleague of some years' standing, and with all the Puritan preachers. Those same ministers beheld an English Bartholomew in the wake of all Valois marriages. They took up their task of protest with such zealous gusto that the Queen found it necessary to censor the Holy Scriptures and define the law which was handed down from Horeb.

Philip doubtless felt a shiver of delight that first Sunday of Lent in the Chapel Royal when a heroic churchman told Elizabeth to her face of the misery her sister Mary had brought on England and herself with a hated foreign lord!

Without waiting to hear the scoundrel out, Gloriana rose
in her glory, glared fiercely at him and flounced away in
dudgeon. The Spanish ambassador Mendoza described the
matter very mildly when he said " this was considered a
great innovation." Innovation? It was cataclysm!

No second snub was needed to convey to the average
truckling courtier the unhealthiness of objections. Leicester saw that all hope of thwarting the marriage lay in the
common people who cordially hated the French, and in the
Privy Council. He and Hatton worked industriously for
a strong Puritan as successor to Sir Nicholas Bacon, the
Lord Chancellor who had died in February 1579. By March
their efforts were crowned with success. Sir Thomas Bromley was named (over the head of Burleigh's man) and they
were sure of one more vote in the Council.

That same Council, on which Philip's father now sat,
debated seven hours on end without stirring from their
places, on May 3d, 1579. Lord Burleigh pointed out the
" Perrells " which would ensue if the Queen failed to
marry. Walsingham admitted the danger from Spain, but
presented " Remedyes " therefor which would serve her
Highness better than introducing a foreigner and a Catholic as her husband. Meanwhile poor Paulet in France was
" quite at the end of his Latin," — in short as close to bad
language as his Puritan standards permitted!

Then at last the Council prevailed with the Queen
against marriage. On May 6th, 1579 Hatton could write
that the French alliance seemed " clearly laid aside." London merchants who had been seeing foreign armies and
rivers of blood in their sleep, settled down to counting
their shillings and pence. Praise God, business would be
undisturbed! Now Leicester breathed freely at last. Like
him, Philip Sidney felt that the danger of Alençon as King
Consort was over.

Simier, to whom tantrums came as easily as to a naughty

child, stamped and cursed at the news. He had thought
the affair was settled, and in his fury he held Leicester ac-
countable. He swore mighty oaths that he would make him
rue his meddling. Moreover he kept them.

He went to Elizabeth with some news which was like to
cost Robin his head. He told her that this Leicester, her
faithful devoted lover, who protested that he thought of
her alone, had gazed on another lady, on a mere ordinary
mortal, in short on the Countess of Essex. Worse than that,
he had married the woman! He had been married for two
years. Everyone had known it, Simier blithely assured her,
but no one had dared to tell her.

Elizabeth was in a towering passion. Never was woman
more vain. And now her pride had been dragged in the
dirt, before the eyes of all the court, even before foreign
envoys! Cruelly, the blow had fallen when she knew herself haggard and worn out by superhuman efforts. At
forty-six she needed more than ever to hear herself praised
as young and blooming. Instead she was cut to the quick,
abandoned by the one person on earth whom she came
close to loving, while he like an ingrate followed the bold
eyes of that pink and white draggle-tail, that hell-cat her
cousin, Lettice Knollys! Her Leicester, her Robin. Fury
and hurt knew no bounds.

In the first hours of her wrath, Leicester was lucky to
escape being murdered in cold blood and buried hugger
mugger. As she strode up and down her long gallery at
Greenwich she threw at the prostrate favorite every insult-
ing word in the language. She swore with thundering oaths
that he should go forthwith to the Tower. His father and
grandfather had died for less. She had been nothing short
of a fool to trust herself to a scoundrel who came of that
traitor's brood. Now she must make full amends. No death
on the block for this dainty Dudley of hers. 'Od's Wounds,
here was one should set a new fashion. She'd have him

taken to Tyburn on hurdles, there to be hung and drawn and quartered!

Generously Sussex intervened. He begged the outraged goddess to send Leicester to prison in the fort of Greenwich Park. Then discovering the Queen could not abide the recreant so nigh to the palace, got him ordered to keep to his house of Wanstead in Essex. When the humbled Earl " retired," Lady Sidney withdrew from court. Belike she, too, had felt the rough edge of Gloriana's tongue. In all probability, spirited young Philip took his leave as well. He had known of the marriage some time, possibly as early as December of 1577.

Yet even if this newest Dudley disgrace had not brought to Sidney a fresh access of the loyalty which gripped him close to the clan; even if Elizabeth had not resented her suffering from one of his kin, the youth would have found the court bitter to him just then. He was too sensitive to brook the ill-concealed gloating of his uncle's enemies. He was too human not to chafe at Simier's aggrandizement, and his air of gusto now the marriage had been " revived." He was too shrewd a political prophet not to see disaster ahead in the visit which the lover Alençon was making to London within a month, strictly *incognito,* to woo his elderly bride!

Some time in this year 1579, Philip Sidney changed his motto. Previously, it had been " I hope." Now it became " I have done with hoping." No one knew exactly why. Camden suggested later, because Leicester had a son born to him and Philip could no longer count on being his heir.

But many disappointments, more noble, had crowded the two years since the young ambassador returned to England in July of 1577. Avidly he had built on plans which without exception miscarried: projects for a Protestant League, for gold in America, for a colony of the faithful, for a brilliant foreign marriage, for service in the Low Countries. Every abortive hope had hurt deeply.

He was now twenty-five. Is it possible that he saw this year 1579 and his own first quarter of a century as the end of the youthful time when life holds glittering chances with a certain triumph to crown them? Did he mean, from now on, to recognize limitations, meet them as resourcefully as possible, to smithy success from the cold fires of disaster? As a matter of fact, he did something very like that in the six brief years which remained to him. To such high aspirations he owed his immortal fame.

But in the meantime one of the hardest problems he had was just around the corner.

THE ELEVENTH CHAPTER
ENTITLED
AUGUST 1579.

OLONIUS himself would have been at a stay to describe the " tragical-comical-historical " romantical farce which now took the royal boards. The time, August 1579. The place, Greenwich Palace. The atmosphere, mysterious and passionate: a lover in disguise, creeping up the privy stairs and hiding behind the arras. And the actors? " The best in the world! "

Gloriana herself, to bring facile technique and natural gusto to the maiden-all-in-a-flutter, full of tender trepidations, delicious fears, coyness and palpitations. Most effective, in scenes *à deux*. Playing the virginals, posing those lovely hands, bestowing a golden key which opened every door in the palace. Lending herself to be wooed, with reserves as became a Virgin, with aggression as graced a Queen.

Never in all this world was a lover like Alençon! Twisted and pock-marked, with a knobby nose and an awkward dwarfish body, he was Frog Prince to the life. (By advice of his stage-manager mother, he abandoned his potent name of Hercules and appeared on the program as François). Rehearsing a-plenty lay behind those lingering glances, that ardor, that ecstasy, that headlong passion which could not bide the change of his traveling clothes before he gazed on his mistress. He threw his very soul into the drama. For at home his répertoire was exhausted. He hoped for a lucrative foreign engagement (Henri III wanted it long, as well!) and the ultimate role of King Consort.

The other parts were ungrateful. The court and Council were restricted to walking on, and as little of that as might be, since they were not even supposed to know that a lover was about! Simier was doubly effective as the Monkey and Sir Pandarus of Troy. But an actor named Robert Dudley who in his day had done wonders as the romantic favorite was condemned to a few very humble lines which he accepted of gladly. However, he still knew more than anyone else of the setting and the script, and without any manner of doubt his presence inspired the Queen to incredible heights in her acting.

No one knew more than Elizabeth how important to a play was plot. In this one there was to be no incident which was extraneous. Court ladies who could not keep a quiet tongue in their heads she sent off to private gaolers. Books against the French which were thrown in at her closet, she threw, in turn, to the flames. Commoners who complained were haled away to the stocks. Ministers were gagged without ceremony. The Queen was writing the play!

At least she thought so. Then Fate took a hand. And strange were the trio of collaborators which Fate raised up. They were the Spanish ambassador, a Puritan lawyer named Stubbe, and the grave young Philip Sidney.

Mendoza's method of stopping the marriage was simplicity itself. He instructed La Motte the Spanish governor at Gravelines to take a shot at Alençon's boat as it passed from France to England. If Monsieur had " dropped out of sight " at that time, there would have been less anxiety in England for years to come — and the world would have lost the *Arcadia.* However the governor " missed." Since

Elizabeth sent her darling home on a ship of war, he had no second chance.

Alençon came on the 16th. Probably a fortnight before in a humble part of London, behind closed casements, Stubbe began on his *Gaping Gulf*. Perhaps Leicester made some suggestions, for the descriptions of Simier show a venomous strength. Possibly Walsingham made others; at all events the Queen gave him credit for it. But the devoted fervor, the vigor, the fierceness of the man's loyal protest against the hated foreign marriage were all his own. Stubbe was writing one of the bravest, the maddest, the most triumphantly tactless books that has ever been produced. He knew his neck was in the noose the instant that he was found to be its author. Nevertheless he went on. For in him was speaking the voice the Queen would not hear, the authentic voice of the people.

Like most commoners of his time, Stubbe profoundly distrusted the French. In terms as pungent and sturdy as the mustard and beef which stood untouched at his elbow as his pen raced on, he described them as "light" and "false semblant," people who made "Macciavel theyr new Testament."

The Valois were the worst of the lot. As the Trojans feared the Greeks when they came with gifts, this man suspected the Valois whenever they went to woo. Look what happened the last time there was a wedding in that dreadful family! How could the English expect less than "Barthelmy murthers" when this very bridegroom's mother was that "Italian of the Toscan florentine Medices"? Triumphantly he produced the poisoning of Jeanne d'Albret and hauled from the Huguenot annals every one of the gory revenges which had been ascribed to the Queen Mother.

With him, Gloriana's pet, the lovely Alençon, cut but a scurvy figure. Stubbe was willing to concede that already he had shown a genius for lying, perjury, treason and debauchery which indicated that in time he would rival Heliogabalus. But otherwise he dismissed him as the sniveling tool of a monstrous mother and that sinister " Guysan Duke " who because of " neer consanguinity " was " fast frend " to Scottish Mary, and by consequence Elizabeth's enemy.

All this was bad enough. However only in direct address to the Queen did Stubbe mount to heights of sheer lunatic indiscretion. Bluntly he told her that she was too old to marry, too old to have a child. He brutally mentioned her years. He mentioned Alençon's. He proceeded to tell her that Alençon did not love her anyhow. He merely wanted to marry her. If he won her, she must like a good wife obey and submit to him in all things. This was proper enough of course — when the husband was worthy. But seeing Alençon the sort of man he was, what would become of the kingdom? It would be swallowed up in France! At best England was only a " molehyll," a " poore Iland " set in seas " which if the Lord did but whistle," could come tumbling in and devour all. Why should not the Lord God whistle when he saw an " oxe joined to an asse? "

He pitied her for a poor weak woman who needed direction. (Gloriana would enjoy that!) He paid his respects to her present advisers who (being very well-advised!) gave her only " smoothe and delicate " words instead of the " playn rough truth " which he had himself unfolded. He prayed God to grant her grace to " smel a flatterer from a loyall counsayler." He besought Heaven to fill her " royall hart with the tractable and easie swetenes of a yelding nature," delivering therewith as strong a challenge to Omnipotence as had ever been made. He begged that she might receive his honest warnings both " readely and humbly," apparently with no idea that the boon he craved was colossal. He ended his pious petition with a veritable fanfare of supplication: The nobles were to " join courage to wisdom." The bishops were to cease to " speke Frensch " and deliver only Holy Writ (presumably on the basis that God spoke only English). All the " meaner sort " were to be moved unceasingly to pray for the departure of this " plague of a Stranger in Christian Israel and a forrein Frenschman in England. Amen. Amen. AMEN." Yet even the courage of Stubbe did not climb to signing the sheets on which he had written his way to ruin.

All through the " wyndy clowdy rayny " weather which marked Alençon's amorous visit, another devoted soul, Hugh Singleton the printer, in his shop in Creed Lane, by Ludgate was setting type in secret. No apprentice for the neat small Roman which he held in his smudgy fingers. For what Singleton was doing defied the Stationers' Company, defied Elizabeth's edict that every book that was printed must pass one of their wardens and belike the Bishop of London (if the matter was at all " tickle "). Tickle this was indeed, yet it was to appear like the manna from heaven, out of the very air. A venturesome Puritan, Page, would see to its secret circulation. Thomas Cartwright would help, who was the leader of the Puritan party as well as the brother-in-law of daring John Stubbe. Elizabeth hated Cartwright and had been heard to remark that the time would come when those Puritan pests would think themselves mightier than the kings whom God himself had appointed. By the end of August when the *Gaping Gulf* was out and doing its work, Gloriana felt that the hour of apocalypse had arrived already, though in reality it waited for a king named Charles and a Stuart.

About the 25th, there was a meeting at Barnard's Castle just a turn to the south and east from Singleton's shop. Much the same spirit which animated Stubbe was in the lords who came to the Earl of Pembroke's by night, in

secret and desperation to confer on ways of blocking the
marriage. Chief among them was the little dark man
whom Elizabeth called her Moor. To-night Sir Francis
Walsingham was graver, more nervous than usual, his
keen eyes bright with apprehension. For like Stubbe, he
linked Alençon and trouble from Scottish Mary. There was
Leicester suffering the additional distress of knowing that
he could do nothing directly himself. In the company also
were Hatton, Sir Henry Sidney, the new Chancellor, Bromley, and a serious young courtier whom William of Orange
had recognized as a statesman though it pleased Gloriana
to keep him for an ornament.

By cresset light, with doors shut and servants barred,
they debated. Here was the Queen, so overseas in love as
to have no eyes for a restive people, no ears for anything
anyone told her which was not in praise of Alençon. Of
course this might be acting. Yet with the meaner sort verging on rebellion to " forestall massacres," the danger was
there even so, such danger as cried for help.

Before they parted a campaign had been determined.
This courtier and that who dared were to write to Gloriana
what she would never have patience to hear if he started to
tell it. Among them, one Philip Sidney was enjoined to
prepare a letter. The Queen might consider a tactful petition from him: he was young and handsome, so more
like to be forgiven; on occasion she called him " hers."
Moreover no pen could compare with Mr. Philip's!

While young Sidney was still busy with his letter, he
had a serious quarrel with my Lord of Oxford. Of itself
this was no particular distinction. Feuds were easily started
in that quarter. While he was still a ward in Burleigh's
house, the captious young Earl had murdered a cook. (It
had taken all Cecil's influence to secure a finding that the
victim " deliberately ran on his lordship's sword," which
was true enough since Oxford drove him into a corner

where he could hardly do anything else!) His contentious-
ness had kept him, and Burleigh whose daughter he married, in a kettle of trouble ever since.

Sidney himself required a real reason to fight. But his
hot blood needed no more. In this instance there was cause
enough in the marriage of the Queen. Oxford favored it
because the Earl of Sussex did. Also for the excellent courtier's reason that it seemed likely to go through. Philip for
his part resented the success which Sussex was building on
his uncle Leicester's disgrace. Logically enough, he resented
Oxford as well.

One afternoon late in August, Philip was on the tennis
court at the palace, playing under the eyes of Alençon's
train who were watching from the galleries. Oxford arrived, high-handedly ordering Sidney away. His tone was
so peremptory that Philip refused, saying proudly enough
that he would defer to courteous requests from one of
higher rank, but never to commands. At this, the Frenchmen who had been bored enough before hung over the very
railings to enjoy the delightful diversion of a fight. They
had been long enough in England to know that these were
not two angry young courtiers squabbling over a tennis
court, but factions facing each other down. Stimulated by
their interest, the Earl called Philip a puppy!

By this time Sidney needed no urging to a thoroughly
kingly wrath. In carrying tones he remarked that his lordship was singularly ill-informed in the realm of natural
history. The offspring of men were called children. Only
dogs had pups! His tone carried with it the justification not
only of a man and a gentleman, but of a Dudley to boot!
Then as the followers of Oxford flocked to his Grace's call,
young Philip who was sparsely attended, withdrew in hau-
teur. But as soon as he could stalk to pen and paper, he
sent the Earl a challenge.

This was directly counter to the punctilio of the duel

which accorded the power of challenge to the man of higher rank. Incidentally it deprived Sidney of his right of choosing weapons. He had acted in a white heat which defied both law and custom. But fortunately the arbitrament was not to be bloody. The affair was too public for that.

The Council interfered. On August 28th, Sidney wrote to Hatton (probably as to the most important councilor who was not related to him), a statement which showed little sign of yielding:

As for the matter depending between the Earl of Oxford and me, certainly, sir, howsoever I might have forgiven him, I should never have forgiven myself if I had lain under so proud an injury, as he would have laid upon me. Neither can anything under the sun make me repent it, nor any misery make me go one half word back from it. Let him therefore digest it as he will!

Oxford proved equally unamenable. With the two unrepentant hot-heads calling for one another's blood, the Council admitted its collective inability to bring about peace. At this point Gloriana took Philip in hand.

Considering that Alençon had just departed, and that among the business which had piled up during his visit there was much which was more important than this affair of Philip's, she was very patient about it! She explained to him that Earls were Earls, and Oxford one of the greatest in the kingdom. For himself, he was merely a private gentleman. She went on to say — exactly what Languet wrote when he heard the tale — that there was no use flying in the face of noblemen. Then she waited for a humble answer.

Sidney was unchastened. Though he was thoroughly respectful about it, he made it clear that he " would not let fall anything of his right." He said that "place was never intended for privilege to do wrong." (Those Puritans must have been bad for him!) Finally, says Greville, he concluded with the announcement that however great Oxford might be, "hee was no Lord over him." It was probably the Tudor emphasis with which the Queen met these remarks when she commanded him to withdraw his challenge on the instant, which led Sidney to write to Languet. Urgently he begged for service under La Noue in Flanders, till the odium of the affair should pass.

Though Monsieur had gone his ways on the 26th, he wrote to his mistress every hour. So did Simier. In mawkish epistles authentically spotted with tears, Monsieur protested that he could not sleep for visions of her. His sobs and sighs kept the company awake as well. As he took his ship at Dover he was agitated lest his tears, added to the watery upheaval of the circumfluent ocean (which had made him so sea-sick coming over) would inundate the craft which carried him! So to endless absurdity.

Elizabeth replied in kind. Although as became the pursued lady she showed a trifle more restraint, she was extravagant enough. She wrote back that she was overcome with impatience to see her dearest pretty Frog swimming again in the Thames, where the loyal wavelets missed him. Even if the lovers were only half as mad about each other as they professed, the situation had need of all the eloquence, all the tact, all the earnestness which Sidney was invoking in his letter to dissuade the Queen from the match.

His *Discourse to the Queen's Majesty touching her Marriage with Monsieur* was a deft piece of persuasive writing which met all these demands. It was intended for Elizabeth's eye alone. The simplicity of the style was a compliment to her which she did not appreciate any more than Philip's assumption that love and loyalty might speak to her frankly. But had she been willing to listen to anything, she would have hearkened to this wise and temperate letter.

However, even the royal eye ran placidly enough over the prosperous start:

Most feared and beloved, most sweet and gracious Sovereign:

To seek out excuses of this my boldness and to arm the acknowledging of a fault with reasons for it, might better show I knew I did amiss, than any whit diminish the attempt; especially in your judgment who are able lively to discern into the nature of the thing done, it were folly to hope with laying on better colours to make it the more acceptable.

Having announced that he scorned flattery, by every canon of court, Sidney should now have proceeded to flatter to the full. Yet with mal-inspired honesty, he did nothing of the sort!

Therefore, carrying no other olive branches of intercession but the laying of myself at your feet, nor no other insinuation either for attention or pardon but the true and vowed sacrifice of unfeigned love, I will in simple and direct terms set down the overflowing of my mind.

Simple and direct terms, forsooth! There was nothing the Queen wanted less. A pox on these people whose minds were always overflowing. She had not lived six and forty years without discovering that when men had a mind to be impudent and interfering, they talked of being direct! From this point she went on with a diminished interest.

Sidney considered three aspects of the subject: the realm, Monsieur and herself. For the realm he told her, it was now consummately happy in possessing an " abso-

lute princess " who was " accordingly respected." It had
two factions neither one of which could well suffer change.
The first was the Protestant party to which he referred (with
restraint extraordinary in one of " religion ") as that she
was " so enwrapped in as it were," that without " excessive
trouble " she could scarce withdraw from a group she had
" so long maintained." The second or Catholic party was
made up of " men whose spirits were full of anguish, being
forced to oaths they accounted damnable; " men of great
numbers and riches who " wanted nothing so much as a
head " to rebel — as witness the plots of Norfolk and " infinite other practices." By marriage with Monsieur she
would weaken this Protestant strength of hers and
strengthen her Catholic weakness.

Courageously he discussed Monsieur. After referring to
his mother as Jezebel and citing Bartholomew with all the
conviction of an eye-witness, he enlarged on Alençon's
" lightness." He had supported the Huguenots only so long
as it suited him. He had made " inconstant attempts " on
the throne of his brother. If he had declined to play second
fiddle in France, would he be content to do it in England?
Would it be wise to put trust in a man who had gone wiv-
ing in so many other quarters and whose gaze might stray
even from the Sun? More restrainedly than Stubbe, but
with deadly obliqueness, Sidney cited Monsieur's de-
baucheries:

*I will temper my speeches from any other irreverent dis-
gracings of him in particular, though they be never so
true!*

In times when ministers spoke " in particular " freely, this
was doubtless discretion in Philip, and not mere delicacy
meet for a lady's eye.

After he had quietly refuted all the arguments for the
marriage, without ostentatious demolishment, but very

thoroughly, Sidney made his final contention. All this, of course, would be nothing, provided the Queen really wished to marry! But often he had heard her say that marriage would be both " unprofitable to the kingdom " and " unpleasant " to her. At such cost the match would be a very " dear purchase of repentance." Then possibly with the thought that it might not be well to close by disproving a lady out of her own mouth, he finished with the sort of thing which Gloriana wanted to hear, except when, as at present, she was seething with fury:

Doing as you do, you shall be the example of princesses, the ornament of your age, the comfort of the afflicted, the delight of your people, the most excellent fruit of your progenitors and the perfect mirror of posterity.

With a resentment not dissimilar, her most excellent progenitor Henry VIII had received unanswerable arguments against marriage plans of his own to which Elizabeth owed her existence.

A pretty tradition records that the Queen wept when she read Sidney's *Discourse.* If so, she shed tears of vexation and rage. Her active annoyance against his father had not been mitigated by Sir Henry's recent opposition to the marriage on the Council. His uncle Leicester had given her every reason for distrust and alarm. In Philip's inconvenient Sidney honesty and his overweening Dudley aggressiveness, she saw him as likely to unite the plagues of both his houses. Such a youth as this who calmly took Earls for his equals, and now had the effrontery to instruct his Sovereign not only on the management of the kingdom but on her private affairs as well, was no lad to be wept over! Nor was she the woman to weep. She either rated him soundly, or decided that it was better still to ignore this proud popinjay who thought himself so important. That would make him smart! Whatever she did, Philip did not go to court for some time after.

Immediately he wrote to Languet to press afresh for command in the Low Countries. Unfortunately, however, copies of Sidney's *Discourse to the Queen* were already in circulation, thanks, probably, to the indiscretion of Burleigh's secretary. One had found its way to the hands of furious Alençon in that very Flanders which Philip had picked for a refuge!

France was closed to him because of his " religion " and his stand against Monsieur. Into friendly Germany he could pass only through Flanders. To England Alençon was expected to return almost immediately for the marriage. That made the court impossible. Going to America not only took huge sums on which he could not lay his hand, but involved securing the royal permission. In her present humor, the Queen was little likely to grant him license.

If Sidney had been restive before under the snaffle of circumstance when he at least had occupation of sorts at court, his proud ambitious spirit now fretted fiercely against the tighter curb of Fortune.

THE TWELFTH CHAPTER
ENTITLED
ASYLUM IN ARCADIA.

OWEVER, if there was anything more bitter than nursing a sense of futility away from court, it was supporting life in it, during the remaining months of the year. As the Queen found opposition growing more solid against the marriage, any doubts which she may have had herself vanished into thin air. She was determined to have her desire at any cost. Mounting to a new pitch of captiousness and unreason she regarded all contrary opinions as misprision in the highest. Everybody who disagreed with her was a traitor.

Hatton, faithful " Sheep " that he was, usually followed her bell in silent devotion. But the strain was too much even for his lifetime's role of patience. He withdrew from Glory for a full week. After that he became so nervous about what Glory might be doing, that he returned to suffer again. He took care to be quiet about it.

Walsingham, on the other hand, found it difficult to stay stifled. Accordingly, in October, Elizabeth sent him packing with the remark that he was of no use anyhow, save to " protect heretics " ! Deeply offended, the best servant she had withdrew to extract what comfort he could from the perusal of Thucydides and the planting of hawthorne at his manor of Barn Elms.

Leicester had been holding on like grim death. Humbly

he endured abuse and vituperation. The Queen held him responsible for the popular animosity which made it impossible for her to embark on the marriage without the consent of Parliament, and at the same time made that consent the unlikeliest thing on earth. Submissively Robin pointed out that this was a " far fetched matter to pick to him." Nevertheless she ordered him out of her sight. For more than a month she kept him confined to his house. That exile cut Philip off from all the news of the court. Like the rest of Gloriana's subjects, he now became prey to cruel anxiety without even the consolation of knowing what was likely to happen.

When she was not accusing Walsingham and Leicester of sowing discord among the people, the Queen blamed the opposition on the " lewd " and abominable slanders in that " croked," dishonest, railing book, the *Gaping Gulf*. The volume had been secretly circulated all over England. By calculation it came to London last. While Elizabeth was on progress at Giddy Hall in Essex, her eye had lit on a copy. She " burned in choller " as she read. For from the first page she foresaw the need of such diplomatic apologies to France as galled an " absolute princess," but had never entered the mind of honest Stubbe. In a fury she summoned her much tried Council.

On September 27th, 1579 she banned the *Gaping Gulf* in a royal proclamation which was sent post-haste over the country. By the next day Philip Sidney and other her faithful subjects were reading the rights of the case from the pen of the Queen herself. She stated that Monsieur was faithful and honest, one who adored her madly. He had risked his life to visit her (that, at least, was true, though the fault was none of his!). The libel itself was the device of filthy traitors to " stir up trouble abroad and seditions at home." Harboring a copy was henceforth treason. Every one of the volumes must be searched out by constables, carted to the cross in the public squares and burned incontinent.

Burned they were, before public curiosity, now roused to the highest literary pitch, could be satisfied. Filched from under people's noses before choice passages could be copied! So zealously did the Queen's affrighted beadles and bailiffs go at their work, so merrily did the flames crackle, that of the great number of copies issued, only five exist at the present day. Every one shows signs of fervid perusal. Probably among them is that carefully guarded volume belonging to Leicester from which Philip Sidney read, with a mighty admiration for the devoted author's courage.

In the hue and cry against them, Stubbe, Page and Singleton could not hope for freedom long. Shortly they were in the Tower. In no time they had been tried and condemned, each to lose his offending right hand, by operation of a law which dated from Bloody Mary and forbade all criticism of " the Queen's husband."

At this point, certain narrow legal minds made annoying objections. In the first place, they contended, Alençon was not yet the Queen's husband. In the second, Mary was dead; the statute had died with her. The judges from whom these unsatisfactory findings emanated, the Queen committed to the Fleet. Not surprisingly she soon found a magistrate of properly elastic mind (or rather, of real learning!) who handed down the statement that " the King of England never dies." So the episode had a happy ending after all: the three caitiffs were to suffer.

Suffer they did, at Westminster, on November 3d, 1579. Somewhere in the meantime Gloriana had discovered that Singleton was a " warm man." She therefore pardoned him on payment of a staggering fine which permanently impoverished him. Her two blood victims paid the penalty for their brave, blind experiment in international affairs before a silent and sympathetic crowd.

Stubbe said he was sorry for the loss of his hand, " more sorie to lose it by iudgment, but most of all with her Majesties indignation and evell opinion." Like Page he prayed publicly that his punishment might not " withdraw any parte of his dewtie and affection." Both protested with all solemnity that they had never supposed their offense " wolde have reatched soe highlie." Even when the mallet and the butcher's cleaver had done their gory work, and hot irons had seared the stumps, both men threw their caps in the air and cried loyally, " God save her Majesty! "

Sensing protest in the people, the royal officers hurried Stubbe away to the Tower. There, poor man, he was prisoner for eighteen months more, though he wrote letters painfully with his left hand, asking for " prince-like, Lady-like, Christian mercy." He signed them " Iohn Stubbe, Scaeva," grimly conscious that *Scaeva* meant both " left hand " and " unlucky."

Pitiful puns meant nothing to Elizabeth. She was having enough trouble through November 1579, without attacks of conscience. Her Council refused to be manoeuvered into advising her to marry Alençon, though the members agreed to carry out her wishes, if it pleased her Grace to announce them. Popular feeling was ugly. She dared not summon Parliament. Simier was pressing for a positive answer, slamming the doors of the Council chamber on the lords who would not give it to him, and stamping off to weep out his woes to Gloriana. She heaved a sigh of relief when she got him away at last on November 24th, 1579. The message which he bore across the Channel to Monsieur was that the marriage must be delayed until Parliament could meet. In her heart, Elizabeth knew that could not be for some time.

This bloody and restless interval Philip Sidney had

passed quietly enough. He was spending his time at Leicester House set in its gardens by the Thames. There he saw something of his uncle's pretty step-daughter, Penelope, who was now seventeen. Evidently he thought her agreeable, attractive and an excellent listener but found no reason particularly to deplore that their match had been broken off. Brave courtiers, who like himself had found the airs of Westminster Palace and Greenwich suddenly too chill, came to visit. But since courage is no courtier's virtue, Sidney was often alone. Then he found solace in the intellectual life which he had practically abandoned in the routine of " attendance."

Just when he had need of stimulus most, Fate again threw him in the way of Edmund Spenser who was now in Leicester's service. As mature men, the two had even more in common than in their student days. So, while Stubbe was suffering and Simier was in his tantrums, two young poets had their heads together over verses about shepherds who sang of " purple Cullambines," cowslips and kingcups and " Daffadowndillies."

Spenser was putting the finishing touches to the *Shepheards Calender* which before the year was out he dedicated to Sidney as to one who was

> *the President*
> *Of Noblesse and of chevalree.*

He had modeled it on the pastoral poems of Virgil, except that his shepherds had English names like Willy and Cuddy. And though it was the bookish first book of a bookish young man, he was so great a poet that in spite of himself he transferred to his page the dim dewy loveliness of actual meadows and hedgerows.

For his own part Sidney needed only leisure and the example of such a rare companion to turn to literary expression. Already he had written a masque called the *Lady of*

May which had been acted before the Queen in the garden at Wanstead, probably in 1578. In it Philip provided the delicate verse and compliment which Leicester wanted for Gloriana. He added as well a country schoolmaster named Rhombus who did not know that there were any words smaller than " plumbeous cerebrosities," and who sent the court ladies into gales of laughter by his misquotations from Virgil.

However, Sidney did not consider his own writing of any particular importance except when he employed his pen to political purpose. Not a bit of his work was printed within his lifetime. As Greville said, " his end was not writing even when he wrote." It was release.

But he took with the utmost seriousness his duty as patron of literature. Even when he was heavily in debt " his bountie blased like Torch at night," dimming the candles of other benefactors. Perhaps on that account, perhaps because in the words of the great Thomas Nash, Sidney knew what belonged " to a scholar, what pains, what toil, what travail leadeth to perfection," he received in this year 1579, four dedications besides that of the mighty Spenser. What he gave was of more value than golden angels. It was the understanding of another creative artist.

On occasion his authors brought Philip annoyance as well as a proud obligation. Such a one was the Puritan, Stephen Gosson, who jumped to the conclusion that because Sidney was opposed to the French marriage he was pure Puritan all compact, who disapproved of plays and poetry as well. Consequently, much to his chagrin, this young man who loved the theatre and counted the actors Tarlton and Will Kemp among his friends, found himself hailed as the patron of the *Schoole of Abuse.* Even more than by Gosson's diatribes against players, Philip was annoyed by his grouping of " poets and pipers and such peevish cattle " !

That remark roused Sidney to action. He answered Gosson roundly. With the same ardent seriousness which had actuated the defense of his father and his letter to the Queen on her marriage, he now proceeded to clear the profession of letters from charges of being immoral. His *Apologie for Poetrie* vindicated the cause, not only of verse but of all creative writing; of everything which the mind and spirit might make and commit to paper.

Racy and vivid was the style in which he discussed his subject. No dead learned language, this! The re-creation of life was itself a living matter. So, too, all talk about it. Even his thinking had a vital freshness. On such beloved ground, Sidney refused to follow too close at heel the great idol of bookmen, the mighty Aristotle.

With gusto he proved that these " making " poets of his did the greatest good of all. Mere historians (whom no one considered naughty) were " captived to the truth of a foolish world," and in fealty to the facts of their " old Mouse-eaten records " must take Man pretty much as they found him. Lawyers, too, had a mundane task. Not theirs " to make men good," but to ensure that " their evil hurt not others." Even philosophers could do no more than fumble after goodness, teaching human beings the while how to endure injustice and evil. Yet of those godlike creatures, the makers, not one from Dante down, but had his " Heaven and Hell under the authority of his pen " !

With Divinity itself, they shared the task of ennobling men, by rousing their high emotions:

Who readeth Aeneas carrying old Anchises on his back that wisheth not it were his fortune to perform so excellent an act?

They need not have the stupendous scope of Virgil to do their holy office, either. For fables *under a pretty tale of Wolves and Sheep can conclude the whole consideration of wrong doing and patience.*

So the poet is really superior to all the world beside, since

with a tale forsooth, he cometh unto you: with a tale which holdeth children from play, and old men from the chimney corner.

Being so eloquent and so fully informed with the quaint and lovely humanistic ideal that books were to make men good, this Sidney could not fail to be a very prince of patrons. No wonder that Spenser who had already envisioned his *Faerie Queene* as an epic to " fashion . . . a noble person in vertuous and gentle discipline," wrote to his friend Gabriel Harvey at Cambridge, to thank God that Mr. Philip Sidney had him " at some use in familiarity " !

While Sidney was busy with such high matters, affairs at court were in no hopeful posture. To be sure by January 1st, 1580 Leicester and Walsingham had returned. On New Year's day, Philip himself appeared at least long enough to tender his gift to the Queen. It was a " cup of Cristall with a cover," possibly intended as a symbol of honesty that was " stopped."

If he was not ready and able to bridle that honest tongue which " ran one way with his heart," court was no place for him. The marriage was now regarded as inevitable. Leicester was meeting Alençon's advances as gracefully as he could, and although he kept it in the back of his mind that they might be " all French chatter," he was professing himself delighted that henceforth he and Monsieur were to labor together in Gloriana's vineyard. He urged a similar conformity upon his nephew Philip.

So did good Languet. A letter from Antwerp written on January 30th, 1580 shows that Philip's old friend was moving heaven and earth in the Low Countries to bring about

a reconciliation between Sidney and Alençon. He had seen
the Prince of Orange who said " there was nothing he
would not do " in Philip's behalf. But even the Prince's
efforts would be futile if the boy should continue to make
himself unpopular by talk against the marriage:

*I advise you to give way to necessity and reserve your
self for better times. . . . The party and influence of the
Duke is on the increase here, and if you should annoy him
by your opposition in England, you will scarcely find a
reception here. . . .*

Languet had been frank in admiring Sidney's courage " in
freely admonishing the Queen " so long as there was hope
of dissuading her. Now however, everybody else was running " to the safe side of the vessel." If Philip was to sur-
vive for future service, he must learn to do the same.

Perhaps the young man felt himself unequal to the task.
Perhaps he considered life at court too expensive as well as
too dangerous. At all events he bided neither in Greenwich
nor London. On his going he asked Hatton to tell her
Majesty that " necessity did even banish " him. Possibly it
was on Leicester's advice that he put his withdrawal on
the basis of poverty. That, at least, meant telling no lies!
In February 1580, he seems to have joined his sister at Wilton. She had retired there some time before to await the birth
of her first child which was expected in April.

When Philip arrived, winter was bleak in the " bos-
cages," and the marl on Salisbury Plain made riding " wett
and dirty." A lace of ice still lay on the " Wyley bourn "
which ran by his sister's gates and on the little Adder which
cut through the park itself. But from the windows of Wilton House he could see over the " floted meadows " and
misty downs, to the great spire of Salisbury Cathedral piercing the sky like a fine Spanish needle. The old monkish
cloister which formed the core of the splendid mansion was

warmed by thin sunshine as well as great crackling fires.
There Philip and Mary, in high carved chairs with the
family dogs at their feet, set to work on the translation of
the *Psalms* which they were undertaking together. There
Philip committed to " loose sheetes of paper " the romance
which he had begun, probably some months before. It was
dedicated to his sister and called the *Countess of Pembroke's
Arcadia.*

As the lovely first sentence announced, " Arcadia among
all the Provinces of Grece was ever had in singuler reputation." In this pastoral antique world Philip was creating asylum for himself, where he could forget dangerous religious
struggles in England, among shepherds who raised unanimous paeans to a " great god Pan; " where he could put
from him the memory of frustrated ambitions, by singing

My sheep are thoughts which I both guide and serve.

He could even become resident there himself, under the
name of Philisides who by " desperate work of Fortune,"
was reduced to be a shepherd!

For this charming world, the disillusioned courtier
could sigh in all comfort as he sat in his furred pantoffles
by my Lord of Pembroke's fire. Meantime, on the rain-
drenched downs, real shepherds with chopped hands, were
tending the heavy ewes. Having no change to their feet,
they found those cold wet meadows most cursedly " in-
commodious." Still Pan was hardly the personage whom
they praised for the cruel climate!

But by first and last intent, this " toyful booke " this trifle
" triflinglie handled," was, as its affectionate dedication
avowed, for the Countess of Pembroke only. We who read
it later do so over the shoulder of that pretty red-headed
creature for whom, to judge by the halts in the plot, her
brother made it to order.

If the sprightly Lady Mary decided she wanted a tilt,

The Countess of Pembroke whose *Arcadia* it was.

he stopped his tale on the instant, and introduced one, as gorgeous as ever was seen at Hampton Court. If her mind ran to a bear-baiting, he obligingly shifted his Arcadians, to whom time and space were nothing, " to a goodly greene two miles hence," and gave her that rural sport. If she cried a hunt would be brave, hunt there was, with horses and *tantartaree!* If it pleased her Grace to shoot birds, when the weather was foul without, she could still shoot while snug in her cloister. For thither brother Philip transported the scene entire, not forgetting that salient figure, her favorite friend from the kennels:

the water spaniel . . . came down to the river, showing that he hunted for a duck, & with a snuffling grace, disdaining that his smelling force could not as well prevail through the water as through the air; & therefore waiting with his eye, to see if he could espy the ducks getting up again: but then a little below them, failing of his purpose, he got out of the river & shaking off the water . . . inweeded himself.

Nor the boy " piping as though he should never be old."

All this he wrote her in mellifluous, balanced language. The style was like the brocade in her gown, rich in design and overlaid with ornament. Like the tiered and priceless laces in her ruff, it was a marvel of airy line and delicate intricacy. The Countess loved its dainty elaboration. It was, in short, a proper book for a lady.

It was also the first of English novels, with a stirring plot. Though Mary's real days might be dull, these her brother made for her were teeming with excitement. Princes in disguise, elopements, shipwrecks and brigands, enchantments, bloody rebellions, murders and magic potions, lions and " ougly Beares " — he heaped them with lavish hand. He gave her lyrics, shepherds' sports, and love-scenes galore. Out of his memories of Kenilworth, he manufactured

Mopsa. Out of Bartholomew, he created the witch Cecro-
pia, who was the stuff of that Jezebel, Catherine de' Medici!

Nor were the lovely young Sidneys, Philip and Mary,
the only great ones for whom the pages of the *Arcadia*
would carry stimulus and comfort. There Shakespeare
came on a blind Paphlagonian King who gave him a Gloster
for *Lear*. There a monarch named Charles Stuart found the
prayer of Pamela, which to John Milton's horror, he used
upon the scaffold.

At last, on April 8th, 1580 little William Herbert was
born. He grew up to be the third Earl of Pembroke and
the patron of Shakespeare (who according to tradition, acted
at Wilton a role in *As You Like It*). Even within his own
right, this nephew of Philip's would prove a person of distinction. For when Countess Mary died, in 1621, her epi-
taph would record, not only that she was " fair and learn'd
and good," but that first of all, she was " Sidney's sister,
Pembroke's mother."

Just now this " subject of all verse," a happy little mother
of nineteen, was, in her brother's phrase, recovering " both
of her pain and her disease." Philip himself was riding
afield in the Wiltshire spring. All about, the meadows were
white with ladysmocks, or golden with butter flowers. In
the fallows was fragrance of saffron, maiden's honesty and
wild strawberries of an " innosent flaver." Hedges were
smothered in may.

Stragglers on Salisbury Plain saw him as a handsome
horseman, to whom " the Muses appearing, he wrote down
their dictates," like Hamlet, on his tables. Home, with a
brace of bustards, he brought a poem on Stone Henge, to
edify his sister and very new nephew withal:

> *Near Wilton sweet, huge heaps of stones are found,*
>   *But so confused, that neither any eye*
> *Can count them just, nor reason reason try,*

What force brought them to so unlikely ground.
To stranger weights my mind's waste soil is bound,
Of passion hills, reaching to reason's sky . . .

Whether he was at Greenwich, or on Salisbury Plain, Sidney's problem of personal adjustment was still to be worked out!

As summer wore on, it became increasingly clear that he must return to court. Leicester sent down discouraging news. In late May 1580, Monsieur wrote the Queen that although he was encountering opposition at home, he was determined to have her. Meantime he was cherishing her night-cap! (Evidently one which Simier stole before he left for France.) By July, Fortune smiled on the lovers again. August 12th was the date set for the arrival of the French Commissioners who would draw up the marriage contract and work out details for the wedding. In view of this last, Uncle Robert told Philip to come to Greenwich as soon as he could. Then when " changes " went into effect, he would be solidly established.

Sidney answered the letter on August 2d, 1580. He said he was too " full of cold " to speak. He would wait for a cure, since his " only service " was speech and that " stopped." (Did he mean in more senses than one?) Sturdily enough, he contended that since he had left in the first place, ostensibly for lack of funds, it would be better for him

either constantly to [attend], or constantly to hold the
course of poverty, for coming and going neither bre[d]
desert, nor witnesse[d] necessity.

However, since Leicester advised otherwise, he would follow his " judgment and command," and come as soon as the cold permitted, " within 3 or 4 days."

Shortly after he left his Arcadian world, where he had

that blessed poet's control over the last chapter. He was traveling to Gloriana's domain, also of "singuler reputation," where the courtiers prated almost as much of love as his shepherds. There and at Leicester House he would try the truth of one of his pastoral sayings: "Love one time layeth burdens, and another time giveth wings." Both were waiting for Philip and Penelope Devereux.

THE THIRTEENTH CHAPTER
ENTITLED
ASTROPHEL AND STELLA.

 HEN Sidney came back to London in the early autumn of 1580, he carried with him certain sugared sonnets, probably begun at Leicester House at the end of the year preceding and continued at Wilton. So far, they were purely conventional.

Every proper courtier wrote such to his mistress. So Petrarch had written to Laura. The divinity thus " adored " need arouse no particular feeling. (Meter gave trouble enough without unnecessary complications from passion.) For her part, the lady was grateful for the fame assured to her charms. Hence she was content (sometimes because she must be) with lavish verbal affections. On this perfectly safe understanding, even married women were like the rats in Ireland, almost rimed to death!

In Penelope Devereux, Sidney found a convenient little luminary to worship in this wise. He called himself Astrophel, a shepherd. She was his Star, his Stella. When she raised her honey-colored head from the tapestry she was working, it gave her a gallant comfort to know that Philip, who was waiting impatiently for his uncle, would do her a poem. And in it, he would swear that he had been slain by the god of love himself who lay intrenched in her provocative black eyes:

Fly, fly, my friends, I have my death's wound, fly!
  See there that boy, that murdering boy, I say,
Who like a thief hid in a bush doth lie,
Till bloody bullet get him wrongful prey.
So, tyrant he no fitter place could spy,
Nor so far level in so secret stay,
As that sweet black which walls thy heavenly eye;
There he himself with his shot close doth lay.
Poor passenger, pass now thereby I did,
  And stayed to see the prospect of the place,
While that black hue from me the bad guest hid,
But straight I saw motions of lightning's grace,
  And there descried the glisterings of his dart:
  But ere I could fly thence, it pierced my heart.

Such poetic attentions were the more flattering, from a man to whom she had been betrothed, but whom she could never marry. The look of it was so faithful! No matter that only a few months after her father's death the treaty was broken off because they were both so poor. No matter that Philip had since been pursued by a princess, whom he would have wedded if he could. Behold, three years after his hopes of Stella had vanished, Astrophel — still devoted — was writing her lovely sonnets.

Just now in August 1580, Stella was both the coquette and the eager child. Secretly agog, she watched Astrophel's man unpacking her shepherd's wallet and tar-box (or rather his pile of trunks). She was longing to read the charming things her poet had thought up to say about her while he was off in Wiltshire. That would be more exciting than all this chatter about the baby! She would copy these new ones out fair and show them to all her friends — for their literary style. So would Leicester and her mother. In a purely private way, those innocent sonnets would be almost as public as Elizabeth's proclamations!

No harm done, either. For of the hundred odd poems which were published unofficially in 1591, from copies then in circulation, none hint at anything but a perfectly proper relation. Indeed, the first thirty, written before Stella's marriage in April 1581, reflect the usual conventional court affair — save for one detail. Defying the usual literary fashion, this honest Astrophel went to the trouble of saying in his second sonnet, that he was not in love at all!

> *I saw and liked, I liked but lovéd not.*

After this neat knock at sentimentality, he came nearer doing what was expected of him. For some thirty sonnets he rang all the proper changes on the compliments common to sonneteers since Petrarch, achieving nevertheless a charm and freshness of his own:

> *You that do search for every purling spring,*
>   *Which from the ribs of old* Parnassus *flows,*
> *And every flower (not sweet, perhaps) which grows*
> *Near thereabout, into your poems wring.*
> *You that do dictionary method bring*
>   *Into your rimes, running in rattling rows,*
>   *You that old* Petrarch's *long deceaséd woes*
> *With new-born sighs, and wit disguiséd sing;*
> *You take wrong ways; those far-fetched helps be such,*
> *As do betray a want of inward touch,*
> *And sure at length stolen goods do come to light.*
> *But if both for your love and skill you name,*
> *You seek to nurse at fullest breast of Fame,*
> Stella *behold, and then begin to write!*

Even at that, he could forget his dutiful posing, off and on, to produce verses on the political state of Europe in October 1580, which paid tribute not to Stella but to his hero, William the Silent:

Holland *hearts, now such good towns are lost*
Trust in the shade of pleasing Orange *tree.*

Or to talk of love in general, without reference to any particular goddess:

With how sad steps, O Moon, thou climb'st the skies,
  How silently, and with how wan a face,
What may it be, that even in heavenly place,
That busy archer his sharp arrows tries?
Sure if that long-with-love-acquainted eyes
  Can judge of love, thou feelst of lover's case,
  I read within thy looks thy languished grace.
To me that feel the like, my state descries.
Then even of fellowship, O Moon, tell me
Is constant love deemed there but want of wit?
Are beauties there, as proud as here they be?
Do they above, love to be loved, and yet
  Those lovers scorn, whom that love doth possess?
  Do they call virtue there, ungratefulness?

With such completely conventional gallantry, varied by digressions which reveal the charming sham, the series might have gone on till the hundred were done, and Sidney started his second " century " to quite a different lady. But in the middle of March 1581, Fate took a hand in the business and taught the poetic philanderer something of burdens, and wings.

What happened was a marriage. On March 10th, 1581 Sidney's uncle, the Earl of Huntingdon, wrote to Walsingham and Burleigh, who were Stella's other guardians, about a brilliant chance:

God hath taken to his mercy Lord Rich, who hath left
to his heir a proper gentleman and one in years very fit for
my Lady Penelope Devereux, if with the favour and liking
of her Majesty, the matter might be brought to pass. . . .

Burleigh and Walsingham bestirred themselves as became good Christian souls to secure this boon of a rich, that is a "proper" husband, before any other damsel nipped him up. It was pleasant for Penelope that his years were "very fit." Yet even if he had been toothless and cursed with the rheum, her guardians would have hailed him with joy. The fact was my lady was getting on — in her nineteenth year. Soon she would be an "old maiden," who was poor, to boot. When Philip Sidney heard of the astonishing stroke of luck produced by God in His mercy, he was doubtless just as delighted as he had been at his sister's *coup.*

Penelope fettled her joints against a speedy marriage. Probably byApril 1581, the wedding had been concluded, and for the moment Stella passed from Astrophel's ken. His thirty-third sonnet attested a very real sorrow, that, for sordid considerations of pounds and pence, he had lost her:

> *I might, unhappy word (woe me) I might,*
>   *And then would not, nor could not see my bliss:*
> *Till now, wrapped in a most infernal night,*
> *I find how heavenly day (wretch) did I miss;*
> *Heart, rend thyself, thou dost thyself but right.*
>   *No lovely* Paris *made thy* Helen *his,*
>   *No force, no fraud, robbed thee of thy delight,*
> *No Fortune of thy fortune author is;*
> *But to myself, myself did give the blow,*
> *While too much wit, forsooth, so troubled me,*
> *That I respects for both our sakes must show.*
> *And could I not by rising morn foresee,*
>   *How fair a day was near (O punished eyes)*
>   *That I had been more foolish, or more wise.*

Here was deep and affectionate regret, impatience with poverty, some jealousy, perhaps. But so far, no passion.

Penelope was from the start actively unhappy. There is evidence that she

*was married against her will unto one whom she did pro-
test at the very solemnity and ever after; between whom
from the first day, there ensued continual discord, although
the same fears that forced her to marry him constrained her
to live with him. . . .*

This statement is, to be sure, somewhat invalidated by coming from Charles Blount, Earl of Devonshire in 1593. At
that time Lady Rich had just eloped with him, leaving her
seven children behind. (No one would have ventured to
pass on which were little Blounts and which little Riches!)
The open avowal of the *liaison* created the need of an explanation. Devonshire provided the best he could, falling
back on the time-honored excuse that Lady Rich had become his mistress because her marriage was unbearable.
As it happens, however, the Sidney sonnets corroborate
Blount's assertions concerning the conjugal miseries of
Stella.

And by common consent the new husband was called the
" rich Lord Rich " because there was nothing else pleasant
to say about him. Reports make him " rough and uncourtly
in manners and conversation." The Bishop of London complained of the " riots " he kept in his house. Even on his
own showing, he was " a poor man of no language," having only the slightest " oversight " even of French. By consequence, the more vain little Penelope admired the culture and brilliance of a person like Sidney, the less she
liked Robert Rich who despite the university, was " dull
and uneducated."

For a while, however, Astrophel had no inkling of
Stella's unhappiness. His first reference to her new state
was quite without rancor:

> *now long needy Fame,*
> *Doth even grow rich, meaning my Stella's name.*

For himself, he was missing her acutely. She had understood his " melancholy times." She had known for a sensitive aloofness what others took for pride:

> *Because I oft in dark abstractéd guise,*
> *Seem most alone in greatest company,*
> *With dearth of words and answers quite awry,*
> *To them that would make nakéd speech arise;*
> *They deem, and of their doom the rumor flies,*
>   *That poison foul of bubbling Pride doth lie*
>   *So in my swelling breast, that only I*
> *Fawn on myself, all others do despise:*
> *Yet pride (I think) doth not my soul possess,*
> *(Which looks too oft in this unflattering glass)*
> *But one worse fault, ambition, I confess,*
>   *That makes me oft my best friends overpass*
>   *Unseen, unheard, while thought to highest place*
>   *Bends all his powers, even unto* Stella's *grace.*

And now, newly lonely, he found himself conjuring up for comfort a remembered Stella who

> *methinks not only shines but sings!*

This dangerous and romantic state was only part of a general sense of frustration. With Penelope's marriage, all Sidney's troubles took on acuteness and pressure. From the middle of April to the middle of June 1581, he was harried by the presence of the French Commissioners who had come at last to debate Gloriana's articles of marriage. At the same time he was being bludgeoned into gracious adjustment to the match by a constant, commanded attendance both on the Queen and her foreign guests. Never had he seen things look blacker for his beloved Protestantism; not only in England, but in Scotland, France and Flanders. His uncle Leicester was desperate, reduced to tears with the Queen, to fisticuffs with Sussex.

Crowning complication to these difficulties, and itself at the core of his troubled intensity about Stella, was the ever-lasting problem of money. For the entertainment of the French he was forced into terrific expenditures. Even in an age of wide credit (to nobles), he was driven to selling lands. Poverty stood between him and all the lovely things of life — like Stella, like the " bliss of children " which he saw as " unspeakable comfort." At twenty-seven, his chances of founding a family were less than ever. For, lucrative service at home or abroad, such as might come through Leicester's influence and his own desert at the end of patient years, was little likely to be his under a French régime. Now, additionally, he must endure heavy drains on his purse and brace himself to stoic endurance in a court as enervating as ever, which was also the home of Alençon. To cap the climax, there was no longer at Leicester House the understanding alluring young woman to whom he could talk freely.

In short, by mid April 1581, Philip Sidney was in just such a tetchy queasy emotional state as has aforetime minis-tered to passion. Like his mother, he was a person fiercely " racked by native strengths." Obstruction he found a very hell. He had already endured all the balking that he could stand — and more! All he needed to open the floodgates to a passion without restraint was the realization that for Stella her marriage was as " dear a purchase of repentance " as it was for him.

That came soon enough. And when it came, there was no mistaking the quality of his reaction:

> *My mouth doth water, and my breast doth swell,*
> *My tongue doth itch, my thoughts in labour be:*
> *Listen then, Lordings, with good ear to me,*
> *For of my life I must a riddle tell.*
> *Toward* Aurora's *Court a Nymph doth dwell,*

Rich in all beauties which man's heart can see:
Beauties so far from reach of words, that we
Abase her praise saying she doth excel:
Rich in the treasure of deserved renown,
* Rich in the riches of a royal heart,*
* Rich in those gifts which give th' eternal crown;*
Who though most rich in these and every part,
* Which make the patents of true worldly bliss,*
* Hath no misfortune, but that Rich she is!*

The emotional impact of the discovery was terrific. His suffering ran the gamut of feeling. Bitterness gave way to fury. His whole idealistic universe of truth and beauty came toppling about his ears. In the deepest of his earlier depressions he had never conceived cataclysm like this. Such a fate as in the words of his favorite Euripides, thrust his high things low and shook his hills to dust. Indignantly Sidney hurled on paper his desperate revolt at the whole damnable paradox of living. His agony over the wreckage was dirge, litany, exorcism — all in one:

Ring out your bells, let mourning shows be spread
* For Love is dead:*
*   All Love is dead, infected*
*   With plague of deep disdain:*
*   Worth as naught-worth rejected,*
*   And Faith fair Scorn doth gain.*
*   From so ungrateful fancy*
*   From such a female frenzy,*
*   From them that use men thus,*
*   Good Lord, deliver us!*

Weep neighbors, weep. Do you not hear it said
* That Love is dead?*
*   His death-bed peacock's Folly,*
*   His winding-sheet is Shame,*

His will, False-seeming holy,
His sole executor, Blame.
  From so ungrateful fancy
  From such a female frenzy,
  From them that use men thus,
  Good Lord, deliver us!

Let dirge be sung, and trentals rightly read,
  For Love is dead:
    Sir Wrong his tomb ordaineth,
    My mistress' marble heart,
    Which epitaph containeth,
    Her eyes were once his dart.
    From so ungrateful fancy,
    From such a female frenzy,
    From them that use men thus,
    Good Lord, deliver us!

Then, even from the bottom of despair, leaped hope — insistent, triumphant with consolation: love was not dead!
In a world swept clean of justice, of decency, of every
earthly and heavenly thing of virtue, love alone lived.
Here was the comforting creed to a new and exultant religion, a faith which admitted but one heresy, knew but
one sin — denial of itself!

Alas, I lie: rage hath this error bred,
  Love is not dead.
    Love is not dead, but sleepeth
    In her unmatchéd mind:
    Where she his counsel keepeth
    Till due desert she find.
      Therefore from so vile fancy,
      To call such wit a frenzy,
      Who Love can temper thus
      Good Lord, deliver us!

With love playing devil's advocate in this style, Sidney had only a step to go till he cursed the sacredness of such marriage as stood between him and Stella; cursed that union for a thing unholy, damnable; refused any longer to regard it as the barrier, enjoining reverence, before which his own desires should come to hallowed halt. Coolly he forswore constraint, and prepared to woo in earnest:

For me, alas, I am full resolved,
Those bands, alas, shall not be dissolved,
Nor break my word, though reward come late,
Nor fail my faith in my failing fate,
Nor change in change, though change change my estate.

But always one myself, with eagle-eyed Truth to fly,
Up to the sun, although the sun my wings do fry:
  For if those flames burn my desire
  Yet shall I die in Phoenix *fire.*

Before Stella's marriage, her Astrophel had " suffered " purely conventional pangs which took toll of neither appetite nor sleep. But now with the mounting of real passion, his torturing thoughts kept him awake o' nights:

As good to write, as for to lie and groan,
  O Stella *dear, how much thy power hath wrought,*
Thou hast my mind, none of the basest, brought
My still kept course while others sleep to moan;
Alas, if from the height of Virtue's throne,
  Thou canst vouchsafe the influence of a thought,
  Upon a wretch which long thy grace hath sought;
Weigh then, by thee how I am overthrown;
And then think thus, although thy beauty be
Made manifest by such a victory,
Yet noblest conquerors do wrecks avoid;

Since then thou hast so far subduéd me,
That in my heart I offer still to thee,
O do not let thy temple be destroyed!

This same tormenting restless ardor produced one of the loveliest of the sonnets, on which Shakespeare himself levied:

Come Sleep, O Sleep, the certain knot of peace
  The baiting place of wits, the balm of woe,
The poor man's wealth, the prisoner's release,
The indifferent judge between the high and low,
With shield of proof, shield me from out the press
  Of these fierce darts, Despair doth at me throw;
  O make in me those civil wars to cease:
I will good tribute pay if thou do so.
Take thou of me smooth pillows, sweetest bed,
A chamber deaf of noise, and blind of light,
A rosy garland, and a weary head.
And if these things (as being thine in right)
  Move not thy heavy grace, thou shalt in me,
  Livelier than elsewhere, Stella's image see.

When Lady Rich returned to London from her husband's house of Leighs, she resumed her attendance on Aurora. Agonizingly, delightedly, Sidney was aware of her presence even in crowds. At a tilt for the French Commissioners, on May 15th, 1581, he felt himself victor, solely because she watched. At still another tournament probably about the same time, thoughts of her swept from him all consideration of mere martial matters so that he well nigh disgraced himself:

In martial sports I had my cunning tried,
  And yet to break more staves I did address
While people shout: indeed I must confess,

The Lady Penelope Rich who was Stella.

Youth, luck, and praise filled my veins with pride;
  When Cupid *having me his slave descried.*
In Mars *his livery, prancing in the press,*
' *Now what, sir fool!* ' *said he* (*I would no less*)
' *Look here, I say!* ' *I looked and* Stella *spied,*
Who hard by, through a window sent her light;
My heart then quaked, then dazzled were my eyes,
One hand forgot to rule, th'other to fight,
No trumpet sound I heard, nor friendly cries;
  My foe came on and beat the air for me,
  Till that her blush taught me my shame to see.

Passionately he came to envy the very spaniel who might
be with her constantly. Here at last was one dog he did not
love, an ugly graceless little brute!

Dear, why make you more of a dog than me?
  If he do love, alas, I burn in love;
If he wait well, I never thence would move;
If he be fair, yet but a dog can be;
Little he is, so little worth is he:
  He barks, my songs in one voice oft do prove;
  Bidden, (perhaps) he fetcheth thee a glove;
But I unbid, fetch even my soul to thee!

Meantime Stella noticed her Astrophel's depression. But
actuated either by discretion or coquetry, she affected not to
know the cause. Her lover was moved to protest:

Stella *oft sees the very face of woes*
  Painted in my bewrinkled stormy face:
But cannot skill to pity my disgrace;
Not though thereof the cause herself she knows.
Yet hearing late a fable which did show,
  Of lovers never known a piteous case,
  Pity thereof got in her breast such place,

That, from that sea derived, tears' springs did flow.
Alas, if Fancy drawn by fainéd things,
Though false, yet with free store more grace doth
    breed
Than servant's wreck, where new doubt honor
    brings,
Then think, my dear, that in me you do read
  Of lover's ruin some thrice sad tragedy.
  I am not I — pity the tale of me!

However, Stella's suspicions of his amorous woe rested on an intimate acquaintance with this sensitive melancholy lover of hers. From the knowledge of other ladies who looked only for the conventional signs of love, he considered himself safe enough:

Because I breathe not love to everyone,
  Nor do not use set colors for to wear:
Nor nourish special locks with vowéd hair.
Nor give each speech a full point of a groan,
The courtly nymphs acquainted with the moan
  Of them which in their lips Love's standard bear:
' What, he?' (say they of me) ' No, I dare swear,
He cannot love; no, no, let him alone! '
  And think so still, so Stella know my mind.
Profess indeed I do not Cupid's art:
But you, fair maids, at length this true shall find
That his right badge is learnéd in the heart.
  Dumb swans, not chattering pies do lovers prove,
  They love indeed, who quake to say they love.

When serious siege failed of results, Sidney could turn playful and disprove his lady's protestations out of her own mouth with the school-book maxim: two negatives make an affirmative. In his own graceful phrase the argument ran:

O grammar rules, O now your virtues show,
  So children read you still with awful eyes,
As my young dove may in your precepts wise.
Her grant to me by her own virtue know.
For late with heart most high, with eyes most low,
  I craved the thing which ever she denies.
  She lightening love, displaying Venus *skies,*
Lest one should not be heard, twice said 'No, No!'
Sing, then, my muse, now I do paean sing.
Hearken, Envy, not at my high triumphing:
But grammar's force with sweet success confirm,
  For grammar says (ah, this dear Stella, weigh!)
  For grammar says (to grammar who says nay?)
That in one speech, two negatives affirm!

At last, however, perhaps in her own unhappiness divining the like of him, she admitted to guessing his secret, and in a glorious moment, gloriously celebrated in a series of ecstatic sonnets, she confessed to loving Astrophel as Astrophel loved her! Triumphant Sidney sang the miracle of that hour:

O joy too high for my love still to show,
  O bliss, fit for a nobler seat than me,
Envy, put out thine eyes, lest thou do see
What Oceans *of delight in me do flow.*
My friend that oft saw'st through all masks my woe,
  Come, come, and let me pour myself in thee:
  Gone is the winter of my misery.
My Spring appears, lo! see what here doth grow,
For Stella *hath with words (where faith doth shine)*
Of her high heart given me the monarchy:
And I, O I! may say that she is mine.
And though she give but this conditionally,
  This realm of bliss, while Virtue's course I take;
  No kings be crowned, but they some covenant make!

However, as might have been foreseen, trouble lurked in that same royal covenant. It was well enough for Stella to counsel that whoever

> *a sound affection bears*
> *So captives to his saint both soul and mind,*
> *That wholly hers, all selfness he forbears*
> *Thence his desire he learns, his life's course thence.*

Despite Philip's heroic efforts to keep the faith, he became a little uncertain of his powers:

> *Desire, though thou my old companion art,*
> *   And oft so clings to my pure Love, that I*
> *One from the other scarcely can descry,*
> *While each do blow the fire of my heart;*
> *Now from thy fellowship I needs must part.*
> *   Venus is taught with Dian's wings to fly,*
> *   I must no more in thy sweet passions lie:*
> *Virtue's gold now must head my Cupid's dart,*
> *Service and honour, wonder with delight,*
> *Fear to offend, well worthy to appear,*
> *Care shining in mine eyes, faith in my sprite —*
> *These things are left me by my only dear.*
> *   But thou Desire, because thou wouldst have all:*
> *   Now banished art, but yet within my call.*

Certain sweet contentions developed on this very point:

> *Late tired with woe, even ready for to pine*
> *   With rage of love, I called my love unkind.*
> *She in whose eyes, love's fires unfelt do shine,*
> *Sweetly said: I true love in her should find!*
> *I joy, but straight thus watered was my wine:*
> *That love she did, but with a love not blind,*
> *Which would not let me, whom she loved, decline*
> *   From nobler course, fit for my birth and mind.*

And therefore by her love's authority,
Willed me these tempests of vain love to flee:
And anchor fast myself on Virtue's shore.
  Alas! if this the only metal be,
  Of love new coined, to help my beggary:
Dear, love me not — that you may love me more.

Astrophel still continued to yearn for more than was
nominated in the bond, with a new danger in his old Dudley scorn of constraint:

No more, my dear, no more these counsels try,
  O give my passions leave to run their race:
Let Fortune lay on me her worst disgrace.
Let folk o'ercharged with brain against me cry,
Let clouds be dim, my fate bereaves mine eyes,
  Let me no steps but of lost labour try,
Let all the earth in scorn recount my race;
But do not will me from my love to fly.
  I do not envy Aristotle's *wit,*
Nor do aspire to Caesar's *bleeding fame:*
Nor aught do care though some above me sit;
Nor hope nor wish another course to frame:
  But that which once may win thy cruel heart,
  Thou art my wit; and thou my Virtue art.

A fig for reason, learning, family, pride. This Philip was in
the last degree of love. He was well nigh drowned!

One day coming upon Stella asleep, perhaps in the garden at Leicester House, Astrophel stole a kiss. None of
those chaste salutes which to the amazement and delight
of visiting foreigners, English ladies casually greeted strange
men withal, but a lover's kiss. By his own confession, he
was far from repenting the trespass:

  Have I caught my heavenly jewel
  Teaching sleep most fair to be?

*Now will I teach her, that she
When she wakes is too, too cruel.*

*Her tongue waking still refuseth,
Giving frankly niggard ' No.'
Now will I attempt to know,
What ' No ' her tongue sleeping useth.*

*See the hand that waking guardeth,
Sleeping grants a free resort:
Now I will invade the fort,
Cowards love with loss rewarded.*

*But (O fool) think of the danger
Of her just and high disdain,
Now will I (alas) refrain
Love fears nothing else but anger.*

*Yet those lips so sweetly swelling,
Do invite a stealing kiss;
Now but venture will I this,
Who will read must first learn spelling.*

*O sweet kiss! But ah, she is waking,
Lowering beauty chastens me.
Now will I for fear hence flee,
Fool, more fool, for no more taking.*

On the strength of that kiss, he wrote with greater charm and conviction than ever. What could he not do, with more?

*I never drank of Aganippe well,
    Nor never did in shade of Tempe sit:
And Muses scorn with vulgar brains to dwell,
Poor layman I, for sacred rites unfit.
    Some do, I hear, of poets' fury tell,
But God wot, wot not what they mean by it:*

And this I swear by blackest brook of Hell,
I am no pickpurse of another's wit.
* How falls it, then, that with so smooth an ease*
My thoughts I speak? And what I speak I show
In verse? and that my verse best wits doth please?
Guess we the cause. What, is it this? fie, no.
* Or so? much less. How then? sure thus it is:*
* My lips are sure inspired with* Stella's *kiss!*

But at the same time he could, in fierce remorse, rate himself sharply:

What? doth high place ambitious thoughts augument?
Cannot such grace your silly self content,
But you must needs with those lips billing be?
* And through those lips drink nectar from that tongue,*
* Leave that,* Sir Philip, *lest your neck be wrung!.*

However, other kisses succeeded, bringing fresh repentance — and kisses! Frequent sight of Stella kept Sidney in a tumult. He visited her when she was ill, and found that in her chamber, sickness itself was " graced." From a " happy window," probably at Barnard's Castle, he saw her pass in her barge, with her golden hair blown about her bewitching face by the little river breezes.

There were stolen meetings so far, innocent. Sidney records the tragic miscarriage of one such. Possibly he expected Stella to come on foot that night, and not in one of the rare new " cosches." Perhaps she failed to stop because she missed a signal. We must piece out the scene for ourselves. Astrophel is purposely not specific:

Unhappy sight, and hath she vanished by?
* So near, in so good time, so free a place?*
Dead glass, dost thou thine object so embrace,
As what my heart still sees thou canst not spy?

I swear by her love and my lack, that I
    Was not in fault that bent my dazzling race
    Only unto the heaven of Stella's *face,*
Counting but dust that in her way did lie:
But cease mine eyes, your tears do witness well,
That you guiltless therefore your nectar missed,
Cursed be the page from whom the bad torch fell,
Cursed be the night which did your will resist,
    Curst be the coachman that did drive so fast
    With no worse curse than absence makes me taste.

On still another occasion he was disappointed of a *rendezvous:*

O absent presence, Stella *is not here!*
    False flattering hope that with so fair a face,
Bare me in hand that in this orphaned place,
Stella *I saw, my* Stella *should appear.*
What say'st thou now, where is that dainty cheer
    Thou told'st mine eyes should help their famished case?
    But where art thou? now that self-felt disgrace
Doth make me most to wish thy comfort near?
But here I do store of fair ladies meet,
Who may with charm of conversation sweet
Make in my heavy mould new thoughts to grow:
    Sure they prevail as much with me, as he
    That bade his friend but then new maimed, to be
Merry with him, and so forget his woe.

However, one night after every one else was abed, they had some whispered moments together, probably on the terrace of Leicester House. The garden was drenched with moonlight. Below the river was mysterious in mist. The voices of merrymakers returning by water from the Bankside to the stairs at Blackfriars or Paul's came back dimly to them. Astrophel made a song of the ecstasy and agony of that meeting:

Only joy, now here you are,
Fit to hear and ease my care,
Let my whispering voice obtain
Sweet rewards for sharpest pain
Take me to thee, and thee to me:
No no no no, my dear, let be.

Night hath closed all in her cloak,
Twinkling stars love thoughts provoke,
Danger hence good care doth keep,
Jealousy itself doth sleep.
Take me to thee, and thee to me:
No no no no, my dear, let be.

Better place no wit can find,
Cupid's knot to loose or bind,
These sweet flowers, our fine bed too,
Us in their best language woo.
Take me to thee, and thee to me:
No no no no, my dear, let be.

This small light the moon bestows,
Serves thy beams for to disclose,
So to raise my heart more high;
Fear not, else none can us spy.
Take me to thee, and thee to me:
No no no no, my dear, let be.

That you heard was but a mouse,
Dumb sleep holdeth all the house,
Yet asleep (me thinks) they say,
Young fools, take time while you may:
Take me to thee, and thee to me:
No no no no, my dear, let be!

Niggard time threats if we miss
This large offer of our bliss,
Long stay ere she grant the same:
Sweet then, while each thing doth frame.
Take me to thee, and thee to me:
No no no no, my dear, let be.

Your fair mother is abed,
Candles out and curtains spread;
She thinks you do letters write:
Write, but first let me endite.
Take me to thee, and thee to me:
No no no no, my dear, let be!

Sweet, alas, why strive you thus?
Concord better fitteth us.
Leave to Mars *the force of hands,*
Your power in your beauty stands.
Take me to thee, and thee to me:
No no no no, my dear, let be.

Woe to me, and do you swear
Me to hate, but I forbear?
Curst be my destinies all,
That brought me so high to fall:
Soon with my death I'll please thee.
No no no no, my dear, let be!

Such leaping raptures, such passionate pleadings, such tender (and yearning) denials were shaping inevitable climax. The affair could have but one end — particularly when the lovely young creatures caught up in its ardors were able to come together on terms of such intimacy at Stella's mother's.

Another song records a meeting in Leicester House gardens. May was young. Birds were singing, and soft winds

stirred the leaves in the plesaunce which swept down to the
Thames. Sidney's words about a " room " which was " apt "
for lovers must refer to the little pavilion at the river end.
There on April 27th, 1581 probably not much more than
a week before, Gloriana herself had been served with dinner privately, while the French Commissioners were being
entertained at the house above in splendor, noise and heat.
It overhung the water. It was cool and retired, and in it
Astrophel and Stella found a sequestered world of their
own, sheltered alike from the activities of the house and
the bustling life of the Thames.

There, according to Sidney, they met with tears, for
" great harms had taught him care " and Stella bore a
" foul yoke ":

> *Wept they had, alas the while,*
> *But now tears themselves did smile,*
> *While their eyes by love directed,*
> *Interchangeably reflected.*
>
> *Sighed they had: but now betwixt*
> *Sighs of woe were glad sighs mixed,*
> *With arms crossed, yet testifying*
> *Restless rest and living dying.*
>
> *Their ears hungry of each word*
> *Which the dear tongue would afford,*
> *But their tongues restrained from walking*
> *Till their hearts had ended talking.*

Then, swept out of himself, Philip became fiercely insistent.
Love, he urged, must run its course:

> *Never season was more fit*
> *Never room more apt for it.*
> *Smiling air allows my reason,*
> *These birds sing: now use the season!*

This small wind which so sweet is,
See how it the leaves doth kiss,
    Each tree in his best attiring,
    Sense of love to love inspiring.

Love makes earth the water drink,
Love to earth makes water sink,
    And if dumb things be so witty,
    Shall a heavenly grace want pity?

There his hands (in their speech) fain
Would have made tongue's language plain,
    But her hands his hands compelling,
    Gave repulse, all grace expelling.

In the verses as they were first published, piratically in 1591, Stella cut him short:

Therewithal away she went,
Leaving him with passion rent,
    With what she had done and spoken
    That therewith my song is broken.

However, in the possession of the Countess of Pembroke, and known only to her, like all the more intimate sonnets and songs, were additional verses. These Astrophel with a delicacy unusual in his day set every guard upon. And his sister knowing his mind kept them carefully from all eyes save her own for years after his death. She made them public for the first time in 1598 when Stella's elopement with Devonshire was a scandal five years old, and Philip's little widow, the daughter of Walsingham, had been a second time married — for nine years.

The verses so long withheld complete the scene. It did not end so abruptly:

Then she spake; her speech was such,
As not ears, but heart did touch:
> *While such wise she love denied,*
> *As yet love she signified.*

Astrophel, *said she, my love,*
Cease in these effects to prove:
> *Now be still, yet still believe me,*
> *Thy grief more than death would grieve me.*

If that any thought in me
Can taste comfort, but of thee,
> *Let me feed with hellish anguish,*
> *Joyless, hopeless, endless languish.*

If those eyes you praisèd be
Half as dear as you to me
> *Let me home return, stark blindèd*
> *Of those eyes, and blinder mindèd.*

If to secret of my heart,
I do any wish impart,
> *Where thou art not foremost placed*
> *Be both wish and I defaced.*

If more may be said, I say,
All my bliss in thee I lay;
> *If thou love, my love, content thee,*
> *For all love, all faith is meant thee.*

Trust me, while I thee deny,
In myself, the smart I try,
> *Tyrant, honour doth thus use thee,*
> *Stella's self might not refuse thee!*

> *Therefore, Dear, this is no move,*
> *Lest, though I leave not thy love,*
>   *Which too deep in me is framed*
>   *I should blush when thou art named.*

A last song, also first published in 1598, tells its story of a lover driven by his madness to the dangerous shift of talking to Stella under the window of her husband's house:

>   *Who is it that this dark night,*
> *Underneath my window plaineth?*
> It is one who from thy sight,
> Being (ah) exiled, disdaineth
> Every other vulgar light.

>   *Why, alas, and are you he?*
> *Be not yet those fancies changéd?*
> Dear, when you find change in me,
> Though from me you be estrangéd,
> Let my change my ruin be.

>   *Well in absence this will die,*
> *Leave to see and leave to wonder:*
> Absence sure will help, if I
> Can learn, how myself to sunder
> From what in my heart doth lie.

>   *But time will these thoughts remove:*
> *Time doth work what no man knoweth,*
> Time doth as the subject prove,
> With time still the affection groweth
> In the faithful turtle dove.

>   *What if you new beauties see,*
> *Will not they stir new affection?*
> I will think thy pictures be.

(Image like of Saint's perfection)
Poorly counterfeiting thee.

Peace, I think that some give ear:
Come no more, lest I get anger,
Bliss, I will my bliss forbear,
Fearing (sweet) you to endanger,
But my soul shall harbor thee.

Well, begone, begone I say,
Lest that Argus *eyes perceive you,*
O unjust fortune's sway,
Which can make me thus to leave you,
And from louts to run away.

Certain additional verses leave no doubt of the progressive intensity of Astrophel's feelings. Here is no lover out of a copy-book, or a Puritan's primer. His ecstasy cries down the centuries:

Think of that most grateful time,
When my leaping heart will climb,
   In those lips to have his biding,
There those roses for to kiss,
Which do breathe a sugared bliss,
   Opening rubies, pearls dividing.

Think of my most princely power,
When I blessèd shall devour,
   With my greedy lickerish senses,
Beauty, music, sweetness, love
While she doth against me prove
   Her strong darts, but weak defenses.

Think, think of those dallyings,
When with dovelike murmurings,
   With glad moaning passèd anguish,

We change eyes, and heart to heart
Each to other do depart,
*   Joying till joy makes us languish.*

Exquisite as it might be, Philip Sidney could not live long
in the fool's paradise of illicit passion. With his emotional
sensitiveness sharpened by frustrations to a very agony of
unhappiness, he might in the first place find himself open
to such thoughts as in his own phrase " overmastered " him.
Temporarily, too, he might find justification in an addled
world for what he knew was sinning, no matter what that
sin's pity or glory. But his open nature was natural enemy
to the devisings of duplicity, to the shifts of stolen meetings. Wrong doing, even under the blanket of beauty, with
the stars singing in their courses above his head, was still
wrong doing. Even though it stimulated mind and spirit
to the loveliest expression of lovely emotion in the loveliest
of all sonnets. Wrong doing, moreover, which cut at the
very springs of Life.

External circumstance may have had some part in concluding the affair which certainly did not continue beyond
the autumn of 1581. Hubert Languet died on September 30th. Madame du Plessis, the wife of Sidney's friend the
Huguenot leader De Mornay, was with him at the end.
To her with his last breath, the old man expressed love for
Philip's clear beauty of spirit, and faith in his high destiny.

The news of Languet's going must have been bitter
enough to Sidney without the poignant stab of that last
tribute. Remembrance of assiduous guarding against every
sort of evil, came now to the apostate disciple, not in pride,
but shame. Once Languet had feared the " cursed hunger
for gold," in a mind which had then (happily!) admitted
nothing " save the love of goodness." What would have
been his loathing now of this hunger truly accursed, this
unleashed, dishonored passion?

In bitter revulsion from the wicked devices and desires
of his own heart, Sidney wrote the two concluding sonnets
for his *Astrophel and Stella.* They put a hallowed finis on
the whole affair. They show the depths to which he had
descended in the pursuit of profane love, even as they scale
the heights in their triumphant search for her sacred sister.
Consequently the Countess of Pembroke, sole confidante
of those depths, kept them unpublished till 1598. Nothing
lovelier than the second exists in the language:

Thou blind man's mark, thou fool's self-chosen snare,
 Fond fancy's scum, and dregs of scattered thought,
Band of all evils, cradle of causeless care,
Thou web of will, whose end is never wrought.
Desire, Desire, I have too dearly bought,
With prize of mangled wit thy worthless ware,
Too long, too long asleep thou hast me brought,
Who should my mind to higher things prepare.
But yet in vain thou hast my ruin sought,
In vain thou made'st me to vain things aspire,
In vain thou kindlest all thy smoky fire.
For Virtue hath this better lesson taught,
Within myself to seek my only hire:
Desiring naught but how to kill Desire.

Leave me, O Love which reachest but to dust,
 And thou my mind, aspire to higher things:
Grow rich in that which never taketh rust:
Whatever fades, but fading pleasure brings.
Draw in thy beams, and humble all thy might,
To that sweet yoke, where lasting freedoms be:
Which breaks the clouds and opens forth the light.
That doth both shine and give us sight to see.
O take fast hold, let that Light be thy guide,
In this small course which birth draws out to death,

And think how evil becometh him to slide,
Who seeketh Heaven and comes of heavenly breath.
Then farewell, World, thy uttermost I see,
Eternal Love, maintain Thy life in me.

So Sidney took farewell of a passion which he announced in a Latin motto to have been both " splendid " and " unprofitable." His was no Puritan soul to deny the shining, even when he saw the sin.

Actually, he had won him a greater glory than he knew. Into this grandeur called love, he had ventured in the first place as a mere blurrer of paper. He continued in petulance because Providence had not at his call produced just what he sought, and just at the time when he sought it. Out of his giddy denial of all religion, he had stumbled to shame through a faith that was false, he had soared to the very Godhead, in one which was real. The splendid profit of *Astrophel and Stella,* dear purchase of suffering, sin and loathing, was a radiant selfless glory of the spirit. That, even more than the undying beauty of peerless verse; more even than his deathless death in Flanders, was destined to make him, among the men of his time, immortal.

THE FOURTEENTH CHAPTER
ENTITLED
CHILD OF DESIRE.

 IDNEY had no sense of any kind of splendor before him, when he headed his horse toward Greenwich in August of 1580. He went because Leicester summoned. He thought it was a mistake for him to be going at all.

He had left court for lack of money, yet so long as Her Majesty saw a silken doublet on him, she would think him " in good cace." She would continue to deny him preferment. She would refuse to let him earn money abroad. She would give him no office at home. Let his Dudley pride pay his tailors!

Once, possibly, Sidney had hoped that his absence might impress her. If so, he now knew that it hadn't. He had been gone from town since February. For three months before that he had rarely come to court. However, Gloriana supported the affliction, and with a pointed calm. It took her till midsummer, to notice he was not there! Even then she did not command him back. Had she made up her mind to ignore him? In such an event, he would hardly make hay in the rays of a Sun which was determined not to shine.

As a matter of fact, she was making him suffer — and would — because of his letter. Memory of its logic, its utter reason, still swept her to fury. If Philip had only been obstreperous like Stubbe, being Leicester's nephew, he might have hoped for pardon. Pardon would have been a

virtue in the Queen. Or if, even with all his tact and modera-
tion he could have only contrived to be wrong. Pardon
would then have been pity. But fatally, he had been right.
Gloriana could never be expected to forgive him for that!

Consequently, it was lucky for Mr. Philip that he had
" done with hoping." It would get him nowhere. By the
same token, it would have been still more lucky if he had
also done with resenting, when he could not get the reasonable things he wanted! As it was, he would suffer acutely.
For at enchanted Wilton, he had created his poet's heaven.
He was coming back to a maker who was certainly not a
poet (her verses proved that) but who nevertheless could
shape him a very heaven or hell. With his father in trouble,
and Alençon's Commissioners in prospect, Philip Sidney
knew only too well that it would not be heaven. But would
it be limbo? or hell?

The first weeks after his arrival saw the recapitulation of
all his old problems. Gloriana had fallen on serviceable Sir
Henry for leaving his charge in Wales (he had managed it
even from Ireland) to post to Wilton and back, when his
first grandchild was born. Though that was in April, she
was still harping on the offense in August 1580, when Walsingham warned him that he were best " walk warily,"
since her Highness was most " apt to give ear " to any who
would " ill " him. Of course, she had only to make this
known, to have both of her ears kept busy. Philip was busy,
as well. To his now accustomed task of defending his father
from lies, he now added the new duty of bearing " with
reverence " the " passions " in Sir Henry which such calumnies engendered.

Money troubles were urgent. Robert Sidney, now seventeen, and on his travels, was in direst straits abroad. In
October 1580, he wrote home to his brother. Philip scurried
after funds. He secured something from Leicester. He undertook to get more from Sir Henry, or " jarle." He made

personal contribution for his " sweetest boy " on whom he
preferred to spend, than to have it for himself. Late on the
18th, though he was so " overwatched with tedeous busi-
nes " that his eyes were " almost closed up " in sleep, he
sat down to write to young Robin.

The political situation which he reported to his brother
left Philip profoundly dejected. Here in England nothing
notable happened. The more shame, too, for while Protestantism suffered such perils abroad, England looked on
but " idly." Those were the " Naighbours' fyres " ! There
was, however, one piece of proud and exciting news. He
retailed it a little wistfully. A fortnight before, Francis
Drake had put into Plymouth Harbor. He had been gone
since November of 1577: " about the world hath he bene,
and rich he is returned " !

Just such noble occupation as Sidney craved had been the
lot of that lucky Drake. It united his needs for money, for
action, for what by local standards was Christian service.
Not to mince words, the *Golden Hind* had returned from
the pious and joyous business of " singeing the beard of the
King of Spain." The little matter of the circumnavigation
of the world, was a romantic by-product: Drake had not
dared to go home by the way he had come!

Though ostensibly bound for Alexandria, he had sneaked
up through the terrible Straits of Magellan to attack from
the unsuspected south, a Peru which lay unprotected. His
loot had come to £500,000. Leicester was one of the three
or four persons, including the Queen (she afterward denied
it) who knew of his secret plans. They all realized something like 4700 per cent on their shares in the venture. (All,
that is, save Gloriana who, between presents and seizures,
delighted in even larger profits!)

By the irony of fate, news of these opulent rewards came
to a Philip Sidney who had the greatest difficulty in fetching out of Lombard Street (which was his only Peru) just

enough to meet the most pressing debts incurred on a school-boy's travels. No wonder that in concluding, he told his brother Robin of " melancholy days."

Actually, he had a richer treasure in the continued devotion of Languet. His good friend sent him cheering news on October 22d, 1580. At last the " dislike " and " hatred " which Alençon conceived for Sidney were like to be dissipated. Monsieur's resentment had been rendered the more intense by the misapprehension that Philip had made the *Discourse* public, by way of demonstrating that " he despised him and cared nothing for his dislike." Languet undertook to have him informed that the circulation of the letter had been no fault of Sidney's. Moreover, that Philip wrote in the first instance, only because he was " ordered," by those he was " bound to obey." These two points were to be conveyed to the Duke by the Prince of Orange, St. Aldegonde and du Plessis, all of them " friendly " and eager to help. Languet concluded by saying:

If others should fail, perhaps I could do something in the matter, for when I was with him last summer, he conferred with me in as friendly a manner as yourself.

Though the friendly Hubert found matter for rejoicing in his Philip's return " from that hiding place " of Wilton " to the open light of the court," the transition gave little satisfaction to Sidney. Between the lines of his letters which attest so freely his " melancholy," his giving over of all " the delight of the world," one gathers that the royal light might be open, but it was certainly very cool. In warmth alone could ambition shoot up and flower. His despair cries out from one of the sonnets:

I cannot brag of word, much less of deed,
Fortune's winds still with me in one sort blow;
My wealth no more, and no whit less my need
Desire still on stilts of fear doth go. . . .

(To such frustrated desire as this was desire for Stella conjoined.)

It was not remarkable, therefore, that Sidney should fall in with the suggestion made by Languet in his letter of October 28th, 1580: he must come over to the Low Countries. Even if his remaining in England was useful to his father, Philip must remember that he had a duty also to his country. Nothing would help her more, nor be more useful to him at this juncture, than acquiring military training under La Noue and Orange.

However, Sidney was allowed to proceed no further than ordering from Plantin in Antwerp, books on the towns and harbors of Europe, and a fine new Map of the World. For months yet, his universe was to be bounded on the east by Greenwich, on the west by the royal manor of Richmond; with Wanstead its northern limit, and escape on the south only so far as to Penshurst or Wilton.

Under such circumstances, even the circumscribed powers of one who sat in Elizabeth's Parliaments must have seemed to him scope and " landscape." After postponements over more than a year, the Commons and Lords were at last permitted to convene on January 16th, 1581. That day the Queen opened Parliament. She sat at the top of the tapestried chamber upon a throne in her crown and mantle, bearing the scepter in her hand. At her left stood Walsingham. Lining the wall beyond him were all the Earls of the realm. At her right stood Burleigh. Ranging the wall beyond him, stood all of the lord bishops. Before Her Highness, in the center but keeping their distance, were the masters of chancery, with the barons banked behind them. At the very bottom of the room, in close order were massed the Commons. This position, far from the Sun, was one to which Sidney was now accustomed.

Her Majesty made matters clear to them from the start. They must think no thoughts on her marriage. They must rule no rulings on the succession. Then she swept off, leaving the Parliament to the unrestricted enjoyment of constitutional freedoms.

Despite these understandings, the Commons got into trouble. Overcome by the conviction that only God Himself could save their country, they piously voted a day of fasting and prayer. In so doing they infringed the Prerogative of the Queen, who was the head of the Church. They were soon told as much. Elizabeth sent Hatton to convey to them her " amazement " at their " rashness "! Her humbled Commons (including Sidney) sent back apologies and reconsidered their vote on prayer. Perhaps not even that would help!

One stout soul did his best to make a motion " regarding the Freedom of this House." However, the Speaker was too well instructed to hear or to see him. He sat down unrecognized. Innocuous measures were voted thereafter, such as the question of paving the street beyond Aldgate.

As Sir Walter Mildmay's opening speech made evident, there was desperate call for a program. Coast-towns and fortifications, many in bad repair, needed strengthening in view of the attack which Spain had made on Ireland four months before. The Border should be protected now that the Guises were fomenting trouble in Scotland. Something must be done by way of protection against the Catholics both in view of these foreign dangers, and the presence in England of Jesuit missionaries.

The matter of ways and means was referred to various committees which discussed them for seven weeks. On two such, Sidney sat. The more important considered the Catholic question. It formulated a law which by Protestant theory was a masterpiece. Such Catholics as this statute did not " reform," it would turn to good use in filling Elizabeth's coffers for it enjoined that hereafter, every recusant who did not attend the English Church must pay the enormous

ne of £20 a month, in lieu of the shilling a Sunday which
ad been levied till then!

Having passed this and other bills to the number of
iirty, Parliament was prorogued on March 18th, 1581.
he Queen graciously " acknowledged its labours," taking
are to specify that she " did not comprehend in her thanks
uch members of the House of Commons as have this ses-
ion more rashly dealt in some things than was fit for them
o do "!

In the midst of the deliberations there was diversion of a
lt on January 22d, 1581. Sidney took part, running
gainst the chief challenger who was another of the King
f Spain's godsons, Philip Howard whose father had been
)uke of Norfolk. He would soon be " restored in blood."
Already he was Earl of Arundel (succeeding his grand-
ather, the Queen's old suitor) and in high favor. In time
e would be a saint.

Anxiety about the French marriage was now at fever
itch among the Puritan group. For in March 1581, news
ame to England that the Commissioners were gathering at
Boulogne and Calais. This time fears were not confined
o Walsingham, Leicester and Hatton, or even to unre-
arded Sidney. Gloriana herself was frightened. In reality
narriage was something she dreamed not of, except in a
iightmare.

What she wanted was alliance with France. Discussions
f marriage kept diplomacy pleasantly lively, and in mo-
nents of pressure might even lend a touch of romance, such
s Alençon's visit had furnished eighteen months before.
Marriage itself was too dreadfully definite for her taste. Yet
narriage was certainly likely, with four hundred French-
nen in the offing, waiting the turn of wind and tide. Mariage it must not be!

In that case, advised Leicester, better not to let them
ome. She might blow hot and cold with a single envoy,

not with four hundred! However the Queen feared to for
bid them. Henry III was seriously ill. He might die. In
that case, placating Alençon would become more important
than ever. Who else would support her against the Guises
who managed the French court? Who else would stand
with her against a Spain furious at Drake's " services " in
Peru? She dared do no more than urge the ambassadors to
wait a while. " She must make preparations proper for so
honourable a throng." Meantime she did some sober thinking.

The first idea she fetched up owed something to Leicester. (He had told her the charges would be terrific for enter-
taining such a host). By a master stroke of economic genius,
she now commanded all sellers of silks, satins and cloth-of-
gold, to vend their wares at a discount of 25 per cent! This
enabled her to refurnish the shabbier portions of Somerset
House where most of the Frenchmen would lodge. Thanks
to these substantial savings, she could pay their mighty
board-bill.

The second idea was just as simple and quite as extraordinary. She confided it solely to Leicester, whom in her
desperation she had fallen to trusting again. If things went
" badly," with his aid, she would bring over Alençon in
secret. When he had once arrived she would tell him in
private conference that she could not marry. Her people
would not allow it. By promising him money to pursue his
career in Flanders, she could bribe him to consent. The man
was easy to handle. And when Monsieur himself told the
Commissioners that the match was off, what could they
do about it? Of course the scheme should be used as a last
resort. For one thing, it would cost a good deal. For another,
Henry III would be annoyed if she went over the heads of
his Commissioners to deal with his brother. It would not
do to antagonize Henry — least of all if he should live!

With matters thus arranged, early in April, she signed

he Frenchmen's passport. She did it with sufficient re-
uctance to set Walsingham and Burleigh to concocting
ittle plans of their own for her diplomatic extrication in
:ase she demanded rescue. That done, Gloriana seems to
lave set to work on another design which involved a con-
'erence with the neglected Philip Sidney. Why might not
he devices in the tilt for the Commissioners give them
omething to think about, as well as entertainment? Mr.
²hilip was famous all over Europe for his skill in shaping
levices. Just now, had she known it, she was doing the
roung man a kindness by keeping him busy. For Stella was
,urely married. Astrophel may even have known that she
vas unhappy, too.

The Frenchmen arrived in London at a most inauspicious
ime, on April 22d, 1581. When the bells of the Tower
were ringing and a hundred parish steeples joined in the
welcoming clamor, England was celebrating the Eve of
St. George. On the morrow came the national feast of the
conquerors at Crécy and Agincourt.

London found them very French indeed, these brilliantly
clad foreigners who lodged all over Fleet Street, the Strand
and Chancery Lane. They kept Somerset House a babel of
highly cadenced talk. However, London held its collective
tongue, for a royal proclamation of April 18th forbade
all comment under the severest penalties. What was to be
done to the French, the Queen would do herself!

She did it by postponing negotiations till the delegates
were desperate. After three weeks of it they wrote to their
King in premature triumph: " We think there is nothing
more that she can put us off for " ! They did not know the
Queen. Her resource was a marvel. All through these deliberate delays, she loaded the Commissioners with compliments. She provided diversions with a free and liberal hand,
from her own purse but chiefly from that of her highest
nobles. She sent them to bear-baitings. She showed them

her palaces. She commissioned Leicester and Pembroke to take them to Hampton Court.

At last the Frenchmen were driven to doubt her " frank ness." They wrote in humiliation and despair to their King begging for recall under some " honest colour." That was on May 13th, 1581. Two days after, the Queen decided the time was ripe for the greatest entertainment of all. It was the tilt of the Four Foster Children of Desire. In there was a device.

The tournament was set in a story which Sidney may have written. Four knights who had been fostered by Per fect Beauty, claimed her as theirs " by right of inheri ance," and with many pretty speeches they announced their determination to defend her against all comers.

Of course, Perfect Beauty was the Queen. Two of the Children were Philip Sidney and Fulke Greville who were well known for Protestants. The other two were the Earl of Arundel and Lord Windsor, both scions of Catholic families. The balance was hardly accidental.

All rode very gorgeously into the tilt-yard of Westminster that Whitmonday afternoon. Perfect Beauty was enthroned in her Fortress surrounded by her maids, a new Lady Rich among them. Past the Fortress, past the bewildered French men, past the common people who in their desire to see were some of them jammed to death, paraded the Foster Children. Arundel's armor was gold. Windsor's train wore coats of orange tawny with the symbol of virginity on them, a silver unicorn. Then in costly glory came Mr Philip Sidney:

in very sumptuous manner with armor part blue and the rest gilded and engraved . . . having caparisons and fur niture very rich and costly, as some of cloth of gold em broidered with gold and silver feathers, very richly and cunningly wrought. He had four pages that rode on his

ur spare horses, who had cassock coats and Venetian hose
ll of cloth of silver, edged with gold lace and hats of the
ime with gold bands and white feathers, and each one a
air of white buskins. Then had he thirty gentlemen and
eomen and four trumpeters who were all in cassock coats
nd Venetian hose of yellow velvet, edged with silver lace,
ellow velvet caps with silver bands and white feathers, and
very one a pair of white buskins. And they had upon their
oats a scroll or band of silver, which came scarf-wise over
he shoulder and so down under the arm, with this posy or
ntence written upon it, both before and behind OURS BUT
NOT FOR US. (*Sic Nos Non Nobis*)

The words of that device OURS BUT NOT FOR US were
uitable enough to the gallant complaint of a dejected Child
f Desire disappointed of his role of guarding Beauty for
is exclusive devotion. Nevertheless there was more here
han met the eye, inescapable literary associations. Therein
iy Gloriana's point, made all the more safely because it
vas also ambiguous. (This Sidney had his uses!)

No one in that throng, save possibly the townfolk, but re-
alled on the instant the phrase on which this of Sidney's
vas modeled. It came out of a Virgil universally known and
oved: YOURS BUT NOT FOR YOU (*Sic Vos Non Vobis*).
t was part of a famous poem in which Virgil proved
is authorship of lines which another had claimed, to-
;ether with the reward. In a fury the true poet had posted
ome incompleted verses which he dared the thief to
inish:

I wrote the other verses, but another took the credit
Yours but not for you, ——
Yours but not for you, ——
Yours but not for you, ——
Yours but not for you, ——

Of course the thief could not. Virgil filled them out in tri
umph. " And," concluded the gospel according to Donatu
(as Virgil's biographer he was only a little less familiar than
the mighty man himself), " Virgil was more highly ex
alted than ever. But the false poet became the laughing
stock of Rome."

The Commissioners sat in their seats in the sunshine
They were somewhat puzzled (as Gloriana intended they
should be). Their eyes followed those cryptic words OURS
BUT NOT FOR US which shone in silver on the backs and
breasts of the thirty gentlemen and yeomen. They fol
lowed the little-loved figure in blue and gold at the head,
that Philip Sidney who had written an impudent letter
about Monsieur. His uncle the Earl of Leicester was the
person whom, not yet plumbing Gloriana's depths, they
held chiefly responsible for the " lets " and " stays " of four
weeks. They, too, recalled their Virgil. They, too, remembered Donatus. Were they by any chance the laughing-
stock of this scurvy English Rome?

Meantime Perfect Beauty sat bland and unconcerned in
the shower of rose-petals and perfumed waters with which
her Fortress was being besieged before the tilting began.
If the Commissioners chose to do anything so far fetched
as to go back fifteen hundred and thirty seven years for the
meaning of Philip Sidney's device, it was no fault of hers!
How could she be expected to know what the boy had in his
head? The Frenchmen could read, couldn't they?

At dusk the tournament ended. The Commissioners
went back to Somerset House. Of one thing only they were
sure. The studied ambiguity of that device might be owing
to Sidney or to the Queen. But it was all of a piece with
everything which had happened since they had come to
London.

In his library at Burleigh House in the Strand, the Lord
Treasurer began to compose a suave, impassably final state-

ment which would force on the French all responsibility for the failure of their mission. He would read it to them with quiet force on the morrow. After that, they would all return to the tilt-yard. There the Commissioners would hear their answer in different words, in lines addressed to the humbled and broken Children of Desire as they knelt before Beauty to ask pardon for their presumption:

This Fortress is to be reserved for the eye of the whole World.

None might possess the Sun, was the drift of that final speech. And " while this realm is thus fortified with Perfect Beauty, may Desire be its chiefest Adversary "!

If Lord Burleigh's pen was busy, so was Philip's as well. He knew much of a real desire which cried out for comfort like a child left alone in the dark. He had settled himself in his poet's pavilion at the misty end of the garden at Leicester House, Astrophel writing to Stella:

Having this day my horse, my hand, my lance
  Guided so well, that I obtained the prize,
Both by the judgment of the English eyes,
And by some sent by that sweet enemy, France;
Horsemen, my skill in horsemanship advance,
  Townfolk, my strength: a daintier judge applies
  His praise to slight, which from good use doth rise:
Some lucky wits impute it but to chance:
Others because from both sides I do take
My blood from them that do excel in this,
Think Nature me a man-at-arms did make.
How far they shoot awry! The true cause is —
  Stella looked on, and — from her heavenly face,
  Sent forth her beams which made so fair a race.

It meant little to Sidney, these days, that his service to Gloriana was one that she could not acknowledge, nor that

policy enjoined her to more than usual remoteness. It was
the mere lovely shell of him that walked through the court
in white shoes, and knelt with the golden cup at the proper
times and places. For Astrophel was living in a universe all
his own. It was a world of mist and moonlight and Stella,
of rapturous meetings and headlong despairs, of ecstasies
and pain. A mad world, my masters! Thence his mind
reached home to an actual earth only through the Countess
of Pembroke. Thence he sent her the glorious sonnets which
she soberly locked in her coffers.

The Commissioners left at last. In spite of Lord Burleigh
they had lingered till the middle of June. Elizabeth was in
a panic. She followed her secret plan and sent for Alençon.
He started, was seasick, put back to await fair weather —
and did not try again. Nevertheless, however, she got the
Frenchmen away without really committing herself. Too
afraid of Spain to protest, France was quiescent. It was a
triumph for the Queen. Sidney was doubtless relieved. But
chiefly, he was in love.

Just after the Frenchmen left, Don Antonio, the Pretender to Portugal arrived on the scene from Stepney. A
month before he had written to Sidney, a letter which began
" Most Illustrious Nephew," in which he went on to say
that he would count his cause lost if Philip were not num-
bered among his supporters. Since November of 1580, Sidney had corresponded with His Majesty's agents. But now
his royal arrival was commonplace to the chance of seeing
Stella!

The Don came in unkingly tatters. Before he could see
the Queen, he was forced to borrow a shirt. He found Elizabeth gracious. Because she hoped to make France pay for
most if not all she gave him, she promised him aid, not to
get his throne, but to fall on the Spanish plate ships as they
passed by his Portuguese Azores. Though Drake and Hawkins should go along, in command of English ships, by a

bit of subtle distinction they sailed them not under her flag
but his. She took the Braganza jewels in pawn for the
money she loaned against his own equipment. He started to
fit his vessels. Here was a scheme to garboil Philip of Spain
which was after Sidney's own heart; or rather after his old
one. The new was full of Stella.

In August 1581, Elizabeth changed her mind. France
had refused to pay for the expedition unless she would
marry Monsieur. She told Don Antonio that she dared
not risk war with Spain. She ordered Drake and Hawkins
back to the court. While they seethed with disappointment,
she sold the ships which they were to have sailed in. She
made His Majesty buy back the flags. Pray, what use were
Portuguese flags to her? In September she sent Philip Sidney
to Dover, with orders to see His Majesty off to France.
If he could not otherwise get rid of him, Sidney must go
along too.

On September 26th, 1581 a desperate Philip wrote to
Hatton. He begged a " singuler favour," that under some
pretext, he might be recalled to court from Dover. There
was no wind to " waffe " His Majesty off. Sidney had no
more money, and there was divers business of his own and
his father's which " something imported " at home.

Whether it was Hatton or the fair wind which fetched
him, he must soon have returned, for, on October 1st, the
King of Portugal was in Paris, alone. Philip was no longer
looking at His Majesty's melancholy dark face, with its
green eyes and the shock of gray hair above it. Instead he
was gazing at Penelope, golden, seductive, joyous at the
sight of him as he at the sight of her. He would not so see
her for long!

By the end of the first week in October 1581, Sidney
knew of Languet's death. In the bleak white light of his
sorrow, passion paled like a star in the dawning. He saw
those sweet meetings as lies, his " love " itself as decep-

tion, all his late manner of life as denial of the native honesty in him. Madness would sway him no more.

Desire, in the sense of ambition that leaped up to noble employment he would know as he always had. For if it were sin to covet honor, he was the most offending soul alive. But even that old desire now took on a luminous beauty as he recognized that his will and the will of Heaven might not be one, and that where they were not, he must submit. In this hard-won mood of acceptance came the ultimate " lasting freedom " for which his soul cried out in the prayer which was also his sonnet-farewell to Stella.

He was already revising his sister's *Arcadia,* making it something even more lovely than the short first version of Wilton. On certain sheets which he gave her not long after this, was a shepherd's song about Languet. It was heart-felt simple tribute to simple goodness and truth. It was also dedication:

The song I sang old Languet *had me taught,*
  (Languet *the shepherd best swift* Ister *knew*
For clerky rede and hating what is naught,
  His faithful heart, clean mouth and hands as true).
  With his sweet skill my skilless youth he drew,
    To have a feeling taste of Him that sits
    Beyond the heaven, far more beyond our wits.

He said the music best those Powers pleased
  Was jump concord between our wit and will,
Where highest notes to godliness are raised,
  And lowest sink not down to jot of ill.
  With old true tales he wont my ears to fill:
    How shepherds did of yore, how now they thrive,
    Spoiling their flock, or while twixt them they strive.

He likéd me, but pitied lustful youth,
  His strong good staff my slippery years upbore,

He still hoped well because I loved Truth
   Till forced to part with heart and eyes even sore,
   The worthy Corydon's care, he gave me o'er
     But thus in oak tree shade recounted he,
     Which now in Night's deep shade, sheep heard of me.

THE FIFTEENTH CHAPTER
ENTITLED
CHAMELEON'S DISH.

IDNEY certainly had need of his new philosophy which had sudden test when, on October 31st, 1581 Monsieur landed at Rye. Richmond Palace was in a rare bustle. Alençon was to be lodged in a little house which communicated by a gallery with the Queen's own quarters. The Earl of Arundel was supervising the airing and warming of the delicate nest, while Elizabeth hovered in the doorway to see to the proper setting up of her own great bed for him. Romance filled the air. However, everyone knew that this time Alençon was coming to screw out of the Queen what money he could to pay his armies in the Low Countries. (His brother was tired of it.) Love was not to be reckoned with. At least nobody thought so.

Leicester made himself so charming that Monsieur thought he had conquered his heart. " My lord is my best friend in England! " — Such are the uses of duplicity. Sidney had no such to fall back on. He saw Monsieur when he bore the cup, for the royal pair dined together. The two men doubtless had converse, and such of Monsieur's resentment as had not given way before the explanations in Flanders was now dispelled by Philip's cordial uncle.

Sidney remained at court till some time after November 17th. That day saw the annual tournament in Elizabeth's honor, in which he took a prominent part. It was his third tilt within the year. Each had demanded new gear for his yeomen attendants, new " furniture," and sharing expenses on such " shows " as might precede. Even with the reductions enjoined by Perfect Beauty, the bills which the rascally silk merchants had sent her Child of Desire, had staggered him. When he craved the royal indulgence for withdrawing to Wilton for Christmas, he could again in all honesty plead poverty as excuse.

There was doubtless another reason. If Gloriana were guilty of half the common carryings-on set down to her in the diplomatic correspondence of the day, court was now no place for a disciple of truth and honor. She carried bouillon to her Frog before he was up. She was with him for hours on end. " The Devil alone knows what they do," wrote one amiable envoy. If souls less pellucid than Philip were moved to horrified speculation, he was doubtless profoundly shocked by the royal freedom of Elizabeth's behavior. Yet neither of the frantic lovers was the slightest particle in love. Under the cloak of scandal, each hid a deep design to which kissing was incidental.

It was play-acting on both sides. Monsieur decided that an emotional approach would most surely wangle him money. Being vain and very unintelligent, he thought the Queen had a heart, and that he was its lord. By consequence, he languished after her like a sick puppy. She responded for all she was worth. For only by the degree of her ardor could she disarm the mighty annoyance of France which would follow another disruption of the match. Since she had less intention of marriage than ever, it behooved her to mount to new heights in her acting. In all conscience she had gone far enough before. The results now, were foreordained to be startling! Still she could assume the role with gusto and assurance, knowing full well that she had only to consult Parliament to effect dramatic rescue from any wild commitment to which she might be driven.

Sidney, of course, did not fathom her inscrutable mind. Indeed so fanatic was the quality of her amorous transport that Alençon was not the only person convinced. The whole court was fooled as well. Even the Privy Council!

There was consternation in her long gallery on November 22d, 1581 when the Queen announced in carrying tones, " The Duke of Alençon shall be my husband! " and kissed him full on the mouth. Leicester was frantic, good Sheep Hatton, reduced to tears. Walsingham protested with such effect that she sent him after Monsieur to unsay her words. Thereupon Monsieur went into a tantrum in which he cursed and swore, and threw her ring away. When she came to soften the blow, she found him blubbered and petulant as a child. Affectingly she wiped his cheeks, and petted him. When she blamed the breaking up of their beautiful romance on her unromantic jealous people, Monsieur turned haughty and said he would return to Flanders. But he did not go. Upheavals continued. No wonder that Sidney sought peace in the cloisters of Wilton!

Things were still worse after he left, for Alençon decided to capitalize his sorrows. In vain Leicester and Burleigh pointed out he was needed in Flanders. Confidentially Sussex told him to go — to no end. Under English urgings, William of Orange wrote and begged his immediate return. All was labor lost. Alençon was holding out for as large a sum as possible as balm for his wounded feelings.

The scenes which now racked Richmond and Greenwich are almost beyond belief. Simier appeared to weep on Eliza's bosom (and to find out for Henry III what it was she was really up to). Ever since Alençon discharged him some months before, without paying his wages or mentioning the debts he owed him, her Monkey had written her naughty gossiping letters, with crosses for kisses and other private signs. He now came to court to spy on Alençon. (Henry III did not trust his dear brother.) Naturally Alençon resented his presence. With hysterical insistence he told his doting lady that the man had wrecked their first romance by falling foul of Leicester. He would do something awful again. To quiet her fretful suitor, the Queen said the Monkey should go, and set about to arrange it.

But it was not merely the French King's business which had brought Simier back to England. He came to challenge Fervarques who was in Alençon's suite. When he did so, Fervarques, who was a Gascon, announced a pitched battle between himself and six friends, and Simier and six. However no battle took place since Simier had not six friends in all England! Meantime there was an attempt to " remove " the Monkey in broad daylight in the 'Change. Being warned, Simier escaped. Next day with drawn dagger, Fervarques pursued into Elizabeth's very presence the man he suspected of telling. No sooner was that riot put down than Simier and Alençon came to blows within the palace. Gloriana, who was keeping up her end of the drama with some difficulty, found this too much and yearned to get rid of the whole quarrelsome crew. It was worth the " loan " of £10,000 which it cost her on February 2d, 1582 to secure her darling's promise to go away. His romantic blackmail had succeeded very nicely!

To some of these exciting moments Sidney was witness, for he returned fairly early in the year 1582. He may even have heard that the enemy Howards were giving Leicester credit for that little business in the Royal Exchange!

On February 7th, 1582 he set out from London with his uncle and other nobles who were charged with escorting Monsieur overseas (privately, too, with seeing he stayed there). Elizabeth herself went with them as far as Canterbury. Up to the very end she sustained her role to a marvel. Even after the company was on the road for Sandwich, she sent Sussex after them to beg Monsieur to come back. (But by now, Sidney and all the others knew they were not to let him go!)

While Gloriana the poet was composing verses " on the Departure of Mount Zeur " in which she described herself for Posterity as " soft and made of melting snow," the party made its way across the Channel in ships well ballasted with the 50 beeves, 500 muttons and potables in proportion which Leicester found necessary to supporting Monsieur's presence for a fortnight more.

To all the pageantry with which the Low Countries welcomed Monsieur as Sovereign, Sidney was witness. It was the usual late Renaissance hodge-podge. There were elephants made of papier mâché with limbs which did not co-ordinate. All the Virtues, with labels and their hair down stood at the city gates. The visitors rode under triumphal arches decorated with Alençon's posy, *Chaseth and Cherisheth*. On February 22d, 1582 Monsieur took his oath of allegiance to the Dutch Estates. In the bald light of the Public Square in Antwerp, he made a grotesque figure in his robes of crimson velvet and ermine, and his gold crown set awkwardly atop the Dutch cap of red woolen. But he was very grand. Moreover so long as William of Orange lived, despite industrious effort, he would do the Dutch no harm.

Before the English left two days later, Leicester had conference with Orange. Monsieur was not to escape again! At that time Sidney heard more of Languet's last days, and of the funeral in which the Prince had walked before the corpse. Previously all his visits to Flanders had been brightened by meetings with Languet, and he had returned to his problems in England, heartened by the old man's affection, his wise and kindly advice. Now however he was going back to meet even greater troubles more gallantly and alone.

Money matters had driven him to sheer desperation. A group of letters to Leicester and Hatton in the last two months of 1581 show that with painful clearness. The Queen had made him " offers " touching the " forfeiture of papists' goods," which his friends urged him to " stand upon." Chief of such counselors was Leicester. Sidney wrote him:

I think my fortune very hard that my reward must be built upon other men's misfortunes. . . .

And in a bitterness unusual to him:

Well my Lord, your Lordship made me a courtier. Do you think of it as seems best to you. . . .

To Hatton he expressed scruples as creditable as they were unusual to the day:

Truly sir, it goeth against my heart to prevent a prince's mercy. My necessity is great. . . .

Yet at last Leicester's arguments that every man's hand was in the dish and that impoundings would not stop for all his nephew's nice scruples, had their effect. Sidney's letter to his uncle on December 28th, 1581 shows an altered and interesting view:

I beseech your Lordship, without it be £3000, never trouble yourself in it, for my case is not so desperate that I would get clamor for less. . . .

The cursed hunger for gold had made a strange Philip ready to suffer the clamors of envy and conscience for much, but not for a little! His reasons are shamefaced enough, a " cumber of debts " and need which " obeys no law and forgets blushing." If his denial of lucrative occupation was costing him dear, unlike his fellow courtiers, he knew it!

Moreover, he was redoubling his efforts to secure the paying post which the Queen had hitherto denied him. He scorned to dance his way to favor like Hatton. He shrunk from philandering like his uncle Robert.

Increasingly there are tiny evidences (his loyalty precluded more) that Philip was growing aware of dissimilarities between Leicester's standards and his own. This was inevitable to the maturing of his excellent mind. In any but a Dudley he would have seen it sooner. Such a realization explains his closer touch with the steady, sober Walsingham. In part, of course, the new connection was the result of Philip's betrothal to Mistress Frances, the Secretary's daughter whom in prevision of a delightful relationship, Sidney described to her father in December of 1581 as " my exceeding like to be good friend."

Still hint of a possible shift of feeling within the family is revealed by Sir Henry's addressing his many requests for the next few years either to Burleigh or Walsingham. Moreover there are very frank words which seem to refer to Philip's uncle in Languet's letter on the *Discourse* under date of October 22d, 1580:

I suspected that you had been urged to write by persons who either did not know into what peril they were thrusting you, or did not care for your danger provided they effected their own object.

If it was by Leicester's insistence that Sidney wrote the letter which practically ended his chances of favor at Elizabeth's hands, Sir Henry's resentment was bitter. Philip himself would have thought at worst that he suffered from an error in judgment. As a matter of fact, in August 1580, when the young man pitted his opinion against his uncle's in the matter of going to court, he gave a clear indication that he was no longer accepting Leicester's ideas without question. Leicester's thinking was so undeniably shallow that inevitably the time must come when Sidney knew it. The lengths to which the nephew would go in loyal support of the uncle without sacrifice of ideals were yet to appear when the two men worked together in Flanders in 1586.

Through the summer of 1582 Leicester was too busy with plans of his own to have much leisure for the boy whom, truth to tell, he loved dearly. (He would have probably sacrificed him the last, or just before the Queen!) His newest aim was dynastic and a pretty duplicate of his father's. Ostensibly his personal agent in Scotland was assisting Her Highness in a scheme to expedite the departure of one Esmé Stuart, Lord d'Aubigny who had been sent over by the Guises to make trouble in 1579. He promptly established a sinister ascendancy over his young relative, King James who had made him Earl of Lennox. So much so that in August 1582, a group of lords including Mar, Gowrie and Angus had descended on James at Perth and carried him off to holier associations among themselves at Ruthven Castle. However, the situation was still dangerous to England because Lennox was free. Although the good citizens of Edinburgh marched past his house singing the 124th Psalm in four parts, they did nothing worse to him. Elizabeth wanted him out of Scotland.

Yet while Leicester's man was supposedly busy removing Lennox, in reality he made soundings with regard to a marriage between Lady Arabella Stuart and Leicester's young son. The prospective bride had just as good a claim to the English throne as King James of Scotland. Elizabeth had not yet signified that James should be her successor, and Leicester knew she did not want him. It was Northumberland's project all over again!

Under the circumstances, it was well that in February 1582, Sidney set very seriously to work on the problem of his own future career. His first choice was for service in the Low Countries which he looked to more eagerly than ever after March 18th, 1582 when at Alençon's birthday feast Philip's friend the Prince of Orange was shot. The wound was serious but not fatal. With it the anti-French feeling which had smouldered in Dutch bosoms flared up on the sudden. Had not Orange controlled the situation, the panic of his good burghers lest they be left to the mercies of the tennis-playing " Sovereign " might have cut off Monsieur in his glory. An Englishman in some sort of command would have stabilized matters. On April 10th, 1582 request was made to Walsingham for

a certain number of cavalry led by some honourable gentle-men, recommended by Her Majesty . . . Philip Sidney would be well suited for this. . . .

Ten days later one of Alençon's gentlemen wrote to Greville that the Duke wished Sidney to come. However, the Queen had no mind to pay for cavalry. Besides, since that letter of Sidney's upon her marriage, Elizabeth who suspected nothing so much as honesty, had decided that the young man would bear watching. She was keeping him under her eye.

Sidney's next hope was for Ireland. Though Sir Henry was ill and weary, he was willing to return to the ungrateful charge there if by so doing, he could help his son. Accordingly he caused Molyneux to draw up " Certain special notes to be imparted to Mr. Philip Sidney " which he signed on April 27th, 1582. They make the terms of the compact clear. If Philip

will assuredly promise him to go with him thither, and withal will put on a determined mind to remain and con-tinue there after him, and to succeed him in the govern-ment (if it may so like Her Majesty to allow him), he will then yield his consent to go; otherwise he will not leave his quiet and contented life at home. . . .

Nothing came of this second plan either. Elizabeth continued too much annoyed with Sir Henry to fall in with any scheme which was calculated to give him satisfaction. And in November 1582 she answered a request of his with such tart finality that the poor man never made her another. So far as Philip was concerned, the loss was *nil*. True, he would have seen plenty of active service. However he had too good a mind not to have worked out a program for Ireland. Nothing was less desirable in Elizabeth's underlings than ideas of their own. Anyone, therefore, with an average amount of system, no particular convictions and a sweet recognition of the impossibility of doing an efficient job anyhow, could, if he had also infinite capacity for accepting blame, manage quite nicely in Ireland. It was no haven for a sensitive creative artist.

Nothing daunted, in July 1582, Sidney put in an appeal to Burleigh and Walsingham for a place on the Council in Wales. He was doubtless looking forward to association with his father in the management of that stout little kingdom which Sir Henry found the most delightful charge in the world. Such a position would have enabled Philip to see something more of Thomas his younger brother, now thirteen and just entering Shrewsbury School. That project, too, proved abortive. There again, considering that it involved a routine task of adjudicating petty quarrels and minor business, he was scarcely the loser.

Flanders. Ireland. Wales. Sidney had nicked them off on his tally. They held nothing for him. America alone remained. It was in an American project that he saw an opportunity obliquely to serve " religion," and directly to aid the expedition which his friend Sir Humphrey Gilbert was intending for Newfoundland.

In 1578, the Queen had granted to Gilbert the first letters patent for such portion of the North American continent as was not already possessed by any Christian monarch. But his right extended only six years. Already four had passed, through which Sir Humphrey had fed on that same chameleon's dish which had perforce satisfied the fierce appetite of Philip Sidney. It was " air, promise cramm'd." Proverbially, it fattened no capons. It bought Sidney neither doublets nor books. It bought Gilbert no ships, no tackle. In 1582, grown a bit desperate, Sir Humphrey conceived the idea of disposing of his lands in spacious snacks of a million acres, to anyone who would outfit a vessel, go over and make a claim. Only by such means could he hope himself, to gain sight of his wonderful holdings.

Walsingham who was his patron, seems to have been the first to see political profit from sending the Catholics thither. The " undiscovered lands " of the patent were too remote to offer to recusants the mischievous exile which treasonous centers like Paris and Rome afforded the " disaffected." Moreover, in America, impoverished Catholics who now " pestered " the gaols (for lack of that £20 fine) would at least be earning their keep!

The scheme for a colony found favor with Sir Thomas Gerrard and Sir George Peckham, wealthy recusants who had been imprisoned for their faith. In June 1582, they took title from Gilbert to " any two islands " which they might like off the coast of " Florida " (the present North Carolina). Peckham alone secured a million and a half acres on the mainland. By July 11th, both leaders had been assured that

the Queen in consideration of their service, might be asked to allow them to settle there in the enjoyment of freedom of conscience and of their property in England, for which purpose they might avail themselves of the intercession of Philip Sidney. . . .

Thus encouraged, Peckham obtained more land. By April of 1583 several Catholic ships sailed

Sidney was busy, not only with intercessions, but with

Sir Walter Raleigh for whose " Virginia " Sidney helped to plan.

a mysterious opposition which came out of the very air. For the wily Mendoza was blocking the scheme. He saw, as well as Walsingham and Sidney, that through it the Catholics in England would lose both grievance and organization. Those were necessary elements to a project in religion which was envisioned by his master, the King of Spain. Therefore no more ships set forth.

In the meantime Sidney himself took title to some of the Gilbert lands. On July 7th, 1582 he acquired possession of an estate of " thirty hundred thousand acres " somewhere in America. With it came " power to inhabit and people," together with all " jurisdictions, privileges and emoluments whatsoever." In return he undertook to "manure " it, for Englishmen had yet to encounter the marvel of virgin soil. He promised to lay it out in parishes three miles square, each with a church in the midst and a vicar in every church. He agreed to give each bishop 10,000 acres, each archbishop 20,000. For every 2000 acres of his own he was to provide a mounted soldier for the army.

Such were the rules of Gilbert's Commonwealth. There was little Sir Humphrey had not thought of in the four years of his waiting. Excepting, of course, what he would actually find in a Newfoundland which would for years be too bleak for bishops. The stipulation that one fifth of the yield of gold and silver should come to the Crown, was Gloriana's contribution.

Of course it is possible that Sidney secured the lands as evidence of good will to the Catholics whom Mendoza was stimulating to all sorts of suspicions. More likely, however, he intended to take possession. At home he had systematically exhausted every avenue which might lead to occupation. Though he was, to be sure, betrothed, he could not aspire to marriage without some source of income. Moreover, the little lady was only but fourteen. While she was growing up, he could make his start in the

New World, which could scarcely treat him worse than the Old!

Before the end of 1582, Philip, his father and three of his uncles had joined in backing Sir Humphrey Gilbert. In return they were to receive right of free trade with any land he discovered. At last on June 11th, 1583 Gilbert started with five stout little ships, to the blare of trumpets and a litter of Latin hexameters. On August 5th, while fisher boats stood about in respectful circle he made claim to St. John's for the Queen of England. But anarchy soon developed in the Commonwealth, and the expedition started home. On the way back his ship the *Squirrel* foundered in terrible seas. As the *Hind* was blown over against her, the crew had last sight of the " General sitting abaft with a booke in his hande and crying ' We are as neere to Heaven by sea as by lande! ' "

Sidney had not even seen Sir Humphrey off because the Queen had sent him to Oxford to squire a visiting prince. He must have found this biding at home a test for his new-found patience — particularly when a packet came from the Continent from his old friend Étienne, which contained the first Renaissance edition of the historian Zozimus, addressed to Philip. The breezy first sentence caught all the zest of the man: " What fine thing is Sidney doing now? " What, indeed!

Eighteen months of frustration lay behind him. He had failed of everything he wanted, from the impropriations of the papists which the Queen had suggested herself, to his own reasonable plans for placement. Philip might well conceive that the answer to Étienne's question must lay in two other dedications. Both came in 1582: Michael Lok's strange provocative *Map of the Western World;* and a book which gave England sleepless and thrilling nights, questing days — Hakluyt's *Divers Voyages Touching the Discovery of America and the Islands Adjacent to the Same.*

However, in July of 1583, he gave up his thirty hundred thousand acres! Peckham would be able to claim them sooner than he, since in September Philip would be a married man. As such he must abide for a while in England. However he still remained " half persuaded to enter into a journey." Thereto Mr. Hakluyt " served for a very good trumpet," a trumpet which Sidney would hear for the rest of his life.

THE SIXTEENTH CHAPTER
ENTITLED NEIGHBORS' FIRES
AND HIS OWN HEARTH.

I N A certain letter which annoyed the Queen, Sidney described her England as a peaceful realm " where our neighbors' fire giveth us light to see our quietness." That was in the early autumn of 1579. A year later when he wrote to his brother, he used the same phrase, though this time not so complacently. He had become apprehensive lest the flames might spread to his own country with any brisk breeze. Walsingham was also alarmed. He knew that fire travels underground as well, that then it is hardest to fight.

In this year 1583 which would see Sidney established under his roof as a son, Mr. Secretary Walsingham was busy tracking down a dangerous conspiracy. Since 1582 he had known that something was afoot. Intercepted letters gave hints of a " great and hidden plan." Though he knew nothing definite, on general principles he mistrusted Scottish Mary, the Guises, the French ambassador. Oddly enough, he did not suspect a certain dark gentleman who could smile and be a villain still, Bernardino de Mendoza. Yet he sensed enough to be doubly anxious about the results of Elizabeth's policy of playing by-courses, of taking desperate chances to save a few hundred pounds.

Sidney, now entering on his twenty-ninth year, and Walsingham, fifty-three, were to hold great comfort for each

other. Through years as Resident in France and again in
the Low Countries, to say nothing of a dozen special missions, Walsingham was convinced that England should
ally herself frankly with the Huguenots and the Dutch. To
these same conclusions, Sidney had come six years before
out of a less extensive experience.

America was another subject on which they saw eye to
eye. Walsingham's concern was, perhaps, rather more in
the development of trade routes; Sidney's, in active venturing. Yet the Secretary kept in his personal service one
Simon Fernandez, a Portuguese, so that whenever need
arose, a pilot might be available in England who knew
the " Florida " coast-line. He had financed Frobisher with
heavy loss to himself. He helped to equip Drake for the
sally on Peru. He had backed the scheme for Don Antonio's
assault on the plate-ships in the summer of 1581. He was
Humphrey Gilbert's patron. Through the early months
of 1583, he was working out with that other half-brother
of Raleigh's, Adrian Gilbert, a scheme for finding the
elusive North-west passage. It was Walsingham's step-
son, Christopher Carlisle, who printed in April 1583, a tract
to whet public interest in Sir Humphrey's Commonwealth.
However it was probably Mr. Secretary himself who spoke
against immediate citizenship therein for his son-to-be, the
eager Philip Sidney!

Meantime Europe held excitements enough, in all conscience. The fires were crackling with new violence in
Flanders, in France, in Scotland.

Flanders was literally aflame. Early in January 1583, the
treacherous Alençon led off with the Antwerp Folly.
Though Sovereign of the Low Countries, he conceived the
disloyal ambition to seize for himself such cities as the
Spanish had left the Dutch. What with his perfidy and
Parma's besieging armies, the burghers were desperate.
However, so furiously did they defend their holdings that

only in very small places did the conspiracy succeed. Fortunately for them, Alençon made a complete fiasco of his own part of the business which was the reduction of the essential city of Antwerp. He was glad to scuttle off to Dendremonde for safety — lucky to get there.

Immediately suspicion of collusion with Spain came into the minds of both Elizabeth and Orange. As it happened they were mistaken. Monsieur was merely bearing out the judgment of Philip Sidney; the opinion of Navarre that he was as " double-minded and malicious " as he was " ill-formed in body." Henry III disclaimed all responsibility for him. Even the Queen Mother disowned him. Between sniffles, resentful Monsieur wrote to Elizabeth for money. He whined that she was his " wife before God and Man." She must do her duty by him!

Poor thing that he was, he still had uses for Gloriana. He fought her battles more cheaply than anyone else. Consequently in March 1583, she was trying to reconcile the Dutch States to their " lord." William of Orange was helping. He, too, found a kind of value in this Alençon who was the French King's brother. So it was that the States in the south and west were cajoled to a kind of toleration. Only the stubborn northern burghers decided to deal with the Queen of England directly.

In August 1583, they sent over an envoy named Ortel. He came after funds, of course. For once, there was some justification in the round refusal of Her Grace. The Dutch still owed her the £65,000 she had loaned them four years before, as well as £28,000 they had borrowed on her credit from Genoese bankers. Meantime the thrifty souls were waxing rich on the results of the embargo which they had placed on Antwerp thanks to which their own Amsterdam had piled up an enormous trade. In fact, just before Ortel came, she had dallied with the idea of seizing Amsterdam cargoes until such time as she had " borrowed " her own back! Though she had abandoned the project, she was in no mood to be asked for money.

Economically, she was right. Politically, she was wrong. It would take her two years to see what Walsingham and Sidney saw now: that inevitably she must make common cause with those folk who were just as shrewd about spending as she. For in those same Low Countries the armed menace of Spain was strongest and nearest. There Sidney himself would die, fighting the menace at Zutphen.

Though Walsingham had not foreseen the humiliation of Ortel, both he and Sidney had anticipated the disappointment of De Ségur. He had come in July of 1583 as envoy from Henry of Navarre to urge support for the Huguenots as well as the Dutch. His failure touched Philip Sidney closely for De Ségur had brought him letters from Navarre and Du Plessis de Mornay. In eager hospitality, Sidney tried to make up for the Queen's defections. He entertained the Frenchman not only at Wilton, but at a house of Pembroke's in Ramsbury. There he, De Ségur and Archibald Douglas kept bachelors' hall. There they could discuss in safety their common fears of the Guisan plots in Scotland, Guisan persecutions in France, fears of the Guises in England. At the time, this Archibald Douglas was professing his Scottish friendship for England, acting as a kind of informal agent for Elizabeth between the two countries. If he was neither honest nor loyal, like Alençon, he had his uses.

The more so, because " Scotland's Burning " was no gay song but very heavy truth. That northern kingdom was too near for England's safety, too far for efficient watching. Moreover, control there was possible only through plotting and bribing. At the first, the Guises were as good as Elizabeth; at the second, vastly better. Their incentive was strong. They sought to release their kinswoman Mary Stuart, restore her to her throne, and drive out the Presbyterians. That done, they aspired to remove the " heretic

Tudor " (they did not call Elizabeth " Queen ") and annex her realm to Mary's. Such were the dangers to Gloriana which lay beyond the Border once the Guises were intrenched.

And intrenched they were, more firmly than ever. To be sure, on December 29th, 1582 their agent the Earl of Lennox had been hustled out of the country. Yet before a month had passed, they had a new man in! It took Elizabeth's servants till May to get rid of him. Already though he had finished his work of arousing the Scotch lords to " rescue " King James from the English sympathizers (Angus, Mar and the rest) who had snatched him away from Lennox at the Raid of Ruthven. Thus urged — and paid! — the lords " released " their stripling monarch on June 27th, 1583. The Ruthven party fled for their lives.

James was now seventeen. His first act was to recall the Earl of Arran, a facile, amusing, graceless person who came of the Stuart kin and played the game of the Guises. He had been right hand man to Lennox. He was right hand man to James.

Such was the situation which Sidney and his friends discussed after their Wiltshire hunting. Archibald Douglas was related to Angus, whom Sidney had probably known at Greenwich as early as 1581. Now that the English party had retreated, neither Douglas nor Sidney had any hopes for the future. Even Mr. Secretary said God alone could help Scotland — a Protestant God, of course!

Such was the situation which at long last impressed the Queen herself as crucial. Having denied Walsingham all funds when bribery might have served, she now decided to send an envoy to James — not with a " pension " but with an appeal to His Majesty's higher nature. For this thankless task, she was considering Lord Hunsdon, Walsingham and this same young Sidney. To be named in such company was itself an honor. Lord Hunsdon had for years been

Governor of the Border town of Berwick, and had a special knowledge of Scotland. Sir Francis was the best ambassador in Europe. Yet for the present mission, Sidney would probably have succeeded better than either. He was closer to James in years. Both were restive young men and poets. Sidney wrote of loving James " well." The words argue a charitable and understanding disposition, a commodity more acceptable than political shrewdness at this dangerous juncture.

Hunsdon and Sidney were probably ruled out because they were thought to have irons of their own in the fire. Hunsdon had. For a year or two he had planned to marry his daughter to James. Philip failed of the appointment on the strength of Leicester's latest project: to match the Scotch King to his step-daughter, Dorothy Devereux. " She-wolf " was the sweetest name Elizabeth bestowed on her mother when first she heard about it! For the girl herself, she predicted a career of crime even more lurid than that of Lady Lettice on which she enlightened the court. If James took a quean of that clan to his bosom, let him look to her well! Of this newest Dudley devising, Sidney himself probably knew nothing. However, the Queen had come to regard him as somewhat dangerous in himself. Moreover, she knew that the Dudley kin had worked together before. It was not unnatural to suppose that they might do so again.

Consequently the lot fell upon Sir Francis. He begged her not to send him, protesting that he would go " with as ill a will " as ever he went anywhere, that he was not well and should not travel. Elizabeth commanded. Hopelessly enough, he set out, in a " cosche " because the " colick " would not allow of horseback. On August 17th, 1583 he left on the slow northward journey, knowing that he would probably miss the marriage of his daughter and " son Philip " which was set for Michaelmas, only a month away. Walsingham had experienced too many diplomatic delays to look for a speedy return. However, at that, James and Arran would surprise him!

At Berwick eleven days later, he halted for his passport. In that amazing document, James limited his train to sixty, though he was amply aware that Elizabeth's envoy had eighty attendants, and he stipulated that the party might stay for the term of its " good behaviour " ! The affronted Walsingham demanded another passport. In time, it came. In time, too, the King condescended to name a day for the first audience. The sick man's temper was not improved by these signs of Guisan aggression.

When he finally saw young James on September 9th, he gave him a royal scolding. He rated him on his ingratitude to the Queen, the low company he kept, his neglect of his kingly business. All this was hard enough for the conceited boy to support. But when Walsingham said that the Scottish folk would be justified in rising up to depose him, James could endure no more. There should be no loose talk about Divine Rights! Where under Heaven, he asked Sir Francis, had he come by such mad opinions? When he had answer, in de Mornay's book *On Tyrants,* his outraged Majesty sniffed. Coldly enough he terminated the interview. He hoped the ambassador did not often waste his time on such arrant trash?

With Arran, Walsingham refused to have any dealings at all. He told him in explanation that he was " a scorner of religion, a sower of discord, and a despiser of true honest men." Though this was all too true, it was hardly diplomatic. Arran threatened to report him to Elizabeth.

Shortly, however, he conceived a revenge which was more annoying. He shut the palace gates in the faces of Walsingham's suite. He took a rich diamond from the ring James gave to Sir Francis in parting and put glass in its stead. For the price of a new plaid and £6, he hired a talented scold named Kate the Witch to sit outside the palace and make personal remarks whenever the envoy appeared. Needless to say, he blocked all his business with James. When Mr. Secretary left for home on September 15th, he was profoundly discouraged.

Though Sidney might have handled the King with more tact, any real understanding between them would have been balked by Arran. From that personage no one English could have hope of more than sneers and stays. Sidney's year had been bitter enough, so far, without them.

Even his knighthood had come, not as an honor — like Francis Drake's on the deck of the *Golden Hind* — but as an accident and a convenience. His friend, Prince Casimir, could not come to receive the Order of the Garter for himself and appointed Sidney his proxy. No one under the rank of a knight might serve. By consequence, plain Philip became Sir Philip of Penshurst Place on January 9th, 1583 merely that he might sit next day in Casimir's stall in the Chapel of St. George at Windsor and receive the Garter in his stead.

With every prospect of success, Sidney had begun in January to sue for the office of Joint Master of Ordnance. His uncle, the Earl of Warwick, who was Master, was not well and found it hard to get about. With foreign dangers increasing, there was a great deal of travel involved in fitting coast-wise forts. For this and the active work in general, Warwick wished Sir Philip's help. Though Leicester does not seem to have appeared in the business at all, Sidney's request had strong enough backing in Burleigh and Walsingham. Indeed on February 24th, 1583 the book of his patent was by way of being engrossed, under conditions of secrecy which hint at some opposition. Whatever it was, the opposition won out. A small post in the Ordnance seems to have been provided. But for the office of Joint Master, Sir Philip was forced to wait till 1585.

He was probably less disappointed when he failed to

secure the Captaincy of the Isle of Wight. That, he knew, depended on a shift in personnel. It did not take place for years. Still Dyer, at least, was sure Sidney would have the place, in March of 1583!

Some of his greatest inquietudes of spirit grew out of the supposedly " comfortable business " of his marriage. The Queen took it into her head to oppose. That, however, was usual. Then Mr. Secretary was paying his debts as a wedding present. Still, husbands were such all-desirable commodities in Sir Philip's world, that he found that usual, too. What undeniably distressed him was the fact that Sir Henry was ill content. It was not the great match on which the father had built hopes for the tottering family fortunes. Moreover, though only fifty-four, he was " toothless and trembling," and already suffered the depression of old age. His lifetime's service and that of his wife " old Moll " had been laid out for Gloriana, a Gloriana who not only failed of common thanks but blandly " paid " £20 a week for an office which she knew cost £30 a week to maintain! Philip was too devoted a son not to have been deeply unhappy at his father's general discouragement, and at his own inability to improve matters.

On March 1st, 1583 Sir Henry wrote to Walsingham about the match in a way which reveals mixed emotions. Even as he hastened to clear himself of the appearance of " coldness," and protested his " joy in the alliance," he confessed that he " might have received a great sum of money " for his " good will " of his son's marriage in other quarters, " greatly to the relief of biting necessities." Then he launched into the " tragical discourse " of his " unfortunate and hard estate " :

If I die tomorrow next, I should leave [my children] worse than my father left me by £20,000. I am £5000 in debt, yea and £50,000 worse [off] than I was at the death

*of my most dear king and master King Edward VI. I have
not had of the Crown of England of my own getting so
much ground as I can cover with my foot. All my fees
amount not to 100 crowns a year. . . .*

Clearly his distress was due to his inability properly to
provide for his wife, and to further the fortunes of his
three boys. He described them to Sir Francis as " of excellent good proof " — that was Philip; " of great good
proof " — that was Robert; and " not to be despaired of
but very well to be liked " — that was young Thomas.

The arrangements made by Sir Francis were generous
in the extreme. He took it upon him to pay Sir Philip's debts
to the amount of £1500. He also agreed to provide the
young people and their servants with " diet," if they would
" take it with him and in his house." Proud and ambitious
as he was, Sir Philip was not to have the common consolation of supporting his own wife!

Elizabeth kept him from too much meditation on that
score by making herself thoroughly disagreeable about the
match. Perhaps the cause lay in her old irritation at Sidney;
perhaps in anger at Sir Henry, now somewhat musty, too.
Perhaps, as Walsingham guessed, it was pique at not having been consulted. At all events, her " misliking " continued through April 1583. Finally though " somewhat
troubled " he asked Hatton to convey to Her Highness discreetly that the affair was " held for concluded." That
brought her round. In May she deigned to " pass over the
offence " with Walsingham. By June she had " forgiven "
Sir Philip.

In that same month, just before Sir Humphrey Gilbert
sailed, she sent young Sidney to Oxford in the train of
the Polish Prince Lasky. There they heard the philosopher,
Giordano Bruno. On his first coming to England three
months before, Sidney had met him at the house of the

French Ambassador, Castelnau, in Butcher's Row hard by Leicester House. Sir Philip was Bruno's earliest patron in England. He was also one of the very few persons with whom the philosopher did not quarrel. Though before Bruno left England, he dedicated two of his books to Sidney, probably no more than his contemporaries, did Philip recognize in him the most wonderful mind in the whole century.

Indeed, it was very easy to forget Bruno's intellect, shining like gold in a world of pinchbeck and glitter, so querulous and conceited was the man's unlovely soul. He had burst upon the cool culture of Oxford with a letter in which he arrogantly recommended himself to the Vice-Chancellor as one

known, approved and honourably received in all the universities of Europe. Nowhere save among barbarians and the ignoble a stranger. The awakener of sleeping souls. The trampler upon presuming and recalcitrant Ignorance, who in all his acts proclaims a Universal Benevolence towards Man.

By Giordano's own modest account, this debate of his before Prince Lasky in St. Mary's marked an epoch in the history of the world. It is certainly to be hoped that Sir Philip was not allowing his mind to wander to De Ségur's coming visit, or any other common concern! Bruno said that the Oxford doctor who opposed him got " stuck fifteen times " in his own arguments " like a chicken in the stubble." Moreover, though he was manifestly ignorant, the Englishman objected to being trampled upon even in the spirit of benevolence. In fact he proved himself a " rude, discourteous Swine." Giordano, on the other hand, behaved as behooved one " reared under the kindly Neapolitan sky," utterly reducing his savage antagonist by quiet reasoning, " patiently and humanely," using bland words.

After such harmony as this, the delicate music of Her Majesty's viols sounded thin indeed, on the deck of the royal barge in which Sidney was taking the guest to Mortlake! Prince Lasky, who dabbled in the occult, was eager for talk with Dee. In the little house where (to the horror of the neighbors) Dr. Dee raised up spirits by night, the Pole remained for the evening of June 15th. During that time, Sir Philip may have availed himself of a chance to slip the short distance to Barn Elms, for a sight of the pretty young woman who was shortly to be his wife.

Possibly under the very moon which had proved so fatal to Sidney, in 1581, little Frances had also met Romance. She was then only thirteen. Without asking her parents' permission, a certain John Wickerson gazed devoutly upon her. She gazed back. He was a most unsuitable person and a fortune hunter to boot. By consequence, Master John soon found himself prisoner in the Marshalsea whence he besought the lady's irate father for freedom. Naïvely enough, he urged a " perpetuall scruple " in favor of marriage with Mistress Frances! For two years he had continued to cherish it, in durance vile. Well after Michaelmas, when she was safely married, her father might release him. Even with a handsome husband in prospect, she thought of John somewhat sadly — though not very often. Sir Philip had had his own experience with mist and moonshine. It left him more tenderly understanding of a young maiden, wistful over romance.

The wedding took place on September 21st, 1583. The Bride was a vision of springtime in a trailing white gown with her hair hanging over her shoulders. To her tiny puffed sleeves and demure little bodice were stitched blue and white ribbands, the true love knots at which bachelors snatched for luck. She was led to church by two fair youths in rich raiment. After her came the Bridegroom, in gayly embroidered doublet and a ruff of rare lace, convoyed by pretty Bridemaids. Then, borne in state, the Bridecake, with its gilded ears of wheat and sprigs of rosemary. Last, the Bridecup from which the couple would drink before the altar.

After solemn words were said, the procession re-formed outside the church to the strains of merry music. Through lanes lined with admiring rustics who blessed them with gusto and jest, Sir Philip walked beside his wife of fifteen. With the grace given to men in those times of pageant, he bore a bouquet of rosemary tied with a true love knot:

Doth not rosemary and Romeo begin with the same letter?

The courtyard was strewn with flowers. Over a door-sill whisked with perfumes, he led Lady Frances Sidney into her father's house which henceforth was also his. The wide low rooms were pointed bright with candles, full of bustle and music and friends. At the head of the table her husband placed her for serving of comfits and wine. He watched with tenderness and amusement her happy air of pride as she cut into the towers of marchpane which told in frosting an edible tale of Troy.

Rosemary stands for remembrance. In all that merry din, Lady Ursula was wondering about her husband. How was he bearing up under colic and young James? Sir Philip had thoughts of Languet who had often urged him to marriage. There was memory, too, of gustier days which had brought him little but heartache, a turmoil mistook for love.

Here was a simple, quiet feeling; joy as innocent as the shepherd's song out of Virgil. That song might have been made for this bridal, so well did it suit the cherishing poet-husband, the Lady Frances he had known from a little lass:

Within our orchard walls, I saw thee first,
A wee child with her mother — (I was sent

To guide you) — gathering apples wet with dew. . . .
Now know I what love is. On hard rocks born. . . .
No child of mortal blood or lineage. . . .

Now know I what love is . . . and lead a wife
Home. . . . There peers the evening star!
Begin, my flute, a song of Arcady.

THE SEVENTEENTH CHAPTER
ENTITLED THE GREAT
AND HIDDEN TREASON.

OR a year and a half after Sir Philip's marriage, England was constantly in the grip of some terror engendered by the Catholics. Of these alarms, the Throckmorton Plot which revealed the " great and hidden treason " was only the mightiest. The successive upheavals touched Sidney as they touched the average Englishman, to a panic of fear and horror. But " in particular " also. He was Walsingham's son-in-law.

He shared his roof on Tower Hill and at Barn Elms. Thither in the nature of things came the men of that strange half-world of spies thanks to whose unlovely profession, Mr. Secretary was able to piece together the plan for the Guisan invasion while it could still be quashed. Thus Sidney may have met Nicholas Berden who with a chameleon's personality and many aliases, managed to worm his way unto the confidence of Catholics at home and abroad for years, without exciting suspicion.

On the other hand at least one Catholic informer, Robert Poley, was deliberately quartered on him. The canny Morgan wrote in triumph to Mary Queen of Scots when Poley had been " placed to be Sir Philip Sidney's man " that he might " more quietly live a Christian life under the said Sidney." However, another letter makes it clear that this was not purely out of tribute to Sir Philip! The duties of the Christian life involved spying on Walsingham's movements, a task all the easier since Poley was " ordinarily in his house and thereby able to pick out many things to the information " of the Scotch Queen. (Despite Sidney's ennobling influence, Poley was among the crew in whose company Christopher Marlowe was done to death in May of 1593 when a great reckoning was made in a little room at Deptford.)

The disease in the body politic to which such men as Poley and Berden ministered in their several capacities of aggravation and relief, had been diagnosed by Sidney in his *Discourse to the Queen's Majesty* in 1579. Not unsympathetically, either, did he speak of the unhappy Catholics:

their ambition stopped because they are not in the way of advancement; some in prison & disgrace; some whose best friends are banished, practisers; many thinking you are an usurper; many thinking the right you had, disannulled by the Pope's excommunication; all [men] grieved at the burdenous weight of their consciences. Men of great number; of great riches, because the affairs of the State have not lain upon them; of minds united as all men that deem themselves oppressed naturally are.

Here he saw " an evil preparative for the Patient (I mean your State) to a greater Sickness." In four years the sickness had grown apace.

The first of the frights which it provided came from a distraught youth named John Somerville. He was a Warwickshire gentleman who happened to be visiting his father-in-law, Edward Arden, on October 22d, 1583. At that time he heard a large amount of scandalous talk about Leicester from the priest, Hugh Hall. In fact what Hall recounted of Sweet Robin's undue familiarity with the Queen, and his intimacy with Lettice Knollys while she was still Countess of Essex, drove poor Somerville entirely out of his wits. Two days later he slipped away from his wife's restraint in the early morning hours, and started for court. At a country inn along the way, he announced that he was going to London to shoot the Queen with his pistol, that she was a serpent and a viper, and he hoped to see her head on a pole!

He was arrested in short order, lodged in the Tower, subjected to endless examinations which only increased his confusion. His wife's parents were haled from Warwickshire. All three were tried in the Guildhall on December 16th, 1583 and condemned to die as traitors. The mother-in-law was pardoned. Somerville himself was found on December 19th — mysteriously strangled in his cell at Newgate; by friends, it was thought, who would spare him the agonies of disembowelment. On December 20th, 1583 Arden was put to death.

From the point of view of danger, this was the mildest scare of the lot. Poor Somerville was as mad as a hatter. What threw his case into a lurid light for the government was its menace to the Queen's personal safety. What brought it home to Sir Philip was its circulation of aspersions on Leicester. Moreover, out of it, came a new and specific charge. The condemnation of Arden was " commonly imputed to Leicester's malice." According to rumor, the Earl was revenging himself, not only for the " detractions " to which Arden had hearkened, but for his constant and " rash opposition."

How Sidney received these scandalous revelations of 1583 may be gathered from his swingeing reply to the book published by Catholics on the Continent in September 1584, under the title of *Leicester's Commonwealth.* This libelous tract asserted that the Earl had England so definitely in his pocket, that he could do anything he wished without let or hindrance. In support of the contention, the author listed every offense in the calendar. Never were calumnies more unrestrained or inconsistent. Though popularly the production was fathered on the Jesuit Parsons, Sidney did not know the writer and haughtily refused even to guess his identity.

But in his *Defence of the Earl of Leicester,* he replied to him nevertheless; and in no uncertain terms. Whatever Sir Philip's disillusionment about his uncle, he rose nobly to his support under attack. Discreetly as well, for he made no real attempt to refute specific accusations. Perhaps in some cases he felt them unanswerable. Perhaps both policy and good taste forbade serious consideration of charges which also involved the Queen. Perhaps his proud scorn of an adversary who was anonymous and a proved liar, was, as he inferred, his true reason. In any event the attitude was well taken. And for what he lacked in particularity, Sir Philip made up in fury.

Contemptuously he dismissed the " whole dictionary of slanders," comprising " dissimulation, hypocrisy, adultery, falsehood, treachery, poison, rebellion, treason, cowardice, atheism and what not," all " upon the superlative." They were " such railings " as might come " from the mouth of some half-drunk scold in a tavern," who did not care what she said, so long as " evil was spoken." He pointed out that the Earl was accused of so many " horrible villainies " as " no good heart " would think possible " to enter into any creature, much less to be likely in so noble and well-known a man." He spoke sarcastically of the " good nature " of the author who " all this while would never reveal " these matters (most of them from ten to twenty years old), till now when "for secrecy sake," he put them " forth in print." As he said, " no man bears a Name, of which . . . by an impudent Liar, anything may not be spoken " !

True as all this was, it was hardly " defence." Such vindication as Sidney undertook was found in two small bits. One was the deft statement that Leicester's " faith " was "so linked to her Majesty's service" that whoever set about to "undermine the one," resolved "withal to overthrow the other." And it was with regard to the utterly preposterous story that Leicester was intending to depose Elizabeth and make himself King that Sir Philip elected to reply:

Being to him as I am, I think I should have [had] some air of that which this gentle libel-maker doth so particularly and piecemeal understand. And I do know the Earls of Warwick, of Pembroke, my Father and all the rest . . . will answer the like. And yet such [treasonous] matters cannot be undertaken without good friends, nor good friends be kept without knowing something!

A good half of Sidney's answer to the *Commonwealth's* "most vile reproaches" and "wicked and filthy thoughts" was given over to proving that the Dudleys came of noble stock:

He saith they are no gentlemen affirming that then Duke of Northumberland [John Dudley] was not born so. In truth if I should have studied with myself of all points of false invections which a poisonous tongue could have spit out against that Duke, yet would it never have come into my head, of all other things, that any man would have objected want of gentry unto him. But this fellow doth like him, who when he had shot off all his railing quiver, called one cuckold that never was married, because he would not be in debt to any one evil word! I am a Dudley in blood. . . . I say that my chiefest honor is to be a Dudley and truly am glad to have cause to set forth the nobiltiy of that blood whereof I am descended. . . . No man but this fellow of invincible shamelessness would ever have called so palpable matter in question!

And at last, he concluded with a fierce challenge:

To thee I say: thou liest in thy throat; which I will be ready to justify upon thee, in any place of Europe, where thou wilt assign me a free place of coming; as within 3 months after the publishing hereof I may understand thy mind. . . . This which I write, I would send to thine own hands, if I knew thee. But I trust it cannot be intended that he should be ignorant of this printed in London which knows the very whisperings of the Privy Chamber!

However, the *Defence* was not published. Perhaps Leicester desired a vindication which was as specific as it was spirited. Perhaps the Queen considered that her two proclamations banning *Leicester's Commonwealth,* met the situation adequately, and that further publicity was inexpedient.

At all events Sidney's reaction to what he called the " stinking rumours " of 1584, indicates the pain and resentment which he experienced at the amount of common talk that followed the trial of Somerville and Arden. All the more so, because in the late autumn of 1583 gossip against Leicester took on new and dangerous value. Only three months before, Sussex had died at Bermondesey House with his famous warning against Robin on his lips:

Beware the gipsy, or he will be too hard for you!

And so Sir Philip felt no great pity within him as he rode across London Bridge on December 21st, 1583 and saw the bloody heads of Somerville and Arden on pikes above him. He could hardly be expected to understand the ardor of the one, nor the madness of the other. The land was well rid of them both!

Particularly in view of the terrible revelations of the Throckmorton Plot. In the course of following up a tip from one of his spies who called himself " Fagot," as far back as April of 1583, Walsingham had begun to watch the house of the French Ambassador in Butcher's Row. Thither, according to his informant, " le sieur Frocquemorton " came secretly, and always late at night.

Finally on November 4th, 1583 the house of Francis Throckmorton at Paul's Wharf and his country place at Lewisham were simultaneously searched. Although a green casket was mysteriously whisked away (and into the hands of the Spanish ambassador) under the noses of Walsingham's agents, the papers they seized yielded sufficient evidence to warrant Throckmorton's arrest. Under the first application of the torture, the prisoner was steadfast enough. But Thomas Norton the " rackmaster " was a famous " pyncher of paynes " who took a craftsman's pride in his task. (Indeed, he vaunted that he had pulled the Jesuit Briant " one good foot longer than God ever made him " !) In the second " examination " at the hands of this worthy, the wretched Throckmorton confessed everything.

The magnitude of the plot left the Queen and her Council gasping. It involved invasion of the country, deposing Elizabeth, putting Mary on the English throne, Romanizing the realm. One foreign army was to descend from Scotland. Simultaneously, under the leadership of the Duke of Guise himself, a second force was to land in the south of England and proceed directly on London. Meantime a Spanish fleet was to harass the coast and meet any English ships which might be sent out against it.

If Lennox had remained in Scotland, the scheme would have been put into effect at the end of 1582 or early in 1583. Again, if Throckmorton had proved " constant " under the torture, the plan would have been carried out anyhow, for since all the incriminating documents had been filched away by Mendoza, Walsingham would have discovered nothing save that Throckmorton owned some Catholic books and a list of English harbors! Moreover, only by the merest chance had Mr. Secretary run down a clue which eventually led to the Spanish ambassador. Never had he suspected him. The French envoy on whom he had been concentrating his attention, knew nothing whatever about the great and hidden treason. Distrusting him as altogether too friendly to the English, the Guises had worked solely through Mendoza.

However, if the hand of God was everywhere visible in the timely disclosure of the dreadful business, so was the patience and careful work of Walsingham. It was he who had sensed the need of eliminating Lennox from the Scotch scene. It was he who for months had watched for some sign of the conspiracy. Now the plot revealed exactly what he and Sidney had feared: that the King of Spain, the Guises and the Pope were all banded against Elizabeth. In collusion with them were prominent English Catholics, two of whom made off to the Continent at the mere news of Throckmorton's arrest. His confession implicated two others, the Earls of Northumberland and Arundel, who had engaged to assist the invaders in the north and south respectively. Both were confined to their houses. Arundel who was related to the Queen secured his release not long after. Poor Northumberland was found dead in the Tower after a year of close imprisonment.

On December 20th, 1583 Sidney wrote to his friend the Earl of Rutland the news of the court. He reported that the Queen was " well, but troubled with these suspicions " of her disloyal lords. There were rumors that the Scotch Queen was to be shifted to a stouter lodging and a stricter guard. Most alarming of all the ambassador of Spain had been discovered " for a great practiser " !

In the question of what was to be done with Mendoza, Sir Philip had his part. He it was who persuaded Alberici Gentilis, the great foreign expert on Civil Law to investigate the whole subject of ambassadors' rights and privileges. Through Leicester, Gentilis had been received at Oxford.

Though he was not yet recognized as the Father of International Law, he was even then held for an authority. This was the man whom the Council consulted about Mendoza.

The Italian doctor gave it as his opinion that though the ambassador had conspired against the life of the Queen, she had no power to punish him, since he had in effect, accomplished nothing. But she could, without consulting his master, order him out of her realm. After he had " discussed the matter before the illustrious Earls of Leicester and Pembroke," Gentilis went home to the parish of St. Helen's Bishopsgate where his family was then residing and began a book on the obligations of ambassadors both to their masters and the monarchs of countries to which they were sent.

In 1584 he finished the epoch-making volume which represents the first systematic work in the Law of Nations, and dedicated it to Sir Philip Sidney with words which made the gift more rich. After speaking in terms of the highest appreciation of his "intimacy" with Sidney who as a mere lad " had discharged the duties of an envoy with the highest distinction," Gentilis acknowledges that in his statements about the origin of legates he has been influenced by Sidney's arguments. He goes on to say that this whole book *On Ambassadors* represents his " persistent and determined effort " to transmit

a pattern of the perfect ambassador. I am sure that this excellent pattern can be found and demonstrated in one man only — a man who has all the qualities which are needed to make this consummate ambassador of ours, and has them indeed in greater abundance and on a more generous scale than is required. That man is Philip Sidney.

Since Sir Philip had " previously induced " him to investigate the whole matter of envoys, and had aided him " in threshing it out with every variety of Socratic device," the famous civilian concluded his preface by saying:

The book was desired, prepared, elaborated and labored over for you, and so far as lay within the power of an inexperienced craftsman modelled upon you. It cannot therefore be dedicated to any one but you!

But though the writing up of Mendoza's case might formally wait till this treatise by Gentilis issued in July 1584, the Privy Council took action just as soon as they had the support of his learned opinion. On the evening of January 19th, 1584 the Council met the Lord Chancellor, Bromley. Then they sent for Mendoza. When he arrived, they solemnly ushered him into an inner room where Sidney's father-in-law, who spoke Italian better than the rest, addressed him. Briefly he informed the suave Spaniard that the Queen was well aware of his plots to disrupt her kingdom: his connivance with Mary, the Guises, and her own disloyal subjects. She gave him fifteen days in which to leave the country. In vain did Mendoza protest innocence, assert his " rights," grow vituperative. However he might bluster, he knew he was fortunate to escape so easily. Walsingham's agents thoughtfully accompanied him to the very port of embarkation. Shortly he was established as Spanish ambassador in Paris where he continued to conspire with Elizabeth's " disaffected " lords. King Philip had no representative in London for years.

Even with Mendoza dispatched and Throckmorton locked safely in the Tower against his trial the coming May, there was still ground for anxiety. The Queen's emissaries were scouring the town after forbidden persons and books. One Carter was executed at Tyburn on January 10th, 1584 for printing seditious pamphlets. Moreover, in that same month Dr. Parry appeared on the scene.

In private conference with Elizabeth he " confessed " to

having agreed to kill her, under the urgings of Thomas Morgan abroad. The Queen was deeply impressed by his tears and penitence; most of all by his having revealed the matter to her in the course of an audience which might otherwise have cost her her life!

She gave him some sort of employment. Surprisingly enough, he had a seat, with Sir Philip, in the Parliament which met in November of 1584. On December 17th, a bill was read which called for the sterner treatment of recusants, to which Parry made such impassioned objection that he was promptly committed to Sergeant's Ward. However, he stood so high in the royal favor that on promise of amendment he was released. On the next day he was in his place again and took a quiet part in the debate. It was the last time that he had (or merited) Elizabeth's mercy.

Just what happened after this, it is hard to say. Certain it is that Parry, who was a confirmed spendthrift, had run through his money and needed more. Perhaps that drove him back to the service of the Catholics whom he had betrayed. At all events early in February 1585, he approached Edmund Neville, one of the Northern family which had been involved in the Norfolk plots, suggesting to him that the Queen be put out of the way. Neville promptly reported the interview to the Council.

Walsingham summoned Parry to his house in Seething Lane on February 8th, 1585. When he arrived, Mr. Secretary told him that the Queen had some inkling of a plot against her. Had any word of such come to him through his Catholic friends? At this point, Parry had every chance to report the talk with Neville, particularly if, as he afterward contended, he had merely been " testing " the man out. Instead, the doctor told Walsingham that he had heard nothing at all! When he was asked to consider if he himself had let fall some words which might draw suspicion on him if incorrectly reported, he " denied it with vehement protestations." When he was informed that a gentleman of good quality was prepared to accuse him to his face, he still " would not in any respect yield that he was party or privy to any such enterprise or intent."

That night he remained in Walsingham House. An extra guard was set about the chamber in which he slept as upon the staircase leading to it; and however much Sir Philip's young wife was kept in ignorance of the serious business afoot, it is inconceivable that her husband was not privy to the matter, and ready to assist at need.

Early in the morning of February 9th, Parry sent for the Secretary betimes. During the evening, it appeared, he had bethought himself of a conversation with one Neville about a Catholic book which discussed the question of the Queen's murder. He still, however, persisted in disavowing all knowledge of any specific plan against Elizabeth. That night he was taken to Leicester House, where to Leicester and Hatton, as well as to Walsingham, he renewed his denials. He continued in them, even when confronted by Neville.

Nevertheless, on February 8th, 1585 a full confession was elicited from him in the Tower. The fact that it was se-cured without resort to torture, makes it the more likely that the man really intended mischief; that if Neville had fallen in with his proposal, there would have been an at-tempt on the Queen's life. He was tried on February 25th, 1585 and less than a week later, hung at Westminster.

When Gloriana was convinced of his guilt, she retired to her garden and wept because her subjects did not love her, and wished her out of the way. Well could she afford the luxury of woe, for she knew that all these upheavals had gripped the nation to her. There was now a Bond of Association, by which her loyal lords went on record as im-placably vowed to destroy anyone who intended harm to her person.

Specifically they meant the Queen of Scots. At the time of the Throckmorton trial in May 1584, both Leicester and Walsingham begged that Mary be put to death. She was deeply involved in this, as inevitably she would be, in all plots against Elizabeth. So long as she lived there was danger. This Gloriana understood as well as they. But she also knew that what great ones do, the less will pattern by. Accordingly she evinced the greatest respect for the blood royal. After all, Mary was a queen.

Being a queen, and without throne or crown, it followed that Mary must conspire. Her next scheme was one in which Morgan, Poley, and Babington all took a hand at Chartley with the aid of a brewer of small beer. Its menace failed to touch Philip Sidney. By the time his indefatigable father-in-law had laid bare its dangers in August 1586, he was himself busy in the Low Countries, with only two months to live.

These traitors from Somerville to Parry with whom he was in touch over the period from October of 1583 to March of 1585, confirmed Sir Philip in two opinions. One was, that what happened to Protestants in other countries was of enormous importance to his own. They must be assisted, — though assistance meant heavy costs! The second was, that from now on, little England must defend herself against the secret or open attacks of a declared and active enemy, in the person of mighty Spain. By assuming the offensive, she might at least choose her time and place, and stand some chance of emergence. There, again, — aggressive war was expensive! Quite apart from the fact that the Queen had a rooted aversion to spending money, she had very little to spend.

What better solution to the everlasting problem of " charges," than to fall on that bottomless store of riches in the New World which King Philip had claimed for his

Sir Francis Drake, " the fellow traveller with
the Sun."

own? To " garboil " him there would have double value. It would strip him of funds. It would replenish Elizabeth's coffers.

Again the ways were pointing Sir Philip, westward over the sea.

THE EIGHTEENTH CHAPTER
ENTITLED APOLLO
AND THE WESTERN WAY.

N MARCH of 1584, Sir Philip and his cherished little lady came to Wilton. The dreadful excitements of December 1583 had probably stood in the way of a wedding visit at Christmas. Just now Sidney's sister was particularly glad of the company of the pretty new wife. The two husbands had business together concerning the cargo of a vessel which had been wrecked off the coast of Wales three months before. Sir Philip had put in a claim which Pembroke was supporting.

Moreover, there was to be a music meeting in neighboring Salisbury, already famous for its composers and performers of note. On the present occasion Sidney himself was sponsoring a kind of harp with " wyar stringes " which produced delectable harmonies, as played by Sir Edward Stradling's man, Thomas Richards. Since the audience to which he discoursed his " musick " was described as an " honorable assemblye of many gentlemen of good calling," presumably the ladies were not included.

While the March winds were sweeping the misty downs, the young wives spent their time happily enough in the low arched cloister. They chatted merrily as they stitched at the elaborately fluted and flounced, tucked and beribboned garments which heralded the arrival of hapless Tudor infants. If the baby were a boy, his name should be

Philip Herbert. That meant that the Sidneys must return in the autumn for a christening!

About them played Lord William now four, and his sister Katherine, three. " She promised much excellence if she might have lived " her affectionate grandfather wrote wistfully in the Sidney *Psalter* before the year was out, for she died in the same October to which the Countess was now looking forward with such anticipation. The new Philip was born on the 17th, the day they buried the little lass.

Prisoners alike to " shamefastnes " and the weather, the two women let their thoughts range to far countries and distant prospects. For some time the Countess had been patron to Adrian Gilbert who came to Wilton to conduct his experiments in the " chimistry " of the occult and to shape his plans for the North-west passage. Since the time of Frobisher, she had " ventured." Her beloved brother, for whom she was naming the baby, made her his confidante both in love, and his schemes for the New World. And down with her from London, little Lady Sidney had brought a book of sketches of the birds and flowers in the American land called " Florida," which extended north-ward from the present St. Augustine to a place the French called Charlesfort (Beaufort, North Carolina). The volume had been given to her in the early days of her marriage by the artist himself, Jacques Le Moine de Morgues who was living now in London under the name James Morgan. Some of the drawings he had made on the ground and brought back with infinite peril. Others were done from memory of the sights he had seen in Florida with René de Laudonnière and the fated Huguenot expedition of 1564.

This same Morgan's adventures made a proper story to tell by a sea-coal fire in a snug low chamber with mulled wine on the hob! Lady Frances had heard them often. How on September 3d, 1565 the artist had gone to sleep with some forebodings of evil, in his hammock inside the fort, dressed in a " single chemise " against the Florida heats. Suddenly on his half-slumbers had come the sound of shot and tumult. The Spanish had fallen on the Protestant plantation they hated! By great good fortune, he escaped the general massacre by eluding the notice of two of the invaders, and dropping over the ramparts into the ditch below. Thence he had crawled on his stomach to safety.

It was dangerous safety in the trackless virgin forest but, by climbing a tree at daylight, he managed to get his bearings and make his way through the tangled woods. There on the outskirts he found Captain René and a few of his other comrades. However, between the fugitives and the French ships which had been run up into an inlet, were two days of wading through water and reeds waist-high, two nights of not daring to stop lest they be sucked under. When at last they came within hailing distance of their vessels, they were so famished and weak that the sailors were constrained to carry them aboard. Just as the Spanish discovered the whereabouts of the boats and began to rain shot upon them, the company pulled off!

In the storms of the Atlantic the pinnaces lost each other, but that in which Laudonnière and Le Moine had sailed, came safe to port at Swansea on November 11th, 1565 after a voyage of almost two months. English gentlemen gave the battered and starving sailors their carriage to London. There Le Moine had been living ever since in St. Anne's parish in the Blackfriars, part of the thriving Huguenot colony which flourished under the wing of the Puritans. In time Philip Sidney had befriended him. His other patron was Walter Raleigh for whom Le Moine drew pictures of native houses, of Indians in their war-paint, and such spirited scenes as the crocodile hunt! However, the Lady Frances preferred her own dainty sketches of blossoms strange to the English eye: a beautiful thing called *petunia,* a weed with a great lovely flower which the Indians called *tobaco,* and a plant that traveled underground which the natives named *potato,* and ate in the rainy season.

While the ladies were busy with their great and little worlds of the future, their lords and masters went racing, for the Earl had arranged a course which started at Chalk Farm. Annually he offered a golden bell to the worth of £50 to the fleetest rider. Sidney may not have raced himself this year, because he was disappointed in the loan of a horse from the Earl of Rutland which he thought would bear away the bell. His judgment proved correct. Under the Earl of Cumberland (to whom he had first been promised), the steed of his choice won the race. Poor Sir Philip! All too often it was his lot to see someone else riding his chances, through to a golden success.

Not so his brother. When Mr. Robert wished to enter a race, he rode. Moreover, he rode to win. In September of this same year, for instance, he carried away the prize in a matrimonial steeplechase where the running was eager, swift and very close indeed.

On September 8th, 1584 John Gammage died. His daughter Barbara, of " the age of 22 years and upwards," was as richly left as any young mistress in decades. For some time, to the disgust of several other suitors, she had been betrothed to Herbert Croft, the grandson of the Comptroller of the Royal Household. That pre-contract gave no pause to Robert Sidney. Before Croft could claim his bride (which he started to do with great expeditiousness) Robert arranged with her uncle, Sir Edward Stradling, to have her removed some distance from his rival, and very close to himself!

Violently Mr. Herbert complained to the Queen. So did the Howard kin of Mistress Barbara. So, even, Sir Walter Raleigh. Nevertheless on September 23d, 1584 Philip's brother married her. None too soon, either, for only two hours after the wedding, came a messenger from the Queen expressly to forbid it! Even by contemporary standards, it was a rare piece of wife-snatching. It set Robert Sidney on the high road to fortune, though incidentally, it saddled the Sidney family with the problem of raising the £6000 for the lady's jointure. To clinch the alliance, the bridegroom and the Earl of Pembroke had gone bond for that amount. Poor Sir Henry's burdens were heavier than ever.

And though Sir Philip was increasingly busy with public matters, there is no indication that any of them added to his income. He was acting as representative for Sir Francis during the periods when, as in February 1584, he was laid up at Barn Elms for as much as a month. Moreover, the work of the Ordnance was more heavy (fitfully, at least) since the uncovering of the great treason. In June 1584, for example, Sidney was scheduled to go to Dover to survey the defenses there, and recommend improvements. There were constant visits to Minories House, once a nunnery of St. Clare and now headquarters of the Office which had long since outgrown its original abode in the Tower hard by.

The Mulcibers who then sweated in the Minories had picturesque workshops in the old bakehouse, the brewhouse and the abbess's lodgings. The sisters' chapel was now the parish church. (Sir Philip would yet lay there in state!) In the Close which was embowered in gardens, one of the Queen's oldest musicians, Marco Antonio Galliardello, still lived in the house which her father had given him shortly after the Dissolution. As Sir Philip checked over his lists of powder kegs, the air might at any time become lovely with the harmonies of old " Mr. Markantry's " viol. And he shook his head over Gloriana's rotting gun-carriages, in an upper chamber where the good nuns, thrifty to loftier ends, had combined an oratory with a place to dry their clothes!

Despite the deadly and now demonstrated danger which lurked in Scotland, Elizabeth's policy through 1584 was

still marked by what Walsingham wryly referred to as
" good housekeeping." Inevitably, too, a rare haggis was
seething there. Robert Bowes, her ambassador, was trying
to build up a party against Arran without any money. His
deft hand was in two conspiracies against the Earl. When
they proved abortive, the Queen decided to play a by-course,
and rather than fight Arran, make friends with him. Thus
quite as surely might she control young James — and at
infinite saving.

There were plenty to agree with her that the idea was
inspired, including Lord Burleigh, whose mind like her
own, ran to indecisive moves and attacks by indirection;
as well as Hunsdon, who backed a by-course as most
likely to serve a marriage he had in mind. In fact, the op-
posers were practically limited to Leicester, Walsingham
and Sidney who all felt that Arran, whatever his protestations of friendship, was not a man to be trusted, one who
played the game of the Guises. That was also the judgment
of Davison whom the Queen sent to Scotland in June 1584,
to explain that she could not return to the vengeance of
Arran, the " rebel " lords of Angus and Mar who had fled
into her territory for asylum.

In August 1584, King James announced that he would
dispatch an envoy of his own to continue the subject.
Though Walsingham promptly forwarded a passport, the
Master of Gray who was named as the ambassador did not
arrive till October. Then he came with many warnings
from Hunsdon who had coached him as he passed through
Berwick. He was to deal with the Queen and Lord Burleigh only. Leicester, Walsingham and Sidney he was to
keep away from, as persons opposed to " peace " with Scotland!

But in the course of delivering a letter from James to
Walsingham, which he had not thought it necessary to
tell Hunsdon he carried, the Master of Gray let it slip that

he was not himself altogether devoted to Arran. Mr. Secretary set about to widen the breach thus providentially disclosed. It was probably at his suggestion that Sir Philip began to see a great deal of the Master of Gray, — to keep the handsome Scot out of mischief. Still, a very real friendship between the two young men grew out of their daily contact of six weeks or more. Whatever his own insincerities, the Master of Gray was devoted to Philip Sidney. Shortly it became evident that James's envoy was intrenched in the very camp which he had been warned away from.

The result was that when he went back to Scotland early in January of 1585, he was eager to win his king to a personal alliance with Elizabeth as " the other great Protestant monarch." Soon after his return he wrote Walsingham a letter which was to be " participated " with his " sone Sir Philip Sidnie." In it he reported that there were in Edinburgh a thousand lies current about his *volte-face,* including one to the effect that he had " promisit in England to kill the Earle of Arrane " !

Gray's mission bore immediate fruits in a new friendliness from James. For her own part, Elizabeth was so delighted with the " proper gentleman of trim spirit " who was her dear brother's envoy, that she yielded a point, and ordered the rebel lords away from the Border where they were a menace to the Scotch King. Instead she brought them down to Oxford where, in the witty phrase of the Master of Gray, they were " put to school."

This *entente* with Scotland, though neither so cordial nor so solid as Walsingham thought, was desperately necessary. He and " sone Philip " had labored to good purpose in a crucial time, for since June 1584, the future of Protestantism had looked black indeed. In that same month both Alençon and William of Orange died. The one Sidney deplored not a whit. The other he mourned as a hero and a friend. For both, Elizabeth wore black impartially — the same mourning dresses, supplied by Catherine de' Medici. Moreover for three weeks she bravely wept for her sweetheart every day. To the Queen Mother she wrote words meant to express overwhelming sorrow, but inadvertently true:

If you could see a picture of my heart, you would see a body without a soul!

In some ways her regret was lively enough, for without any more money than ever, she was at last forced into the policy of open support of the Huguenots and the Dutch to which Sidney and Walsingham had been trying to persuade her for years. Henry of Navarre, who with Alençon's passing, became the logical successor to childless Henry III, was not, as a Protestant, acceptable to a preponderantly Catholic land managed by the Guises. That very fact forced Elizabeth into the Huguenot camp. With Orange dead, she could no longer resort to the old trick of assisting the Dutch " underhand " in the Low Countries. She must now send over armies and fight her own battles.

However, it did not necessarily follow that she must pay the bills alone! Before she went any further in the business, the Queen determined to discover how much, if anything, Henry III might be minded to contribute to the support of forces in Flanders. Therefore she decided to send an envoy to him, under color of bearing her condolences on the death of Alençon. Not without intent she chose the person in her court to whom the role of bearing them would be most ungrateful — Sir Philip Sidney!

On July 6th, 1584 Walsingham wrote to Stafford who was Her Majesty's representative in Paris. He asked him to sound out the King, to discover whether he was " disposed to enter into some good course for the curbing of the King of Spain's greatness." This, by way of preparing for Sidney's real mission. Two days later, Sir Philip received his instructions.

His first audience was to be devoted to high-flown regrets on Monsieur's demise. In the second, he should secure a definite statement from the King about the assistance he would provide in the Low Countries. This he must do, without himself " descending into any particularities." If pressed, he might say that the Queen would do " anything which would stand with her honour " and " due consideration of the future." However, if Henry should prove insistent, he was to terminate the interview by saying that the Queen had found His Majesty so " cold " and " changeable " in the past that she had not thought it wise on this occasion to send a plenipotentiary!

No commission was ever more unpromising. Dubious and discouraged, Sir Philip asked Castelnau, the French ambassador in London, how, in his opinion, the King would receive so " general " a proposal. Badly, said Castelnau, frankly! Still Gloriana insisted.

Sir Philip started out on July 10th, 1584. Some of his carriages had gone over ahead, and he himself was awaiting a wind at Gravesend, when a messenger arrived from Stafford. The French King, it appeared, was going into retirement for a while and asked therefore that Sir Philip might be stayed until the " latter end of September." In less diplomatic language, he did not care to talk about the Low Countries at all! By July 18th, 1584 Sir Philip was back at court and deeply relieved. For once, a stay was welcomed.

Through the summer, matters went from bad to worse in Flanders. The Dutch offered the Sovereignty to Henry in that same July. When he refused, they tendered it to Elizabeth through Ortel in August. When she refused, they renewed their proposals, on more favorable terms, in September, to Henry — only to be denied again.

The fact was, that neither England nor France wished to

undertake the financial responsibility for the Dutch alone. At the same time, each profoundly distrusted the other. Consequently, though there was a good deal of diplomatic chatter about sharing expenses and authority in the Low Countries, each monarch was quietly undermining the other for all he was worth.

Meantime the Dutch lacked a leader, a general, funds, even unity among themselves. On their wants, Parma flourished apace. City after city fell before him. At the present rate, Spain would be master of all Flanders in short order, and able to hurl an army thence into England. No wonder that Walsingham, writing on September 16th, 1584 was apprehensive both for the States and for the " continuance of our happy English peace which we have so long enjoyed " !

In October, the Council begged the Queen to send some " wise person " to look into the affairs of the Low Countries. If he found the Dutch had not already allied themselves to France, it was suggested that he be empowered to offer English aid, requiring as security the towns of Flushing, Brill and Middelburg. Still Elizabeth waited a month before she did anything at all. When in November, 1584 she finally commissioned William Davison to go to Flanders, he had orders to prevent the renewal of offers to France, but to do so, without committing England. Though he pressed steadily for permission to close with the Dutch on Elizabeth's behalf, matters continued in this uncertain posture for the rest of the year.

Meantime the sight of the sea at Gravesend had made Sir Philip restless. He wanted to go to America more than ever! Within two days after his return, he was writing to Stafford in Paris, on July 20th, 1584, to say that he was " half persuaded to enter into the journey of Sir Humphrey Gilbert very eagerly." Gilbert had been dead nine months. After the fashion of the time, Sir Philip was speaking in similes. He meant that he wanted to seek the New World, and plant a colony there.

Without doubt his ambition in that direction had been whetted afresh when his friend Sir Walter Raleigh acquired letters patent to lands in America in March of 1584. Settlement was Sir Walter's aim as well. Since he had a genius for saying pretty things to Gloriana, letting her remove imaginary smudges from his handsome face in public and such kickshaws, he had plenty of money! Therefore less than a month after, in April 1584, he sent over a scouting expedition under Barlow and Amadas. Walsingham loaned him the pilot Fernandez. In the autumn the party would return, with the site chosen and such full report as would enable Sir Walter to equip his colony more effectively than any hitherto. Doubtless Sidney and Raleigh talked of " planting " together in Sir Walter's tower study at Durham House, looking down on the ships in the Thames. Nevertheless Sir Philip's ideas for his colony were all his own.

With the piety of a sixteenth-century Boswell, Greville preserved them for posterity. Sidney's colony was not to be " an Asylum for fugitives," nor a pirate state which was a refuge for bandits and such scum. It was rather to be " an Emporium for the confluence of all Nations that love or profess any kind of Virtue or Commerce."

To certain classes, Sir Philip made special appeal. He wanted soldiers, and offered them " Fame and Conquest." He desired investors, to whom (somewhat rashly) " he propounded the hope of a sure and rich return " ! The ambitious he lured with honor; the fortune-bound, with freedom. To " the Religious divines " he promised not only the task of winning the virgin souls of all the Indians in America, but that of " reducing poor Christians mis-led by the Idolatry of Rome." To merchants he extended the inducement of dealing with a " Simple people." Lastly he enticed " rude mechanicals," not as might have been imagined by high wages, but with the hope of new trades and manufactures to work at! For mere travelers, there was the assurance of all sorts of rare sights and new experiences in this " fruitful womb of Innovation."

However, if Greville's account is accurate, Sir Philip's " Heroicall Design of invading and possessing America " though " exactly projected and digested in every Minute," utterly overlooked the need of husbandmen! It was a common omission. The expedition of Laudonnière had been made up of nobles, soldiers, lawyers and a handful of artisans, the one requirement being that all the members should be thorough-going Calvinists who would teach the Indians to sing psalms in the French translation of Marot! At least Sir Philip was planning to do without the lawyers.

Perhaps this was because a peaceful settlement was only part of the plan. His colony was to serve as a naval and military base for operations against Spain in the New World or in Greville's words, as the " fittest Rendez-vous for supply, or retreat of an Army upon all occasions." In short, Sidney was looking forward to a thorough-going and systematic plundering of the resources of Spain, so far only tapped in occasional foray by Drake. The scheme for the " planting " was, therefore, one to combine the profit of the individual and the nation, the activities of war and peace.

All this as Greville tells it, has the specific air of applying to some one special expedition. But though Sir Fulke supplies a welter of metaphor with his facts, he neglects to provide a single date in the course of his life of Sidney! Nevertheless it is reasonably clear that these plans as he gives them refer to the Raleigh expedition which set sail on April 9th, 1585. With that Sir Philip intended to go and for it he deliberately planned. The other voyage in which he was interested, Drake's, which left in September of the same year, he sought to join at the last minute in an impulsive determination to get out of the country which allowed of no time for the recruiting of artisans or ministers. On that account, it seems likely that the scheme of planting which Greville gives us is the very one which was occupying Sir Philip between late September of 1584 when Fernandez returned, and the time when the fleet set out seven months later.

In that period Sidney had fresh hopes of securing money to manage his share of expenses. For one thing, Robert had married an heiress. For another, on July 19th, 1584 Leicester's only legitimate son, little Robert Dudley, had died. Since the child was presumably about five, and no others had followed, it seemed probable that Sir Philip might after all inherit some of his uncle's estate. Both these events had an inevitable effect on " bankers."

If Sidney was " half persuaded " to a voyage before Amadas and Barlow came home, their accounts and Fernandez's official report to Walsingham completed the work. They had explored the Florida coast north of Laudonnière's settlement of 1564, north of an earlier Huguenot colony at Charlesfort. In the present state of North Carolina they had found a lovely island named Roanok in a district which still bears the name of Raleigh and the friendly Indian Manteo who helped Barlow and his crew. They had discovered the mainland which lay just to the west, beyond a straight so perilous that Fernandez almost wrecked a boat getting in and out of it. That extensive and fair country, the Queen graciously consented to christen in her own honor " Virginia." It was a place of " delicate airs " which " abounded with all kinds of odoriferous flowers." The sweet scent of them was borne out to ships at sea to gladden the nostrils of sailors who were used to the high but less lovely savors of Elizabethan London.

The natives were friendly souls. In return for an English shirt and an old hat, one brought Barlow a boat-load of fish. Another had traded " 20 skins worth 20 crowns " for a bright tin dish which he saw in the ship's galley, and coveted to wear on his chest as armor. (No wonder that merchants yearned to deal with such simple folk!) Indeed the people of Virginia were " most gentle, loving and faithful, void of all guile and treason, and such as live," wrote the enthusiastic Barlow, " after the manner of the Golden Age." Yet in another place he admitted that the Queen of the country advised the English to bring in their oars at night " lest they be stolen " ! Thames-side or Wokoken, human nature was much the same.

Lady Frances listened with wide eyes to the account of the Indian Queen. She was " of a colour yellowish " but " very well favoured, of mean stature and very bashful." On her hair she wore a band of white coral. From her ears hung whole bracelets of pearls hanging down to her middle." Yet she looked after men-folk with ·the same whole-hearted devotion as any Tudor wife.

When Englishmen came to her house made of grasses and bamboo, in her husband's absence, she made them welcome with a simple air of trust. She drew their stockings from their feet with her own hands. While their shirts were being washed and dried, she herself made ready the dinner of boiled beef and venison served on platters of " sweet timber." She poured out a drink which they found rather too innocent for their taste, being water boiled with ginger, black cinnamon and sassafras. When they insisted on spending the night in their open row-boats, she sent out her servants with grass mats to protect them against the rain.

The scouting expedition brought back to England two of the virtuous natives. They were " lusty men " whose names were Manteo and Wanchese. Disappointingly enough, only Manteo belonged to the Golden Age. His companion was plain bad Indian. Still London flocked to see them indiscriminately. Lady Frances who had seen Indians in her sketches, now stared at the marvellous reality with the same flutter of fright produced by Her Majesty's lions. Certainly the noble red men must have presented an astonishing picture. Instead of their native habit of rudely tanned skins which had been thought improper at court, they were now decked out in fashionable suits of "brown taffeta" with ruffs. No wonder they made "a most childish & silly figure" in Gloriana's Greenwich.

When Parliament opened in state in November 1584, Sir Philip did not find its most exciting business in the scene which Parry created. Sidney was absorbed in the work of the committee to confirm the letters patent which the Queen had given to Raleigh eight months before. Daily he was working on the "bounds" of this new Virginia. By December 18th, 1584, he and Sir Walter had the infinite satisfaction of hearing the bill voted through the House. Their expedition might now sail — as soon as the weather permitted!

The Parliament season was enlivened by two tournaments. In the first, which was on Queen's day, November 17th, participation was practically obligatory. The second came on December 6th. Sidney's running that day is recorded. On one occasion or the other, he appeared in the guise of Apollo. His device was a leaping flame, with the words *I will make or find my way*.

Some time during 1585, he had his portrait painted in a dress of white satin with trimmings of gold and a scarf of tawny vermilion. The sunny shades suited his blond beauty to perfection. (Men of his time gave proper thought to such matters!) However, his choice of colors had another reason behind it. They were the tints of Light and Fire. Apollo was god of both.

The very handsome youth who held himself so delicately aloof even in the glowing and vital tones of amber and flame, was not merely sitting for his portrait. He was also revealing a project. The clue to it lay in the careful little pictures of Apollo on his shield. In one the divinity carried his sun. The other showed him bearing a flower in his left hand, and in his right a spear.

To the folk of an age accustomed to allegory, the meaning was clear. Sidney intended to travel, like the sun, to the West. There he would plant the flower of his colony, and wield his weapons of war. Moreover, he was there determined to make or find a way for a mounting ambition which leaped upward like flame, no matter what the obstructions.

Were the eyes of our eager Apollo fixed on Raleigh's expedition, as the painter laid on those radiant colors? Or was he looking forward to going with Drake, the more intensely for having missed of that April voyage? Alas, for Sir Philip! Despite his gallant motto, his Way would not be with Sir Francis, either. What a sorry piece of sunshine this canvas must have seemed to him later! How ironic the summons to golden adventure in its project of *Westward Ho!*

THE NINETEENTH CHAPTER
ENTITLED
KNOCK'T ON THE HEAD.

URING 1585, two of the Foster Children of Desire, who once claimed an exclusive right to gaze on Perfect Beauty, made a most ungallant attempt to run away and leave her! One was Philip Howard, the Earl of Arundel. The other was Sir Philip Sidney. Both were namesakes of the King of Spain. One sought escape as a way to serve him and Catholicism. The other tried to get off for the purpose of singeing his beard, in the name of " religion." Regardless of motive, the treatment which they received from the Queen was roughly the same. In her own thwacking phrase, they were " knock't on the head."

On April 11th, 1585 the Earl of Arundel wrote the Queen a farewell letter from his library in the old Charterhouse. In it he told her that he had embraced Catholicism, fired by the shining faith of Campion. He had grown weary of compounding with his conscience, and was therefore leaving the country, to worship in freedom. Putting the message into the hands of his sister for delivery, he made for the coast, disguised himself, and took ship for France. He was, however, recognized, arrested, brought back under guard and confined to the Tower for four years without so much as a formal accusation.

Certainly for the moment Elizabeth had her hands too full to trouble about a lone Catholic lord whom she had in safe restraint. For at the end of March 1585, news came from Péronne that the Catholic powers had joined in a Holy League. Though their avowed aim was the extermination of " heresy " everywhere, they threatened Queen Bess and Henry of Navarre by first and last intent.

Promptly for once, Elizabeth swung into action. She sent one ambassador to Denmark and Germany. A second went post-haste to King James of Scotland. A third was dispatched to deal with Navarre himself. All were to urge the formation of a Protestant League with the utmost zeal. Now at last the Queen was alive to the need for the very alliance which Sidney had urged for eight years. She was thoroughly frightened!

She had cause to be. In the late spring, the Queen Mother and Henry III made common cause with the Guises and joined the Holy League. For more than twenty years, Gloriana had boggled at nothing, to avoid facing Spain alone. Now, with no other power to support her, she was facing not only Spain, but the Guises and the Pope as well.

Meantime through the early months of the year, Sir Philip and Raleigh were busy with the Virginia expedition. Thomas Heriot the mathematician was choosing the instruments which he wanted to take along. Sailors were loading the *Tyger,* the *Roebuck,* the little *Lion* and the four smaller vessels. Heaped on the quay at Plymouth were the axes and saws and nails which would build strong native timbers into the first houses; the harquebuses and powder to defend them. The hundred colonists were chosen. Sidney himself secured the appointment of Ralph Lane as Governor of the new country.

Lane was by now fifty-five, a seasoned soldier and courtier. In 1569 he had fought the Northern lords. Since then he had chased pirates, spent some £1200 of his patrimony on Gloriana's wars, and pretty well " bruised his limbs." In the process he acquired a flaming hatred of Spain and a mighty admiration of Sidney. When the Queen forbade Sir Walter to go, and Sidney was made commander, Lane was delighted. He knew and approved of Sir Philip's scheme for harrying while he planted, and called him "most noble Generall." His chagrin was great when Sidney was withdrawn at the last moment, and Sir Richard Grenville was put in his place at the head of the expedition.

When they sailed away on April 9th, 1585 Sir Philip was deeply disappointed. Just what happened we do not know. Perhaps Elizabeth forced him to stay at home. Perhaps Walsingham's poor health, in combination with the national troubles made him loth to leave England at a time when he might be needed. If he had gone with the expedition, the whole history of Virginia might have been changed. Grenville was brave but tyrannical and tactless, and to a notable degree lacked Sidney's ability to manage men. In short order he was at loggerheads with the greater part of the colony. So fierce were the dissensions that the settlers were glad to return to privations in England.

Certainly the responsibilities which were speedily heaped on Sir Philip left him little time for regrets. In May, his Huguenot friend, De Ségur, arrived in London. The King of Navarre had sent him to ask the Queen for 200,000 crowns to support his armies. At the same time De Mornay sent frantic word to Sidney that the cause of Protestant France was doomed if Elizabeth did not help. Though Sir Philip used what little influence he had with the Queen, the results were poor enough. When De Ségur left in the middle of July he had the promise of 50,000 crowns — a fourth of what he had begged. Even that was contingent on his securing similar contributions from the German princes, which he was most unlikely to get!

Meantime, the private advices which came to Sidney from the Master of Gray in Scotland gave him anxious occupation. The wily young King was threatening to join with the Guises unless Elizabeth sent him 10,000 angels. For the "satisfaction" of various persons who were friendly to her in Scotland, Gray wanted 2000 more. The danger was crucial. On June 18th, 1585 Walsingham wrote that despite his efforts, the Queen could not be "wrought" to "make any more account of the matter." He said that Sir Philip Sidney had begged his uncle to "be content to yield some present support" till such time as she saw the light. The nephew's labors were vain. Leicester knew the Queen too well to risk his money. In desperation Mr. Secretary sent what he could himself — and said his prayers.

The support of Angus and Mar, the exiled Scottish lords, was forced on him or Sir Philip. Not only would the Queen do nothing toward their keep, but until such time as she gave King James the pension of £5000 which he asked for, she was in no position to make their peace for them. She had very little money and the Dutch were pressing her hard.

When Henry III made his final refusal of the Sovereignty of the Low Countries in March of 1585, the question of assisting the States was put squarely up to Elizabeth. On June 29th, 1585 she declined to protect them formally though she said she would help them, provided the Dutch surrendered Brill and Flushing to her.

That meant war with Spain. Leicester, Walsingham and Sidney were delighted to see promise of positive action at last. All through July Sir Philip was particularly busy with the Ordnance, for he had been made Joint Master on the 21st of the month. Now, in expectation of taking 500 horsemen immediately to Flanders, he was setting affairs in order.

Constantly, too, he was occupied with the Dutch envoys who were established at the Clothworkers' Hall in Mincing Lane. Through the most important part of the negotiations, Sir Francis Walsingham was too ill to leave his country house. Consequently, Sir Philip worked with the delegates all day, and at night, he took barge and went the hour's journey along the river to Barn Elms to report. Progress was very slow because the Dutch were just as eager as Gloriana to drive a close bargain.

While the unholy haggling went on between them, Antwerp fell on August 20th, 1585 under the guns of Parma. That speeded up the discussions at Greenwich. The Queen agreed to send over 5000 foot-soldiers, 1000 horsemen and 700 men for the garrisons. The Dutch made over the towns she asked as assurance of good faith and intention to pay their debts.

Again Sir Philip expected to cross the Channel at any moment. His servants were packing. Before long, Lady Frances should come over after him, for at last he had a " charge." He was to be Governor of Flushing, the all-important• cautionary town which the Dutch were surrendering. His father-in-law wrote his friends on August 26th, 1585 of the certainty of the appointment. Leicester was to take command of the English forces. Everything was settled.

Then Gloriana changed her royal mind. She announced that Thomas Cecil, the son of the Lord Treasurer, was to be Governor of Flushing!

The disappointment proved almost too much for Sir Philip. Increasingly he had schooled himself to meeting rebuffs. He had advanced a long way from the impulsive boy who kicked against the pricks with such passion. But this was one frustration too many. In the words of his father-in-law, who was not without understanding, he took

a very hard resolution to accompany Sir Francis Drake . . . moved thereto for that he saw Her Majesty disposed to commit the charge of Flushing unto some other; which he reputed would fall out greatly to his disgrace, to see another

*preferred before him, both for birth and judgment inferior
to him. The despair thereof and the disgrace that he doubted
he should receive, carried him into a different course. . . .*

With his Dudley pride cut to the quick, he made secret
plans with Drake to go on the harrying voyage which was
then preparing. Two of the leaders were Sidney's old
friends. Christopher Carlisle was the expedition's Lieutenant General. Frobisher was Vice-Admiral. There were to
be eighteen ships in all, with mariners and soldiers to the
number of 2300. The previous exploits of Drake were warrant enough for action and excitement. It was settled, says
Greville, that Drake would be chief of the expedition at sea,
but that when they landed, Sir Philip would take command. When the fleet was ready to start, Drake agreed
to send Sidney word. By some means or other, Sidney engaged to get down to Plymouth.

But how? For once, Fortune was with him when news
arrived that Don Antonio was expected to land at Plymouth. Though the poor monarch was reduced to dining
off bread and water through the better part of that year,
he was after all a king, and as such, required an escort.
Without exciting suspicion, Sir Philip managed to get himself chosen as convoy. Then, providentially, just as he had
his excuse to get off, Drake sent him word that they expected to leave at once; they waited him only, to sail.

In a rare state of excitement, Sidney and Greville set out
for Plymouth. They felt the elation of schoolboys, these
two who proposed to play truant upon the Spanish Main.
Right well they knew their danger. The Queen had fetched
runaways back before, like schoolboys — by the ear!

Though when they arrived at Drake's quarters, he received them with a feast, he was clearly surprised at their
coming. Moreover, Greville sensed in him a kind of " depression," as if their company was " beyond his desire." Sir

Philip had noticed nothing. When the two friends were abed and could talk in private, Greville expressed his suspicions. Still honest Sidney refused to credit them. However, says Sir Fulke

some few days after, finding the ships neither ready according to promise, nor possibly to be made ready in many days; and withal observing some sparks of false fire, breaking out unawares from his yoke-fellow daily; it pleased him (in the freedom of our friendship) to return me my own stock with interest.

Presently Sidney had word from a friend at court that Drake had secretly informed the Queen of his intentions to sail. The message went on to say that Elizabeth was sending letters which ordered Sir Philip's arrest, and the stay of the whole fleet, if Drake did not hand him over!

What followed shows the intensity of Sidney's determination to get away at any cost. He disguised certain of his own men as sailors with orders to play footpads to the royal post, hold up the messenger, and steal his letters! When Sir Philip and Greville read them, they found " a contents as welcome as Bulls of excommunication." Sidney's advices had been correct!

However they held their peace and they tried to expedite preparations. Before they had made any headway, Gloriana sent a second mandate. This time she took no chances, but dispatched a " Peer of the Realm." In one hand, says Greville, he carried grace, in the other, thunder:

The grace was an offer of an instant employment under his uncle then going General into the Low Countries; against which although he would gladly have demurred, yet the confluence of reason, transcendency of power, fear of staying the whole fleet, made him instantly sacrifice all these selfnesses to the duty of obedience. . . .

Sidney tarried in Plymouth long enough to do something more typical of him than the desperate and dubious deed of waylaying the Queen's messenger. He was, says Greville, convinced of Drake's duplicity. Nevertheless he made a gallant speech to the members of the expedition. In it he said that his own employment lay elsewhere, that theirs was a noble voyage in a Christian cause, beseeching them to be loyal to Sir Francis and support his service as became English gentlemen.

Then he gallantly watched them put to sea in great galleons, and pinnaces prancing lightly before the wind. When the last sail had passed from that green little harbor, he saw disappearing with it, the last of his chances to carry out his heroical plan for a colony and a military base on the mainland of America. He mounted his horse and started for London. That was September 14th, 1585.

When he arrived, Her Majesty was ill at her palace of Nonesuch. By her bedside, fretting against inactivity as much as his nephew, was Leicester. Just now he was resorting to every persuasion that he could think of, to move her to send him to Flanders. But for the moment Elizabeth felt she could not exist without him. Like herself Leicester was fifty. He was growing bald and paunchy, no longer a romantic figure. Still he understood her, thought Gloriana, better than anyone else. He must not go to Flanders!

Next day she had changed her mind. Robin might go after all. Gloriana was herself again. She had seen young Sidney and told him some thoughts on truants. 'Sblood! Save for her " grace," he might be lodged in the Tower that instant, like the Earl of Arundel! Taking Philip down had given her stimulus and satisfaction. Forgiving him at the end left her feeling merciful and noble. She had even promised him Flushing out of pure delight in having hauled him back, just in the nick of time, despite his careful planning!

She called him that " rash fellow Sidney " who had to be " knock't on the head."

Shortly after, she had a letter from Don Antonio which gave her an infinite satisfaction. In it he said that when he arrived at Plymouth on September 7th, Sir Philip revealed his plans to sail with Drake. The King hailed them with Latin rapture, and decided to go along. In fact, wrote His Majesty, if the peer had not arrived, they would be on their way that instant to America and gold!

The Queen read the letter to Sidney. She smiled.

THE TWENTIETH CHAPTER
ENTITLED
LA CUISSE ROMPUE.

IR PHILIP wasted no time in vain regrets, but began to recruit his horse. Elizabeth's ingenious plan of making recusants supply her cavalry, in lieu of paying their fines, had failed. Therefore Sidney was reduced to soliciting his friends for as many horses, fully accoutered, as their stables might spare. He had not mustered the full number before he left, and was forced to write begging letters from overseas.

His last days in England were busy. Ordnance matters occupied him up to the very end. Sir Francis needed his aid on the Dutch negotiations. From Wanstead Leicester was urging him to come and block out the campaign. At the end of September Walsingham wrote to Leicester in his behalf:

Sir Philip Sidney is greatly busied in preparing himself for Flushing. He desired me to excuse his silence and let you understand that he hopeth shortly to see you in his government.

Still no orders came to sail. Elsewhere however affairs were shaping more briskly. The Guises recalled Castelnau de Mauvissière whom they considered too friendly to England. The new man arrived late in September. Shortly after came news of an edict issued against the Huguenots on October 17th, 1585. It gave the men fifteen days to leave France. Women and children were to follow — within six months at the latest. By October 22d, there was a messenger from De Ségur begging frantic aid for Navarre. But nothing that Leicester or Walsingham could urge in his behalf moved Elizabeth to assist the Huguenots any further. According to Greville, Sidney "reverently demurred" that the French Protestants should be allowed "to vanish and smother out, unactively like a Meteor." The Queen was unaffected. Only fixed stars concerned her.

Largely, the delay in Sir Philip's sailing had been due to the failure of the Dutch to return the Treaty. Held back by heavy seas, it did not arrive till October 21st, 1585. Even then, however, the Queen dallied for Walsingham was preparing his *Declaration of the Causes Moving the Queen of England to give Aid . . . in the Low Countries* which was the opening gun.

At last, on November 9th, 1585 Sir Philip's letters patent as Governor of Flushing were put into his hands. He took leave of his good father-in-law and his beloved wife. He made his proud farewells to his new daughter Elizabeth, whose christening awaited the pleasure of her royal godmother. By November 10th, he was at Gravesend whence he sent Her Majesty the cipher in which she might communicate with him on secret matters. His 200 soldiers took ship shortly. On November 16th, 1585 he left England for the last time. His brother Robert was with him.

Just before he sailed he received a letter from Count Maurice the eighteen-year-old son of William of Orange, and already an excellent soldier. It welcomed him warmly, and assured him of every co-operation. Sidney appreciated the generous greeting all the more because at the last moment Elizabeth had forbidden Greville to sail with him. Both friends were deeply disappointed. Posterity lost as well, for there is no telling to what rhetorical heights Sir

Sir Francis Walsingham, Chief Secretary.

Fulke might have found himself moved by the brilliant botch which the Queen's parsimony, Leicester's ineptitude and the jealousies of the Dutch were to produce in the Low Countries!

Sir Philip's boats were forced to land at the Ramekins on account of heavy seas. Thence he came to Flushing after " as dirty a walk " of four miles " as ever poor governor entered his charge withal." He took up his residence with a Monsieur Gelée since there were no barracks. That same day, November 20th, 1585 the Queen of England had renounced the sins of this world on behalf of his tiny daughter. Across from St. Olave's in Hart Street where the child was christened, there had been high feasting at a Walsingham House bright with candles in the twilight of raw November.

Even before he had taken his oath to the testy citizens of Flushing, Sidney had seen enough of its defenses to be extremely worried. On November 22d he wrote a succinct account of the needs to Leicester. The first requirement was barracks. Realizing that friction between soldiers and townsmen could not be reduced materially so long as troops were quartered in private houses, he begged Leicester to secure the £3000 for which some sort of military shelters might be erected. There were other matters, too, such as the pay of the soldiers which was months in arrears. When the troops were restrained from making it up in unauthorized plunder, they turned insubordinate or deserted. A military of this sort was a poor dependency for an all-important town. In the event of attack Sir Philip suspected besides, that he could trust neither the strength of the " defences " nor the " loyalty " of the townsfolk.

While he awaited an answer he met the needs of his men as best he could. On December 1st, 1585 he wrote Walsingham that in desperate case he had taken advantage of the offer Sir Francis had made before he left England,

and borrowed £300 on the Secretary's bond. It was that which paid his soldiers. Meantime he awaited Leicester with the greatest impatience, for he was without authority to proceed to important changes until his uncle came.

At last on December 8th, 1585 Leicester set sail from Harwich and Gravesend in 50 vessels, bringing 3000 soldiers with him, including Lady Rich's brother, the young Earl of Essex, and Thomas Sidney. The Dutch hailed his arrival with the greatest joy. This was the man who would work the miracle of unity within their ranks. His gorgeous apparel impressed them. So, too, his mighty ways.

While the pageants and banquets lasted, all went well. Uncle Robert received compliments most graciously from ladies who spoke in broken English out of castles of confectionery. He rode gallantly under plaster arches decorated with his cognizance of the bear and ragged staff. He enjoyed the feasts at which pigs were served jauntily standing on their legs and baked swans thrust their heads through rich pasties.

Of all serious business he made a consummate fiasco. Probably no one on earth could have brought harmony into Flanders. However, shortly after Leicester set about his " reduction " of problems, they multiplied a hundred fold. His positive genius for setting the Dutch by the ears produced the greatest problems which Sir Philip had, in all " reverence," to solve. In a few months he managed to infuriate the burghers and alienate the aristocrats by meddling in religious matters and politics. There were constant altercations, even small revolts.

Leicester's greatest mistake came at the start. While he was still looked on as a miracle worker, the States offered him the title of Governor-General. The English on the ground, including Sir Philip, approved. So did the Council at home. But the Queen's instructions were specific. She had made Leicester Lieutenant-General of the English forces only. He might advise the States. Command over them in any degree he was to avoid, since she had no mind to be held responsible for anything more than she had already undertaken. Leicester knew this perfectly. Nevertheless he accepted the title on January 14th, 1586.

He reported the matter to Walsingham afterward. At the same time he promised to send William Davison, his relative, and the Queen's ambassador in the Low Countries, to explain the situation which had forced the honor on him. However, for three weeks he delayed Davison's departure. When the envoy at last reached London, Gloriana was in a towering rage.

In her anger she accused both Sir Philip and Davison of conniving at this game of family aggrandizement. To Leicester himself she wrote at length:

How contemptuously We conceive Ourself to have been used by you, you shall by this bearer understand, whom We have expressly sent unto you to charge you withal. We could never have imagined, had We not seen it fall out by experience, that a man, raised up by Ourself, & extraordinarily favoured by Us, above any other subject of this land, would have in so contemptible a sort, broken Our commandment, in a cause that so greatly toucheth Us in honour. . . .

Sir Thomas Heneage who brought over this haughty epistle on March 3d, 1586 found sweet Robin considerably dashed. He had not realized how little his power to charm would help him at long range. He met the inquiries of Heneage with a deplorable cowardice which blamed everyone but himself. He laid the responsibility for the whole business on the absent Davison, and he appealed to Sir Philip Sidney as witness. So did Davison.

In this delicate situation Sir Philip's behavior did him infinite credit. He made it clear that he would not and could not take a stand against his uncle. At the same time he exonerated Davison completely. For himself, he confessed with high courage that he had not only advised Leicester to take the title, but still considered the step was wise, nay, necessary.

As accusations continued to be leveled at the innocent Davison, Sidney wrote him on April 14th, 1586 a letter in which all his ideals of friendship and family loyalty speak:

I am heartily sorry with the unkindness you conceive of my Lord [of Leicester], and more at the cause thereof. I know by letters thence and some speeches here that he was much incensed because he had heard that you had utterly and with tears disclaimed him with mislike of the acceptation. But I never did think that he had written touching you into England. For my part I will for no cause deny (and therefore you shall have my handwriting to prove I am no accuser of you) that I was ever of opinion that he should accept [the title] without delay, because of the necessity; without sending to Her Majesty because of not forcing her in a manner to be further engaged than she would, which had been a piece of undutiful dutifulness. The odds was that others were of opinion the authority was not enough. You liked of this as it is, and I only lent to your opinion therein. Well cousin, these mistakings sometimes breed hard effects. But I know he in his judgment loves you very well; how so ever in his passion he have written. And so I end assuring you that I am still one toward you as one that know you and therefore love you.

All this magnanimity in the interest of truth was hardly calculated to appeal to Leicester, who had evidently counted on Philip for as much lying as his personal statements called for. It was such a spirit in his nephew which led the stout Earl to bear " a hand over him as a forward young man."

Such scrupulousness did not appeal to Gloriana either. Her fury at a person who had the effrontery to admit to the crime of urging the title, continued unabated for months.

Meantime poor Walsingham was reaping the whirlwind from two directions. Leicester accused him of half-hearted support. The Queen fell on him for abetting his scamp of a son, Sir Philip, and dinning Leicester's defense in her ears day and night. During March she became so angry with Mr. Secretary that before all the court, she threw her slipper at him! Woefully enough, Walsingham wrote to Flanders that he was weary of the place he served in, and wished himself " among the true-hearted Swiss " !

The difficulties which revealed Leicester's smallness of spirit, his captiousness and disloyalty were drawing beautiful things from Philip Sidney. In spite of his own troubles he took time to write to his uncle a word of comfort on February 19th, 1586:

I beseech your Excellency, be not discouraged with the Queen's discontentments. For the event being any thing good, your glory will shine through these mists.

While the Queen was heaping criticisms upon him, and refusing him barracks and men, he could say to Sir Francis on February 2d, 1586:

I am willing to spend all that I can make. My only care is that I may be able to go through with it to your honour and service, as I hope in God I shall.

His greatest concern for " wants " in equipment, was that the soldiers were thereby " so hardly dealt with."

Sir Philip's simple friendliness disarmed even Count Hohenlo whom the English called Hollock. He was quarrelsome, drunken, and as Sidney's account makes clear, opposed to foreigners on general principles! Yet on February 24th, 1586 Sir Philip reported to Davison:

Count Hollock caused a many handed supplication to be made that no stranger might have any regiment. But presently after, with all the same hands protested they meant it not by me, to whom they wished all honour &c. The Count Maurice showed himself constantly kind toward me therein.

Kind is the last word to describe Elizabeth's reaction. She called Sidney " very ambitious and proud." As Walsingham deplored, she showed herself constantly " apt " to interpret everything to Philip's disadvantage. She had done the same with his father. However, for all his gallant spirit, Sir Henry never achieved the lovely poise to which the once impulsive Philip had by this time mounted. On such heights, fair or unfair, Gloriana could not touch him.

This new steadiness of spirit shines out of a letter which he wrote to his father-in-law on March 24th, 1586 when things looked very black in Flanders:

I receive divers letters from you, full of the discomfort which I see (and am sorry to see) that you daily meet with at home. And I think such is the good will it pleaseth you to bear me, that my part of the trouble is something that troubles you. But I beseech you, let it not. I had before cast my count of danger, want and disgrace. And before God, Sir, it is true that in my heart the love of the cause doth so far overbalance them all, that with God's grace, they shall never make me weary of my resolution. If her Majesty were the only fountain, I would fear, considering what I daily find, that we should wax dry. But she is but a means whom God useth. And I know not whether I am deceived, but I am faithfully persuaded that if she should withdraw herself, other springs would rise to help this action.

For methinks I see the great work indeed in hand, against the abusers of the world, wherein it is no greater fault to have confidence in man's power, than it is hastily to despair of God's work.

I think a wise and constant man ought never to grieve while he doth play (as a man may say) his own part truly, though others be out. But if himself leave his hold, because other mariners will be idle, he will hardly forgive himself his own fault.

For me, I can not promise of my course . . . because I know there is a Higher Power that must uphold me or else I shall fall. But certainly I trust, I shall not by other men's wants be drawn from myself. . . .

With such Power behind him, he attained the supreme pitch of philosophy. Even the vagaries of the Queen engendered no bitterness:

I have seen the worst in my judgment before hand. And worse than that cannot be. If the Queen pay not her soldiers, she must lose her garrisons. There is no doubt thereof. But no man living shall be able to say the fault is in me.

This same serious letter contains a reference to "William my Lord of Leicester's jesting player." As he passed through camp on his way back to England, Sir Philip had given him letters to take along. Evidently he made a sorry business of delivering them. But the man was no fee'd post. He was an actor, a rare one, too, the famous William Kemp who later danced the morris from Norwich to London, and (more important), was in time to create the leading comic roles in Shakespeare's plays up to the end of the century. Now he had just returned from Elsinore where, though he spoke no Danish, the people were so enthusiastic over his capers and jigs that they broke a fence trying to see him! He doubtless performed for Leicester. It is to be hoped that Sir Philip was present, perhaps with some of the skittish soldiers whom he reported the worse "for the sound of a harquebus"! Short of receiving the wages Gloriana still owed them, nothing could possibly have cheered them more.

The high and sober tone of Sidney's long letter told Walsingham more of his problems than a list of complaints could have done. Mr. Secretary set about to help by every means in his power. " There was never so good a father," wrote Sir Philip, " had a more troublesome son! " Walsingham was all the more eager to lighten his load because while little Lady Frances and Philip were eager to be together, Sidney had written that unless re-enforcements and money arrived, he was like to take such a course as would not be fit " for any of the feminine gender."

At the end of March Walsingham succeeded in persuading the Queen to send over some men. They were soldiers recently discharged from the Irish service. If she kept them in England, she knew she must needs support them. If she sent them abroad to Sir Philip, she avoided that problem at least. To such considerations Sidney owed his re-enforcements. More he was not likely to get as Walsingham knew, for Her Highness was in secret, and " underhand," conducting no less than three sets of negotiations for peace with Spain!

Though from April 1586 till the time of his fatal wound in September, Sir Philip was largely in the field, even in the course of campaigning, he had his intellectual consolations. He met Justus Lipsius then professor of Protestant Theology at the University of Leyden, who was so proud of his knowledge of Tacitus that he engaged to stake his life thereon. In the day of setting bets up on such matters, he recited passages on demand with a dirk at his bare breast! He and Philip entered into a discussion on the proper pronunciation of the Latin tongue. As a result, in April of 1586 Lipsius sent to Sidney a Latin treatise on the subject with a dedication marked by the engaging simplicity for which the Lipsian style was famous:

Most illustrious Philip Sidney: Do you really want to know what I think about the pronunciation of Latin? Well, then, I'll tell you. . . .

True son of the Renaissance that he was, Sidney read the learned answer by the light of his candle in camp while his soldiers slept about him. The last letter but one which he ever wrote was to thank Justus Lipsius for it.

In March he had written, "I have seen the worst . . . and worse than that cannot be." Yet two months later, in May 1586, he knew things were not at their worst when he still had power so to describe them. For in May came the news of Sir Henry's death. He had caught a chill as he was rowed across the Severn from Bewdley to Worcester, and had died in the Bishop's palace within view of the great Cathedral. In mid-June a funeral procession of one hundred and forty horse took him over fragrant and leafy lanes to Penshurst, home to the " manour " which his " sweet king King Edward VI " had given to his father. Only in the year before had he built there a fair new tower and gateway, as his personal memorial to the little prince who had died in his arms.

The loss of his father was bitter to Philip. He knew his mother was suffering from a fatal disease, and that she was meeting the blow of bereavement without any son to support her. Without doubt also, he guessed something of the utter disorder of Sir Harry's financial affairs. For all these reasons, he sought permission to go home for a brief interval. However, on June 24th, 1586 he had the Queen's answer — No! Three days before in the chapel at Penshurst, the minister had said of Sir Henry: " he consumed himself as a candle in yielding light to other men." It was to be the same with his son " of excellent good proof," though his candle was destined to burn itself out in Flanders.

Some time in June little Lady Frances arrived with her

boxes and farthingales and her merry child's ways. She was the more welcome because Sir Philip was finding his uncle's incompetence hard to support. However, the nearest he came to murmuring were the words to Walsingham, " To complain of my lord of Leicester you know I may not."

At long last Sir Philip saw action. On the night of July 6th, 1586 he and his Zealand regiment met Lord Willoughby and 500 men at Flushing. From there they proceeded in the dark to the capture of Axel. Sidney and Count Maurice had previously worked out the details with great care. The troops rowed up the Scheldt to a point within three miles of the town where Count Maurice met them. Thence in dead silence they moved to a point within a mile of Axel. In the deep blackness Sir Philip addressed the soldiers, urging them to remember the great cause in which they had enlisted, exhorting them to behave like Englishmen, in a simple oration which, according to Stowe,

did so link the minds of the people that they desired rather to die in that service than live in the contrary.

Shortly after midnight the company came to Axel. Thirty or forty soldiers swam the moat, overpowered the guards and opened the gate to Sir Philip and his band. Immediately a guard of English was established in the market place, and the Spanish holders of the town were put to the sword. Thanks to the perfection of the planning, only one of the invading force was wounded, and none killed.

A garrison of 800 was left in Axel to hold it. Count Maurice flooded the surrounding country by piercing the dikes. Retiring with his troops for a little well-earned rest, Sir Philip had the assurance that at last an aggressive step had been taken into the enemy's own country.

For his exploits that night, Leicester made him a colonel, to Elizabeth's annoyance. She chose to understand the Earl's action as a desire to favor a Dudley at the expense of

The Apollo Portrait of Sir Philip Sidney. "That Heroicall design
of invading and possessing America."

people who had done every bit as well. The honor, she said, should have gone to someone else. Still in writing to Sir Francis, Sidney's uncle gave credit where credit was due:

> *We have taken Axel, a town in Flanders, near Ter-nous. . . . Your son Philip with his bands had the leading and entering of the town which was notably handled.*

By Walsingham's report, the Queen had not been mollified by explanations:

> *Her Majesty doth give out that the Count of Hollock's discontentment groweth in respect he was removed from a colonelship of the footmen serving in Zealand, and the same bestowed upon Sir Philip Sidney. . . . She layeth the blame upon Sir Philip as a thing by him ambitiously sought. I see her Majesty very apt upon slight occasion to find fault with him.*

She had no intention of letting this " rash fellow Sidney " forget his ambitious attempt to run away with Drake, simply because he took a town in the night without loss of a single man!

His next military engagement was not so successful. In fact, nothing but discretion and a cool head kept it from being a complete fiasco, for it was the " affair " of Grave-lines.

Through some Walloon captains, Sidney learned that the garrison of Gravelines was ready to surrender the town to the English. This had a queer look since the commander was the shrewd veteran La Motte, who was hardly the person to have conspiracies under his nose and not know it! Accordingly Sir Philip exercised every precaution. He sent back into the town one Nicholas Mordaunt who had been his chief informant, and gave him a fortnight to perfect arrangements with the disaffected garrison. At the end of that time, by a method duly rehearsed with him, he was to communicate with the English forces. Meantime Sir Philip resolved to keep his eyes open.

On July 16th Sidney and his force cast anchor before Gravelines. That was part of the plan worked out with Mordaunt. Signals were exchanged. That, too, had been planned. Then Sir Philip awaited the hostages which in the terms of the plot should at that time have been delivered. Instead came a corporal and a single servant of Mordaunt's. The letter they bore was full of plausible excuses. Mordaunt said that he could not come himself for reasons he dare not set down. The town, though, was theirs for the taking.

It looked safe enough. Still Sidney was cautious, and dispatched one of his captains to investigate. The man reported that all was well. Thus reassured, Sir Philip sent out a small troop of 26 men. Observing their peaceful reception, he told Lieutenant Brown to advance with 50 more.

At the arrival of the second contingent, the garrison threw off the mask and fell on the English scouts. Sir Philip's men withdrew in as good order as they could, supported by the fire which their resourceful chief caused to be directed against the town from his ships. Naturally the young commander felt himself responsible for the fate of the men whom he had sent into the trap. However his handling of the whole business elicited nothing but praise from seasoned soldiers. Certainly except for his restraining, the company with him would have walked into the ambush in full force.

Up to July 1586, there had been a bare possibility of screwing money out of the Queen for an aggressive campaign. It vanished with Drake's return from the voyage which Sidney had thought to join. Gloriana had gambled on such another glorious investment as she had made in the trip to Peru which had netted 4700 per cent. Instead, she found when the books on this new expedition were balanced at the end of July, that she had lost £5000! Consequently, Sidney and his uncle were forced to content themselves with sitting quiet in their trenches and awaiting Parma's attack. Their highest strategy consisted in diverting his attention to places where they were merely weak, from places where they were more than weak. The result was that Parma besieged Neusz and put all the Protestant inhabitants to the sword. Leicester was in no position to make even a gesture of protest.

Such inaction increased bad feeling within the ranks. Philip Sidney shared an unruly mess at Gertruidenberg, by Leicester's report of one unsoldierly rumpus which ensued between Edward Norris and the quarrelsome Count of Hollock:

They all went to supper. And I know not how nor why, but, as it is reported, young Norris carried himself not at all the best towards the Marshall. And being full of words and speeches, the count Hollock found it was some mislike and therefore commanded Norris to silence. He either not understanding the Count, or [taking exception to his interference] in this matter proceeded, which so misliked the Count as he hurled the cover of a cup at his face, and cut him along the forehead as long as half my finger. This Sir John Norris taketh exceedingly and not only toward the count, but by wrong information of his brother, against the Marshall.

On August 9th, 1586 Lady Mary Sidney died a death Sir Philip could scarcely mourn. She had taken Sir Henry's going very hard indeed. In Greville's phrase she was " wracked by fierce native strengths," And life had tried them to the full. Worn out by suffering and sorrow, she made a " godlei and pious end." Although place was provisionally reserved for her burial in the south side of the chancel of St. Olave's in Hart Street, by her son's wishes she was later interred at Penshurst in the Sidney chapel beside her husband.

When the news of her death reached Sir Philip, Leicester had just embarked on his plan to invest Doesburg, with his nephew's assistance. The hope of both was that Parma would stop besieging the weak town of Berck long enough to march to the defense of Doesburg. Though the ruse failed of its purpose, Doesburg was at least reduced. Before it capitulated, however, Sir William Pelham, Sir Philip's associate in the Ordnance, received a bullet in the stomach on August 31st, as he inspected the trenches outside the city.

Also with the idea of diverting Parma, Leicester withdrew to Zutphen, a strong city on the Yssel. On the left bank of the river, across from the town, were two forts. Though for over ten months in the year preceding, they had withstood assault without perceptible weakening, Leicester was now making an attempt to subdue them and the walled town as well. To this end he threw up his own trenches in the meadows across from the town. Norris he established on the Zutphen side, on Gibbet Hill with a bridge of boats to connect the camps.

This done, in mid-September of 1586, with his two eldest nephews he left for Deventer where conditions had been reported as bad. However, he did not linger long enough to improve them, for a captured Spanish trooper told him on the evening of September 21st, 1586 that next morning Parma was planning to throw a large amount of provisions and powder into Zutphen to enable the forts to hold out. Immediately Leicester returned to Zutphen post-haste. His idea was that the provision wagons would be manned by a small force. By his orders, therefore, Norris sent out a party of only 500 to the ambuscade. Of their own accord about 50 young lords, including the Earl of Essex and Sir Philip's brothers stumbled through the fog in the early morning to join them. The two groups found each other with some difficulty, and quietly advanced to the place of ambuscade.

Unknown to this handful of valiant Englishmen, the provision train was supported by 3000 foot and 1500 horse commanded by the Marquis del Vasto. Under the cover of night they had come up and intrenched themselves just beyond the point of the ambuscade. As the Spanish governor prepared to sally out to meet the victualing party, the mist suddenly lifted. Then, and then only, did the English realize that they were outnumbered eight to one!

In the hopeless fight which ensued the valiant 550 demonstrated the most heroic bravery. Though Lord North had a wound in his leg so that he could not wear a boot upon it, he urged his horse into the thick of the fray. Norris and Stanley who had been at swords points through the entire campaign, in the friendship of fight, swore to die together. According to Greville, Sir Philip met Sir William Pelham starting to his horse without his *cuisses* or thigh guards. Scorning to be better equipped than his colleague, Sidney threw away those portions of his own armor in a gallant gesture which was to cost him his life.

The first two charges carried the English well beyond the ranks of the Spanish, where they performed miracles of courage. It was an epic fight. In the second attack Sir Philip's horse was shot under him. Mounting another, he led the advance the third time. Then just as he was turning to give the signal for retreat, a musket-ball lodged about " three fingers above his knee." The pain was terrific and he controlled his frightened horse with the greatest difficulty. Still he refused to let a soldier lead the animal, so determined was he not to reveal to the Spaniards that he was wounded!

It was a " long mile and a half " to camp. Sir Philip rode the entire distance. Leicester came upon him, advancing slowly in the pale light of mid-morning. Quite beside him-

self with fear, the Earl hurried the boy off to his own tent in
the meadows. On the way, in the words of Greville, Sir
Philip was very thirsty " with excess of bleeding " and
called for drink:

*[It] was presently brought him. But as he was putting the
bottle to his mouth, he saw a poor Soldier carried along,
who had eaten his last at the same Feast, ghastly casting
up his eyes at the bottle. Which Sir* Philip *perceiving, took
it from his head before he drank, and delivered it to the
poor man with these words, Thy necessity is yet greater
than mine. And when he had pledged this poor soldier, he
was presently carried to* Arnheim.

The simple selflessness of that toast has given it undying
fame.

The journey to Arnheim was made as easy as possible
in Leicester's barge. Once in the city, Sidney was tenderly
carried into the house of a Dutch lady named Mdlle
Guithuesissens, while posts were sent to bring Lady Sidney
from Flushing.

The real test of Sir Philip's bravery came with the surgeons. Zealously and in numbers they tried their crude art on
him. Though he had seen too many wounds not to know
what was ahead, he unflinchingly urged them to probe for
the ball while his mind was still clear and he had no fever.
However, the bullet had gone upward, shattering his whole
thigh in its passage, and though they tented to the quick,
they never found it.

There can be no doubt of Leicester's anxious affection for
his wounded nephew. His official letter to Heneage testi-
fies as much by its very incoherence:

*If I could buy his life with all I have, to my shirt, I would
give it. Fear I must needs greatly, the worst, the blow in
so dangerous a place and so great. Never did I hear of any*

man that did abide the dressing and setting his bones better than he did.

In the days of agony ahead, Sidney's shoulder blades cut through the very skin as he postured under his surgeons' directions. Still all the while his thought was for Leicester's anguish, for his dear young wife who was shortly to bear another child, for his grieving brothers. As Leicester wrote home: " He comforteth all about him as much as may be."

At first it looked as if Sir Philip would recover from his wound. Walsingham had a letter from the young man's uncle dated September 27th, 1586 which said:

My grief was so great for the hurt of your son, my dear nephew and son also, as I would not increase yours by the discomfort thereof. But seeing this is the vj th day after his hurt, and having received from the surgeons a most comfortable letter of their very good hope they have now of him, albeit yester evening he grew heavy and into a fever about vj o'clock, he fell into an exceeding good rest. And after his sleep found himself very well and free from any ague at all; and was dressed and did find more ease than at any time since he was hurt. And his wound very fair, with the greatest amendment that is possible for the time, and with as good tokens. I do beg his life of God.

The report next day was equally optimistic.

When Leicester went into winter quarters early in October, his news was still cheering:

I trust now you shall have longer enjoying your son, for all worst days be past, as both surgeons and physicians have informed me. And he amends as well as is possible in this time.

However, one of the surgeons had seen from the start that the hurt was like to prove mortal. This man whom Greville called " one Owle among all the birds " was in the service of Count Hollock and had been sent to Sir Philip by his master who was at that moment suffering from a musket shot in his throat.

This surgeon notwithstanding . . . returning one day to dress his wound, the Count cheerfully asked him how Sir Philip did? And being answered with a heavy countenance that he was not well; at these words the worthy Prince (as having more sense of his friend's wounds, than his own) cries out, Away villain, never see my face again, till thou bring better news of that man's recovery; for whose redemption many such as I were happily lost.

On the last day of September Sir Philip had made his will. Though unfortunately it was unsound from a legal point of view and was to give Sir Francis infinite trouble, it affords beautiful proof of the writer's constant care for his servants and household, and his thought for his debts to the end. With trusting affection he devised one half of all his holdings to " Dame Frances Sidney my Wife." He made ample provision for every contingency which might arise in connection with his unborn child. He arranged for his small Elizabeth's dowry. He bequeathed a jewel of price to the Queen. All his books and pictures he gave to Dyer and Greville. To his father-in-law he left £100. By codicil added on October 17th, 1586 he bestowed goodly sums on his doctors and ministers, his sword on Essex and the hangings of his best chamber on my Lord of Leicester.

The news of his wound did not reach England till October 12th. It caught Elizabeth unaware and betrayed her into an access of real feeling. With her own hand she wrote Sidney a letter full of belated appreciation of all his service.

The special messenger who took it to Flanders, had orders to return again with speed, to report on Sir Philip's condition.

Meantime Sidney lay in the great Dutch bed at Mdlle Guithuesissens's in Arnheim. Lady Frances had taken charge of the bare clean room in a trice. Deftly she made him comfortable after the painful attentions of the surgeons. She sat by, while he talked about Plato's theories on the soul, and compared the ancient and Christian ideas on immortality. Her spirit soared the day his thoughts turned to merrier matters and he called for music. He had written a French ballad upon his " hurt " which he called the *Broken Cuisse*. For a while the sickroom was gay with the chittering of the lutes which supplied the accompaniment to his verses. But next day he was worse. In the confusion and panic, the last poem he made was lost.

Though she had increasingly little hope herself, Lady Sidney dispensed hope freely to wilted Robert Sidney, and young Thomas whom everyone liked. She found cheer to bolster Lord Leicester withal, when daily he came from Zutphen with woe in every line of his plump and elegant figure. She had even harder tasks: to smile bravely back into the tender eyes of her husband; to force a quip when he " ordered " her to obey (as a good wife should!) and take her rest. Still the ministers tried her endurance most. They were not like the friendly vicar of St. Olave's in Hart Street, these Dutch and Huguenot preachers who brought her husband such dreary " consolations "! They " examined " him for hours, they exhorted him in Latin and when they left, he was utterly fagged — with strange ideas that he ought to burn his *Arcadia!*

As the end drew near, he called for ink and paper to write a letter to the Queen. For Sidney was a courtier, though one of a rarely honest breed. He must take his last leave of Majesty in fitting and beautiful words. Then he made his farewells to his uncle, to his beloved wife, to his brothers. At two o'clock on the afternoon of October 17th, 1586 he died in the arms of William Temple, the secretary who had recently done a translation of Ramus for him.

His words at the end were set down:

Love my memory, cherish my friends; their faith to me may assure you they are honest. But above all govern your will and affections by the will and word of your Creator. . . .

They recall the *Arcadia's* song of old Languet the shepherd who loved an honest youth through his impulsive and slippery years, and taught him that true harmony of the spirit is

jump accord with Him who sits
Above all reach, above all human wits.

To his everlasting glory, Philip Sidney had learned that lesson, though he died at thirty-one.

Then Lady Frances was suddenly sick and afraid. In Leicester's words, she was "wonderfully overthrown through her long care since the beginning of her husband's hurt." Now she collapsed, a heap of taffeta and wilted ruff, sorrow and racking pain. Tenderly, the stricken uncle gathered her up and called her daughter. As he carried her to her chamber she clung to him desperately, begging him to take her out of that dreadful country, to take her home to her father. Leicester gave her what comfort he could. Then he went down to write to Walsingham of "your sorrowful child and mine," to put stumbling words of affection on paper about his nephew. It was an honest broken letter. Death had cut through to the real man.

On October 23d Sir Philip's body came by water from Arnheim to Flushing. There it lay in state for eight days that the people might pay their tribute to the handsome

young Governor who had guarded them from " outrage "
and won all their doubting hearts. On November 1st,

*he was brought from his house in Flushing to the sea-side by
the English garrison, which were 1200, marching three by
three, the shot hanging down their pieces, the halbert, pikes
and ensigns trailing along the ground, drums and fifes playing very softly. The body was covered with a pall of velvet;
the burghers of the town followed, mourning, and as soon
as he was embarked, the small shot gave him a triple volley;
then all the great ordnance about the walls were discharged twice, and so took their leave of their well-beloved
Governor.*

He went home on his own vessel, now re-christened the
Black Pinnace for its funeral sails of sable. On its sides
hung his Sidney escutcheon: the silver porcupine, the broad
arrow (which is still on the Ordnance stores). There was
also the proud device of the Dudleys, the bear and the
ragged staff. On the deck, draped in black, with battle
flags about it, lay his body, in the uniform of a colonel.

Although the Estates were poor, and at variance on everything else, they had made Leicester a unanimous offer to
defray the expense of public obsequies for their hero. They
promised to erect him a mighty monument if it cost " half
a ton of gold." However in a moment of unguarded emo-
tionalism, which spoke volumes for her grief, the Queen
had announced she would pay for his " funerals " herself.

When the *Black Pinnace* came to Tower Stairs on
November 5th, Walsingham met it. He was still dazed
by his mighty affliction, and could only murmur, " Her
Majesty hath lost a rare servant, and the realm a worthy
member." Words which usually came with such ease to
Sir Francis failed him utterly now. Up Tower Hill and
along Minories Street they bore the body by his orders.
He saw them set it down in the Minories Church under

the window of jeweled glass which Mr. Markantry had given. Philip Sidney had returned to the Ordnance office.

For a strange reason, too. His own and his father's creditors were clamoring to be paid. Some £6000 was owing. The lands which his will had directed to be sold to meet these very demands, were his, but not his to sell. Even then Walsingham was scouring London for money to pay Sidney's debts. Until he could find it, the funeral could not be held. The creditors were so desperate that they had threatened to seize the body! Since by grace of the blessed nuns, the Minories was " sanctuary," in the Minories Sir Philip remained. Through December when his little widow bore her child and lost it. Through January. When at last his obsequies took place in St. Paul's in February of 1587, Walsingham paid the " charges."

The Last Picture of Sir Philip, from the Lant Roll. " Thy
necessity is yet greater than mine."

THE TWENTY-FIRST CHAPTER
ENTITLED
LOVELY IN HIMSELF.

VEN in the days when every funeral was a pageant, Sidney's obsequies passed into history. It was not merely for their grandeur, nor for the poetry which fittingly graced them. It was largely because they were Sidney's.

In that practical grasping age, his chivalrous spirit had a fresh and romantic appeal. His honesty (notable enough in any generation) moved the folk of his wicked time to a marveling awe. In a period which ruthlessly judged of a man's success, by what he got and did, Sidney's triumph was conceded (with wonder) to have been a matter of soul. Though his one and thirty years had been packed with plans and crowded with accomplishment, his fame rested neither on what he did, nor on what he hoped to do. It was grounded on himself.

For the sake of his shining ideals, people jammed the streets to see his corse go by. Moreover they made of him a tradition. They bought Thomas Lant's great *Roll* with its thirty-eight feet of continuous pictures, which showed every scene of his funeral. They took it home and wound it on tall spools which they placed on their chimney pieces. As they unrolled it for their children, they told them of Sidney and Zutphen. So John Aubrey in pinafores, fifty years later, stood on a chair in the house of his uncle at York, to gaze at Sir Philip's cortège as it passed before his eyes — in figures four inches high! So he and countless others unborn in 1587, first sensed the spirit of Sidney through picture and story. They caught his gentle glamour in the Calidore of Spenser, the complete and courteous knight; and in the elegies which continued to be printed for half a century after Sir Philip was dust. The man was a legend in short order. Almost within his lifetime the mold of his fame had set.

For the tributes to him are strangely unanimous. Three volumes of Latin and Greek verses, some hundred poems in all, were produced by the students of Oxford and Cambridge. Two thirds of them praised him as one who followed " where destinies called " with dignity and with beauty. Greville said that his " heart and tongue went both one way "; and in the popular song which Byrd set for four voices, he was Sidney of

that most rare breast, crystalline sincere, through
which like gold, his princely heart did shine. . . .

His father saw in him the light of his line: *Lumen familiae suae,* and Mendoza who hated him, lamented nevertheless " to see Christendom deprived " of so rare a radiance " in cloudy times." It was a courtier who consoled Leicester with the thought that Sir Philip " liveth now in immortality," and the King of Scotland who furnished the echo

he doth in bed of honor rest
And evermore of him shall live the best.

The most royal poet of all time paid him eternal tribute. For he put his sensitive suffering Hamlet in a courtly background of inaction and intrigue shot through with frustration; he let him learn things of his uncle which harrowed his young soul; and he described him as he might have described Sir Philip:

The courtier's, soldier's, scholar's, eye, tongue, sword;
The expectancy and rose of the fair state,
The glass of fashion and the mould of form. . . .

Through Kemp, Shakespeare had his touch with Sidney
the man as well as the gracious figure of legend. And if he
was in London as early as February 16th, 1587 the bud-
ding dramatist of twenty-three surely found some point of
vantage to watch the solemn and stately procession which
passed that day from the Minories to St. Paul's.

The cortège was ordered by the Clarenceaux king-at-
arms, and consisted of some 700 persons in all. According
to Lant the streets over which it passed

were so thronged with people that the mourners had
scarcely room to pass; the houses likewise were as full as
they might be, of which great multitude there were few or
none that shed not some tears as the corpse passed by them.

Leading, were two " conductors " of the poor. They were
a suitable prologue to the honoring of a life which was one
long record of charity that dispensed friendliness with its
shillings and pence. In their wake were thirty-one paupers
— one for every year of Sir Philip's brief life — in long
cloaks of black woolen.

Then, preceded by " fyffes and dromes playing softly "
came six representatives of his foot in the Low Countries.
With them walked " a lovely youth of a gentle figure " who
bore the Queen's own ensign adorned with the phoenix,
that immortal bird of fable which rose from its own dead
ashes to its own new life. The legend was *Semper eadem,*
" Always the same." Strange motto for the variable Elizabeth! But it was known as hers all over Europe, and her
officers carried the phoenix to battle on their caps. Sir
Philip had worn it at Zutphen.

Next following were the officers of his horse to the same

number. Their guidon trailed behind, with stars on it and the words *Pulchrum propter se,* " Lovely in himself." Nothing could have been more appropriate to Sir Philip's personal radiance. After them came the lieutenant of his horse. Then, ushered by two " conductors," the 60 members of his household, who carried a motto out of Ovid, *Vix ea nostra voco.* Sidney had taken it years before to indicate that we can " scarcely call those things our own " which — like wealth and family fame — have come to us by inheritance: only individual worth can make them ours by right. It was the doctrine, *Noblesse oblige.* No one ever professed it more truly. Preceded by 60 esquires of his kindred and 15 knights including Sir Francis Drake, walked the preacher and two chaplains.

Behind the decorated pennon of Sidney's arms, his war horse paced delicately by, bearing a youth who trailed a broken lance. His barbed horse for the field shone in magnificent caparison of gold, led by a footman and guided by a page who carried a battle-ax with its head turned downward. Heralds bore his " hatchments and the dignity of his knighthood ": Portcullis the spurs, Bluemantle the gloves, Rougedragon the helmet topped by the porcupine, Richmond the shield and Somerset the escutcheon. Like Clarenceux who came last, they wore long capes adorned with the Sidney coat of arms.

Then preceded by gentlemen ushers, the high coffin, covered with three-piled velvet on which the Sidney arms were embroidered. The corners of the pall were held by Thomas Dudley, Edward Wotton (with whom aforetime he practised at tilt in Vienna), and by Edward Dyer and Fulke Greville, his " welcome two." The banneroles were borne by four of his kinsmen. Following the coffin walked Robert Sidney as chief mourner, with Thomas behind him. Close after, on sable steeds rode the earls his uncles, Huntingdon and Leicester, together with Essex and

Pembroke. In their wake, a sombre little company of the Dutch States, led by Ortel; alone of their English allies in Flanders, they had trusted and loved Sir Philip Sidney!

Last in the procession was the City's delegation, headed by the Lord Mayor of London in his purple robes. With him rode the Sheriff, followed by eight aldermen and eight knights. Then walking two by two, 120 members of the Company of Grocers, of whose "mystery" Lant tells us that Sidney was "free." Last of all, 300 citizens, practised in arms, and marching three and three.

Through the great west door where the Queen's guard stood glorious in her Tudor green and white, the cortège passed solemnly into St. Paul's. The interior of the great Gothic Cathedral was hung with black cloth. It was filled with mourners who had for months accounted it a sin "to appear at court or city in any light or gaudy apparel." Under the direction of the Windsor and Chester heralds the nobles took their places according to their degree. When the sermon was ended the body was borne on its magnificent hearse from the choir to be interred behind the high altar.

Elizabeth sat alone in that throng. The music was thunderous and gusty. Around her the air was dim and chill with mortality, for in the tiny radiance of cresset and candle those high sable draperies loomed the blacker and the shadows massed to a deep dull gray. From her seat in the choir she heard the muffled volleys outside on the west porch — the final salute of Sir Philip's soldiers; then the slow creaking of the leaden coffin which was being lowered into the dark space below the pavement.

Perhaps her mind was already running ahead to political problems, because England must go on, no matter who died or what happened. What was greater even than she, was greater than Philip Sidney. She had mourned sincerely that

time in November months past when the news came first
of his going. During two entire days she had given no
thought to state. But that was already long ago, to the sense
of her tired mind. Since then, Mary Queen of Scots had
" suffered " for the Babington plot. (She, Elizabeth, had
suffered as well — agonies of indecision, before the execution and after.) Now Philip of Spain was preparing a
mighty Armada. At last she had come to fear what Sidney
had seen and feared since 1577 — and that was ten years
ago.

Did she, however briefly, regret her treatment of him?
She had stopped " her Philip " and stayed him. She had
balked him cruelly and with intent. She knew as well as
Greville (for little escaped her) that there were " sparks of
extraordinary greatness " in Sidney " which for want of
clear vent lay concealed." The rich and varied ability which
the youth had shown in his short and crowded existence,
despite every hindrance which Her Highness could con-
trive, made it clear that England had lost by this constant
frustration. So had Her Highness. For that she might
properly grieve and repent her at length of the evil (though
belike she did no such thing)!

To Sidney himself however she had done nothing but
good. Out of those very obstructions he had shaped his
personal splendor. She had helped him to the immortality
which England guessed at that day and the world has come
to acclaim without any qualification.

Sir Philip's reputation did not hang on his powers as
a scholar or soldier, nor yet as a statesman. With the
facility of the typical Renaissance figure, he had done all
things well. Because he was Sidney, he had done them also
with grace. Still his ultimate fame did not come from the
capture of cities, nor the deft discharge of difficult missions.
Nor — though he left behind him the loveliest of sonnets,
and composed the first great romantic tale in the language

— was his glory in literature. All these added to his luster. But they brought him no deathless splendor.

For his essential radiance of soul, he had chiefly to thank the Queen. Out of the fierce disappointments she had dealt to his mounting Dudley pride; out of his high ambitions which she loved to set so low; out of his sufferings when she gave him that final knock on the head (and the barb of her wit withal) — he had shaped his impulsive self to control and patience. He had fought for and found his poise. It was such shining of spirit as comes to high minds out of shipwreck, the poignant pain and glory which his favorite Greek poet put in the mouth of a mighty Hecuba, humbled, — after the towers of Troy had fallen about her, after she saw Cassandra raving and ravished:

Had He not turned us in His hand, and thrust
Our high things low, and shook our hills to dust,
We had not been this splendor, nor our wrong
The everlasting music to the song
Of Earth and Heaven.

INDEX.

*This book designed by Ronald Freelander,
set in Granjon type and printed on
Warren's paper at The Plimpton
Press, Norwood, Mass.*